THE ORDEAL OF
ELIZABETH VAUGHAN

THE ORDEAL OF
ELIZABETH VAUGHAN

EDITED BY
CAROL M. PETILLO

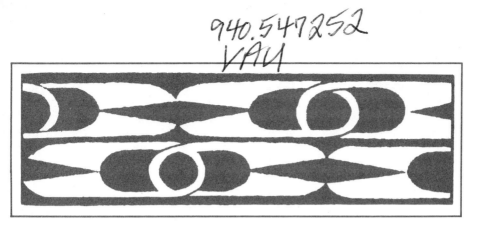

A WARTIME DIARY
OF THE PHILIPPINES

THE UNIVERSITY
OF GEORGIA PRESS

© 1985 by the University of Georgia Press
Athens, Georgia 30602
All rights reserved

Designed by Sandra Strother Hudson
Set in Linotron Joanna with Post Roman Medium display

The paper in this book meets the guidelines
for permanence and durability of the Committee on
Production Guidelines for Book Longevity of the
Council on Library Resources

Printed in the United States of America

89 88 87 86 85   5 4 3 2 1

Library of Congress Cataloging in Publication Data

Vaughan, Elizabeth, 1905–1957.
    The ordeal of Elizabeth Vaughan.

    Includes index.
    1. Vaughan, Elizabeth, 1905–1957. 2. World War,
1939–1945—Prisoners and prisons, Japanese. 3. World War,
1939–1945—Personal narratives, American. 4. World War,
1939–1945—Concentration camps—Philippines. 5. Prisoners
of war—United States—Biography. 6. Prisoners of war—
Philippines—Biography. I. Petillo, Carol Morris,
1940–   . II. Title.
D805.P6V38 1985   940.54'72'52095995   84-16178
ISBN 0-8203-0751-3

CONTENTS

The publisher gratefully acknowledges the contribution of Ernestine Jernigan, who transcribed her sister's wartime diary and brought it to the attention of the University of Georgia Press.

INTRODUCTION

Even before the experiences that she recounts in this diary, Elizabeth Vaughan's life was unusual for a woman of her time and place. Born Elizabeth Head in 1905 in Athens, Georgia, the fourth child and first daughter of a well-to-do Southern merchant family, she seemed determined from the outset to accomplish and experience all that she could. Family stories confirm her adventuresome nature. Following in her mother's footsteps, she attended a private girls' school in Athens where she was no doubt encouraged to think for herself. A good student and outstanding athlete, she was, as one close observer puts it, "always a winner." She enjoyed basketball and track, and under her mother's tutelage became an accomplished pianist. In every way, she sought and achieved the academic excellence and opportunities for success that her family had provided for her older brothers.

The first serious challenge to these efforts developed in 1924 when, due to a failure of the cotton crop, an economic depression hit the South. The family business suffered and for a time it looked as if the three younger children (Elizabeth now had two younger siblings) would not be able to continue their educations. Indeed, Elizabeth was forced to return to Athens from the women's college which she attended in Virginia.

By no means defeated by this turn of events, she entered the University of Georgia in Athens to pursue a degree in journalism. The experience of the next three years reinforced several of the traits which would define her life. She worked very hard, and by dint of this effort sharpened her already acute intellectual skills. Moreover, she contributed financially to her education by taking advantage of whatever opportunities of this nature arose. All this hard work did not, however, diminish the spirit and vision with which Elizabeth viewed the world. Joining with several other journalism students, she helped to publish a newspaper called the Iconoclast. Although the university did not appreciate the effort, the paper reflected the critical attitude common to this new generation of college students in the 1920s, of which Elizabeth Head was very representative.

After graduating with honors, she was awarded a grant by the Julius Rosenwald Fund which enabled her to pursue a master's degree in sociology at Vanderbilt University in Nashville, Tennessee. In the late 1920s and early 1930s she taught courses at the University of Georgia as well as at two private schools elsewhere in the South, while completing the degree at Vanderbilt and beginning a Ph.D. program at the University of North Carolina.

Two particular experiences during these years would later illuminate many of the observations which she made while interned in the Philippines. She worked on the research staff of the Commission on Interracial Cooperation (later known as the Southern Regional Council) in Atlanta, and then, between 1935 and 1937, served as a research assistant to Dr. Howard W. Odum while he prepared *Southern Regions of the United States*, a study of the relationship between the geographic, economic, and general cultural factors within the southeastern United States. Both of these projects emphasized for her the role of race in societal relations, and undoubtedly provided her with a broader understanding of this topic than was held by many of her contemporaries.

In 1936, at the age of thirty-one, Elizabeth Head changed directions. Deciding that the boundaries of her experience were too narrow, she characteristically set out to broaden them. Her immediate goal was to "see the world." With her mother's encouragement, she went to California, and after working at various jobs in order to finance her adventure she sailed alone aboard a freighter for China. A college roommate had married a missionary who was serving there, and in early 1937 Elizabeth visited them in Shanghai.

Following her visit to Shanghai, she proceeded on to the Philippine Islands, probably as part of a prearranged itinerary, but perhaps also because as a United States colony the Islands were America's "outpost in the Pacific." For whatever reasons, she arrived in Manila in mid-1937 and settled into the Manila Hotel, a luxurious hostelry over-looking Manila Bay favored by visiting westerners. At this point, the course of events becomes unclear. Three developments occurred, but in what order and with what causative effect on each other, it is impossible to say. Elizabeth met Milton James (Jim) Vaughan, a young civil engineer from Mississippi working in the Philippines for the Pacific Commercial Company; she was robbed of most of her traveling funds and had to stay in Manila while waiting for money to be sent to her by her family; and she took a position teaching English and sociology at the University of the Philippines (U.P.) in Manila. With her visit extended, she and Jim soon fell in love and began to plan a life together.

After a trip back to Georgia in early 1938 to prepare for the wedding, Elizabeth returned to Shanghai in June. There Jim met her and there they were married by her college friend's husband. After a honeymoon in Hong Kong, they went on to Manila to begin married life. Almost immediately Jim was transferred by his company to Iloilo on the island of Panay, 340 miles southeast of Manila. Iloilo, with a population of nearly 100,000 in 1938, was an old city which had served as the capital of the province of Iloilo since 1688. On the southeastern coast of the island, the city overlooked Guimaras Strait and nearby Negros Island. Because of the strategic location of Iloilo, the U.S. Army had been active in the vicinity since the beginning of the American colonial period at the turn of the century. When the Vaughans arrived, it was the leading sugar shipping port in the Philippines and a bustling modern city.

Here Elizabeth and Jim Vaughan settled with relative ease into the life of the American colonial elite. Like many other young men from the depression-ridden United States in the 1930s, Jim Vaughan chose to work in the Islands because salaries were higher and because most

x   INTRODUCTION

companies offered perquisites which often included a furnished home, a car (sometimes with driver), and travel and entertainment allowances. Although, as the diary indicates, the youthful Vaughans did not perceive of themselves as rich, their life was clearly comfortable. They had a small staff of servants and the opportunity to save for the future—conditions rare among the middle class in the United States in 1938. While, as she suggests in the diary, Elizabeth may have found it a little difficult to adjust to this life of leisure, bridge, and cocktail parties, the transition was eased by her devotion to her husband and their plan to return to the South when they had saved enough money to buy a farm there. Perhaps because she had married later than most women of her generation, she and Jim decided to begin a family soon after their move to Iloilo. In the late summer of 1939 their first child, Beth, was born; a year later a son, Clay, joined the family.

Sometime after Clay's birth in 1940 the Vaughans moved once again, this time to Bacolod, the provincial capital of Negros Occidental, on Negros Island, just across the Guimaras Strait from Iloilo. Negros, the fourth largest island in the archipelago, was, like Panay, a part of the Visäyan sub-group of islands in the mid-Philippines, and the largest sugar producing district in the Islands. Bacolod, a city of approximately 25,000 in 1940, served as a trade center for the sugar-producing communities (sugar centrals) which were sprinkled throughout the island. Like most of the major cities in the Philippines, its foreign population was varied and consisted of European and Chinese merchants, former U.S. soldiers who had stayed on after completing their military service, and professionals from many countries involved in the growth or extraction of indigenous resources. From all accounts, it appears that the Vaughans found a comfortable house in a residential section of Bacolod, joined a social set made up of other colonials in similar circumstances, and continued to live their lives as most of us do, as if the future would pretty much pattern itself after the past. On December 8, 1941, when war struck the Philippines and Elizabeth Vaughan began this diary, it quickly became apparent that this expectation would not be fulfilled.

For some, the war came as less of a surprise. Indeed, some observers had predicted just such a confrontation between Japan and the United States ever since the first decade of the twentieth century. At that time, Japan moved effectively into the international scene by defeating Russia in the Russo-Japanese War, just as the United States finally "pacified" the Philippine Islands after a long and bloody struggle which had begun as part of the Spanish-American War. Although allies in World War I, the two relatively new entrants onto the world stage consistently competed with each other for markets and materials in Asia and for prestige and equality in worldwide diplomatic circles in the 1920s. The Great Depression exacerbated this conflict as Japan, desperate for raw materials to support her expanding industrial base and guided increasingly by a growing militarism, began to move into China and Southeast Asia in the 1930s. The United States, also with interests in China and with its flag still flying over the Philippines, perceived this expansion as a threat to its economic and strategic involvement in the area and began slowly to react.

One phase of this reaction, also encouraged by American sugar producers who saw in the Philippines competition that they could not afford in light of the Depression, was reflected in the United States's decision to grant the independence which the Filipinos had demanded since 1898. A commonwealth government was established in 1935 to ease the transition to nationhood in 1945.

Another phase of the U.S. reaction involved military aid to the Islands. Manuel Quezon, president of the Philippine Commonwealth, understood well the Japanese threat to his country and the extent to which the Philippines would be vulnerable after breaking its ties to the United States. With this in mind, he traveled to Washington in 1935 to negotiate with President Franklin D. Roosevelt an agreement whereby the United States would provide materiél and advisors to a Philippine military establishment to be organized under the direction of General Douglas MacArthur. MacArthur, a longtime friend of Quezon, had served extensively in the Philippines throughout the American colonial period, was fond of Island life, and assured the Filipino leader that together they could without doubt create a military force that would defend the archipelago against any attacker. Between late 1935 and the end of 1941, with uneven American support and frequent Filipino criticism, they tried to do just that. Aided by the American military presence still in the Islands, they attempted to train most of the available young Filipino men, including many who lacked the basic skills and experience which would allow them to participate effectively in a modern army. Ostensibly, these recruits would be briefly trained, then returned to civilian life as reserves to be recalled in a crisis. By the late 1930s many observers predicted that this plan would not work as well as MacArthur maintained. In fact, by early 1941 MacArthur himself had become somewhat disillusioned about his mission and threatened to leave if not given more support by the U.S. military establishment, preferably in the form of an appointment to command in the Philippines the American forces from which he had retired in 1937.

The third aspect of the U.S. reaction to the growing Japanese threat in the Pacific in the 1930s took place on a broader canvas, but with perhaps less clear definition. Directed from Washington, this reaction involved various tactics including tentative support to the Chinese nationalists fighting the Japanese on mainland China, an attempt to enlarge and improve the U.S. military system in the face of Axis expansion in Europe and Africa, and efforts in the United States to discourage widespread domestic isolationism which would not support in Congress the appropriations necessary for even limited expenditures for these purposes. While Roosevelt, Secretary of War Henry Stimson, and Army Chief of Staff George Marshall all understood the difficulties facing MacArthur and the Philippine Army in the late 1930s and early 1940s, in the context of these overall demands on their resources, they could do little but promise aid whenever possible, occasionally urge caution, and convey concern. As a result, when the Japanese began their quick advance into Southeast Asia in late 1941, MacArthur, Quezon, and the Filipino people were almost as vulnerable as they had been in 1935.

The surprise felt by Elizabeth Vaughan when she learned of the Japanese invasion of the Philippines on December 8, 1941, was not an uncommon phenomenon. Many of the Americans living in the Islands chose not to follow or even believe the advice of their more cautious friends who returned to the United States beginning in late

1940. For reasons of faith, convenience, or simple inertia, they remained in the vain hope of fulfilling already set personal goals or to protect their property interests. Not knowing when or where, or even if, such an invasion would occur, they went on with their lives as usual. It is with this in mind that we can understand more easily Jim Vaughan's business trip to Manila the week before Japan's attack. As the diary records, the young husband and father, unable to obtain transport back to Bacolod, remained in Manila, joined the U.S. Army as a member of the Quartermaster Corps, removed to Bataan when Manila was evacuated, fought there with the Philamerican forces, surrendered with those forces in April 1942, and survived the long Bataan "Death March" to the prisoner-of-war camp at Cabanatuan, only to die there of dysentery in July 1942. With astounding suddenness, all the plans and expectations of the young family collapsed.

Although she was unaware of her husband's fate, Elizabeth Vaughan's circumstances obviously and immediately changed after the invasion of the Philippines, even though the Japanese would not reach Negros for another five months. One by one the members of her household staff abandoned her, until she was left with just one houseboy. In addition, her supply of cash rapidly dwindled as local merchants cancelled credit arrangements in the face of the increased demand for their now-limited stocks. As one of the few Americans left in Bacolod, she was invited by the manager of a nearby American-owned sugar central to join their community. Leaving behind most of her household goods, she moved with her two children to a small cottage on the Hawaiian–Philippine Central. From there, as the diary recounts, she and the children in April 1942 retreated with the other Central residents to a hidden camp in the mountains, came down from the mountains two months later and entered a Japanese internment camp in Bacolod, and finally, the following March, were taken on to Manila to the Santo Tomás Internment Camp from which they were liberated by American troops in early February 1945.

As they lived through the experiences that Elizabeth Vaughan recorded in the diary which follows, the larger geopolitical and military forces to which their lives had fallen victim continued to wax and wane. In March 1942 Douglas MacArthur was evacuated from his command on Corregidor to Australia, where he was appointed commander in chief of the Southwest Pacific Area (SWPA). There he began slowly to marshal the Allied forces which would, over the next three years, regain the Japanese-occupied islands in the Pacific and return to liberate the Philippines as he had promised. The effort was slow and costly, hampered by the U.S. policy that the war in Europe should be given first priority.

Added to the uncertainty caused by these factors was the distress resulting from the deteriorating conditions within the Philippines. Predictably, throughout both the Spanish and American colonial periods, the Islands had increasingly been encouraged to grow more products for export (sugar, hemp, copra) and fewer for local consumption. As a result, by the 1920s and 1930s many in the Islands were at least partially dependent upon food imported from the United States and elsewhere. When this supply ceased, the resulting food shortages quickly became apparent. The six months of fighting before the fall of the Philippines interrupted regular planting patterns and added to the problem. Moreover, the occupying Japanese troops required food, and this, too, added stress to the already depleted Philippine stocks. As the war continued (for much longer than the American military, the Filipinos, or the Japanese expected), this growing shortage of food seriously affected the internees. Not only did the provisions which they bought from Filipino suppliers diminish both in quantity and quality, but the gifts of food which their Filipino friends had so generously offered gradually stopped. By late 1944 conditions in Manila were so desperate that hungry neighbors from outside Santo Tomás often raided the gardens inside tended by the internees. By this time the outstanding courage demonstrated both by the Filipinos and the internees throughout the early years of their experience was fading, sometimes replaced by cynicism and corruption occasioned by the constant effort simply to stay alive. As Elizabeth Vaughan reminds us throughout the diary, the stress of sacrifice does not always produce heroes.

It is within this context that she related her own often heroic, sometimes disillusioned, but always human experience of the war. The diary, although not unique in regard to its subject, is particularly significant because its author embodied within her life and outlook so many of the issues and concerns central to understanding the twentieth century. Because of her unique background, she brought to her day-to-day life as an internee analytical skills and particular questions and interests which often translated the personal and the mundane into the representative and the profound.

As a scholar whose past professional experience involved the study of race relations in the American South, she brought to her interracial internment an understanding and curiosity reflected in her accounts of both her Japanese captors and her Filipino, black, and native American companions in the camps. Not always able to rise above the racism of her time and the understandable rage she felt toward the Japanese, she nonetheless tried to behave intelligently and sympathetically under difficult circumstances. In this effort she was not unlike many white, western men and women in the present era who have faced and attempted to adjust to a world far different from the one for which they were prepared.

As a sociologist trained to observe the interaction of groups under various conditions, she was consistently aware of the unique opportunity which this unsought ordeal provided. Although the major part of her subsequent analysis appeared in its most complete form in the book she published after her return to the United States, the diary takes note of many of the same phenomena in a less abstract and perhaps therefore more precise and helpful manner. Elizabeth Vaughan was fascinated by questions of how social class and status were affected by the role reversals sometimes caused by the internment process. Often the most prestigious of the prewar elite could not adjust effectively to the indignities they perceived in their new surroundings. One can sense the diarist's amusement at some of the examples of their discomfort, but this seldom diminished her sympathy toward those she observed, nor her capacity to learn from and use effectively those observations.

As a woman, wife, and mother, Vaughan faced straightforwardly the conflicts and confusions inherent in those roles in the modern age. She took delight in romantic fantasies and throughout her imprisonment longed for the chiffons, lotions, and other luxuries which she had known earlier. These more traditional ideas and concerns, however, in no way contradicted the fact—obvious both in the diary and in her life before and after her Philippine years—that she was a woman determined to move beyond the options permitted by those traditions into a world within which she could use her intellectual powers to their fullest capacity. Although she had readily submitted to the demands of her position as young matron in the prewar Philippines, learning to cook, entertain, and manage a household of servants, she was not unaware of the limits of this life-style, nor was she willing while interned to devote all her time to caretaking responsibilities. She needed her diary, or other reading material, no matter how inadequate, to provide relief from the intellectually stifling qualities of those demands. Finally, as a mother, she proved to be effective, constant, and above all loving toward Beth and Clay. There can be no question that they remained first and foremost among her concerns during the long years of the internment. Nonetheless, and perhaps because of this devotion, she could admit to some ambivalence about the relationship. She, like other women in the twentieth century, could not deny that the demands of motherhood often conflicted with the necessities of fully realized selfhood in other aspects of life.

Finally, as a participant, however unwillingly, in the phenomenon of modern warfare, Elizabeth Vaughan observed and analyzed its impact with the sensitivity and sense of tragedy that it demands. She noted regularly in her observations that, contrary to patriotic myth, the experience of deprivation and terror engendered by war brought despair and diminishment to those it touched as often as it encouraged bravery and honor. It was not without a certain resignation and sorrow that she traced the impact of recent wars upon the women in her own family. And although she could not yet know the full irony of her comment, written as it was before Hiroshima, when she reminded herself "to tell Beth what she will need for the next war," she conveyed, perhaps unwittingly but not unimportantly, the bewilderment and discouraged acceptance that has become so much more widespread in the world since 1945.

The diary ends as the Vaughans are repatriated in the spring of 1945. In its entirety, it not only encompasses the themes outlined above, but is a fascinating adventure as well. Whether it is read as the unique historical document that it is or simply for the interesting story it tells, it contributes a significant personal dimension to our knowledge of World War II.

In mid-March 1945 Elizabeth Vaughan and the two children arrived in California, where they visited one of her brothers before continuing on to Georgia for an extended rest and visit with other family and friends. Characteristically, she soon began to plan for the future and to take steps to rebuild the life so changed by the war. As soon as possible, she re-entered the University of North Carolina, where she wrote a dissertation based upon her experience as "a participant observer" in the internment camp and was soon granted a Ph.D. in sociology. In 1949 Princeton University Press published her work entitled *Community Under Stress: An Internment Camp Culture*. In the same period she taught sociology at Winthrop College in Rock Hill, South Carolina, and Shaw University in Raleigh, North Carolina. She later headed the Department of Sociology and Economics at Meredith College for Women (also in Raleigh), a position she held until forced to retire for medical reasons in 1957.

Throughout these years, Elizabeth Vaughan published and lectured widely, almost always about the topics which had engaged her intellectually throughout her adult life. Increasingly in her analyses she emphasized the changing roles of women in modern society and the strengths and weaknesses they brought, as women, to that transformation. As was true (and probably necessary) for many successful professional women of her generation, her standards were exceptionally high, and she had little patience for the argument that women attempting to enter the world beyond their traditional concerns deserved special consideration and encouragement. She remained throughout her life, in the words one family member used to describe her as a young woman, "persistent, tenacious, relentless."

At the same time she was establishing her career, she undertook the responsibilities of single parenthood with predictable vigor and determination. She believed that the shared experience of internment had created a special bond between her children and herself, and she sought to strengthen that bond while still encouraging independence and self-reliance in Beth and Clay. Aided by a network of family and friends, she supported the interests they revealed, whether intellectual, social, or athletic. When in early adolescence they decided that a trip abroad might be worthwhile, she applied for a Ford Foundation grant to study for a year in Switzerland. When she received the award in 1953, she and her children began to plan the journey. She would study "the internal and external cooperative techniques of the Swiss people, . . . [and] Swiss family living conditions." In other words, she would examine in a new setting many of the social issues which had always interested her. She and the children would also be able to visit the Swiss family who had befriended them in Manila during their time in Santo Tomás, and to share the joy of travel abroad in a way their Philippine experience had certainly not allowed. Although they did not know it at the time, the trip was to be their last big adventure together.

Just before leaving for Switzerland, Elizabeth Vaughan discovered a lump in her breast. Assured by her doctor that it was nothing to worry about, and undoubtedly wishing to believe that diagnosis, she went on with the trip. When she returned to the United States a year later, the cancer had metastasized and the doctors told her that she had only a few months to live. Typically, she refused to succumb easily to the prognosis. She set for herself a new goal: she would live at least long enough to see her two children enter college. Since this meant that she had to hang on until 1958—nearly four years—she was once more faced with an overwhelming challenge. And she nearly met it. She sought and received the most advanced treatment available at the time, spending long months in Walter Reed Army Hospital, teaching when she could, and providing for her children's future, both emotionally and economically, as best she could. In early September 1957 Beth entered Wheaton College and Clay began his last year of high school at Mount Herman Preparatory School. On September 29 of that year, Elizabeth Head Vaughan died.

In one last effort to give meaning to the experience of her life, Elizabeth Vaughan attempted to share her final challenge with others through articles she published in *Religion and Health* (September 1956) and in *Ladies' Home Journal* (December 1956). Well before health-care specialists would recognize the importance of this insight, she advised that some of the agony of cancer victims could be alleviated if those around them would simply recognize and address the reality of the situation. She argued that "articulate cancerous men and women have a peculiar obligation to prod an indifferent public into greater concern." And, of course, as we are now beginning to recognize, she was correct in her analysis.

Beyond this concern for others like herself who had cancer, she sought to leave for her children a message that they could refer to as adults when, perhaps more experienced in living, they might seek her advice. "Never be satisfied to be 'average,' would be my exhortation," she wrote. "It is unworthy to substitute 'I do not' for 'I do.' Friendship is life's greatest reward. Beauty, laughter, love are everywhere. There will be beauty as long as there are heavens and a sunrise and sunset. There will be laughter whenever a heart seeks mirth. And love unfailingly awaits him who gives it."

Although, like the rest of us, Elizabeth Vaughan had not always been able to live by her own advice, she had made a valiant effort in that direction in her youth, during the great ordeal of her internment, and throughout the remainder of her life. It was no small accomplishment, and certainly one which deserves the recognition implied by the publication of this diary. It is the form of tribute which she would have most enjoyed.

Carol M. Petillo
Brookline, Massachusetts
1984

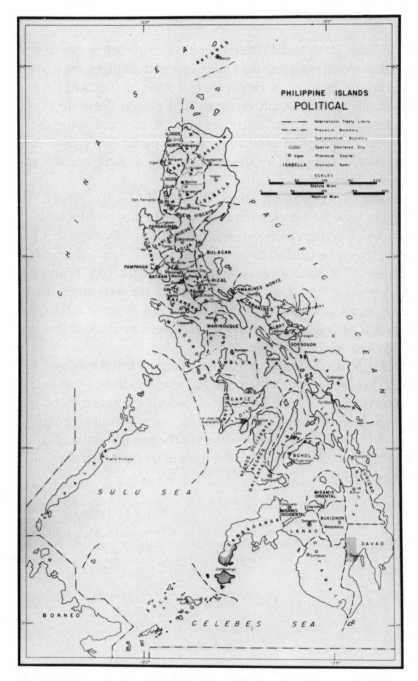

The Philippine Islands, 1942. (Map 775, Record Group 26, Records of the OSS, National Archives, Washington, D.C.)

EDITOR'S NOTE

The diary which follows began as an extended letter meant by Elizabeth Head Vaughan (EHV) to be shared with her husband when they were reunited at war's end. It eventually became a record of her experiences to be saved for her children, as well as a safe receptacle for the strong emotions which she could not afford to vent elsewhere during the long months and years of her internment. As she herself suggested in one part of the diary, the idea of publication was always a possibility. Clearly, the diary served as an important source for her more scholarly sociological work *Community Under Stress*, published in 1949. In addition, however, internal evidence suggests that at some point she attempted a revision of the first entries—accounting for the obvious difference in style and tone of the first few pages, especially of the December 8 entry. Apparently giving up the idea, she stored the diary with her other personal papers where it remained for more than twenty years after her death in 1957. In the late 1970s her sister, Ernestine Jernigan, began a painstaking transcription of the diary, which in its original form resembled, in the words of one family member, little more than a "pile of rubbish." From the disparate pieces (including some typed and pencil-edited pages, thirteen previously used blue examination books, several pieces of torn brown wrapping paper, and many scraps garnered from various notebooks), a typescript emerged which has been edited and published here. Explanatory notes have been inserted where necessary, and possible misreadings of the original have been corrected wherever noted. A minimal editorial effort has been made to ease the terseness of style imposed on EHV by lack of space in the original, but our general intent has been to retain the immediacy of tone which the diary style conveys with as few changes as possible.

THE ORDEAL OF
ELIZABETH VAUGHAN

A WARTIME DIARY
OF THE PHILIPPINES

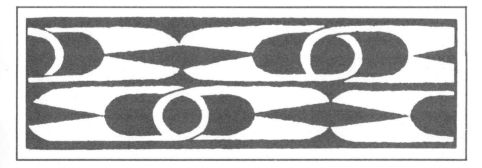

CITY OF BACOLOD 1941

December 8, 1941. On Monday morning, December 8 (it was still Sunday, December 7, in the U.S.), I was up early because my husband was out of town on business and I had gone to bed with the children the night before after a five o'clock supper with them in the nursery. I turned on the radio for the daily 6:15 A.M. news broadcast. My world collapsed. "The U.S. is at war with Japan," the announcer said as calmly as though telling the daily account of news of the battlefronts of Europe. He then told of the attack on Pearl Harbor. I went to the telephone to call my husband in Manila to ask him how this would affect us, and to ask him not to wait to return the next day as planned, but on the plane today, if possible. Telephone connections between the Islands had been closed to all except the army. At 10:00 A.M. a telegram from my husband sending money transfer and three words to torment me for days of waiting, "Other telegram follows." At noon I heard over the radio that Manila, Baguio,* and Davao,† in the Philippines, had been bombed. Then telegraphic lines as well as telephone connections were closed to civilians.

There was absolute panic in Bacolod, Negros Occidental, where I

*Summer capital of the Philippines located 125 miles northwest of Manila in Mountain Province, Luzon.
†Major city in central Mindanao Island in the southern Philippines, 600 miles southeast of Manila.

was living, the only American-born woman in a foreign community. My husband had called me from the Manila Hotel on the Friday before. It was my birthday, and he had telephoned to greet me and to say that he had a nice surprise for me.

"An Ormosolo painting?" I queried, for we had talked of a portrait of a typical Filipino by this most famous of Philippine artists. We wished to put it over the servette in the dining room.

"No, something easier to bring home, but something you want as much," he replied.

How often I've wondered about my birthday gift. What did I want? I could not remember having asked for anything. Jim always loved to surprise me with gifts.

December 9, 1941, Tuesday. No telegram. I waited all day for the "other telegram." I tried again to call Manila; tried so many times that the operator became impatient and answered me that no calls *still* were allowed through, before I stated the purpose of my lifting the receiver. This afternoon a bridge and mah-jongg party at Hawaiian-Philippine Sugar Central‡ at the manager's house. Only one-half of invited guests were there, though written invitations were sent out almost a month before and written acceptances sent in promptly. Regrets were sent by telephone on day of the party.

I wanted to talk to other American ladies and I always feel deep responsibility to put in appearance after accepting bridge date as three others will have ruined afternoon if fourth for game fails to arrive. It was an unhappy group which dispersed early to be home before the blackout. This party was to honor Mrs. Harblentzel, a Swiss, who with her Swiss husband and two daughters had reservations to leave Manila on Clipper,* December 26, for United States on six-month vacation. Honor guest not now leaving, other parties for her cancelled by understanding.

‡Self-contained community built around and peopled by the employees (and their families) of sugar mills—the major industry of Negros Island.
*Pan-American Clipper plane providing commercial flights from Manila to the United States.

December 10, 1941, Wednesday. No telegram. Telegraphed Eddie Best and Mr. Booth. Mr. Wiley telegraphed Mr. Schick (P.C.C.)† to ask about Jim. I sent three telegrams to him asking for immediate acknowledgment. No word. Wagon did not arrive, due each Wednesday 4:35 P.M. Radio reports Manila bombed.

December 11, 1941, Thursday. Servants all said they were leaving, but when I told them there would be no pay till Mr. Vaughan returned, they grudgingly returned to work. At 11:00 A.M. Mr. Serobe called excitedly saying Japanese had landed at Banago pier and were now marching on Bacolod—that roads were blocked, and to leave the house at once with one suitcase. Frantic packing of one case for children with diapers and Carnation milk principally, also blankets (weather cool). Second suitcase with bandages, gauze, iodine, mercurochrome, many bottles of cod liver oil. (Children catch cold easily if not given concentrated cod liver oil daily.) Servants running wildly, children screaming because of noise and excitement around them, my heart missing every other beat with fear for children—thinking of horror stories of torture administered by Japanese soldiers and my lips repeating, "Jim, oh Jim, come home." When we could do no more, I decided to stay in the house because of the physical impossibility of carrying two small children and suitcases. We have no car and taxis have been impossible to obtain since war was declared. When I decided to stay and face what came, a certain calmness prevailed. Then telephone call saying alarm was false, that ship seen from pier was American battleship patrolling area.

Thursday night constantly at radio hoping for some word about passage from Manila that might indicate when Jim would come home or when I might expect a letter at least. Not a word of English on any station, all weird (and at the moment terrifying) Oriental dialect and string music. Thought that "on the hour" or the "half-hour" spot the station announcement, at least, would be given in English, and also some explanation. Went to bed, got up four times to turn on radio,

†Pacific Commercial Company, for which EHV's husband worked as a civil engineer.

but same terrifying programs. Decided it could only mean Manila had fallen into Japanese hands and they were broadcasting in own language from all Manila stations. Terror so great, Jim must be trapped in Manila, nauseated with fear. Finally, in spite of late hour, called the Simkes to ask if Manila had been taken. Mr. Simke said there had been an announcement in late afternoon that the most popular Manila stations, KZRH and KZRM, would be off the air that night and as a result Chinese broadcasts filled the air, the language and music were Chinese not Japanese. I finally could sleep fitfully.

December 12, 1941, Friday. Still no word. Called North Negros to ask Mr. L.O. if he knew whether Jim would be located at Manapla‡ when he did return. (Jim was to decide in Manila where his new work would be.) I was to buy groceries for the future, cases of milk and large supplies of canned goods if we did not move. Mr. O. said he knew nothing of Jim's plans but would try to find out from Manila or Iloilo and would call back. Mrs. O. called at noon to say unable to get message through. So I got a few groceries, powdered milk, canned vegetables, canned meats, matches, flashlight batteries, cigarettes for Jim. Manager of the Chinese grocery, La Pepito de Oro, said they were no longer selling on credit, but when I told him husband was in Manila he permitted this one order. Mr. Kanga, the manager, said that a Mr. Luis Yangco had bought $700.00 worth of groceries, taking every can of powdered milk in the store. They were selling what groceries were left, in small amounts only (for cash) so more people could buy.

December 13, 1941, Saturday. No message from Manila. Afraid at night, servants are always threatening to go and sending clothes away already. When Elsa Huni offered to move in with me I was delighted. Elsa is daughter (19 years old) of a Swiss father and Filipino mother. Mother dead and father now married to red-headed Swiss woman, making Elsa's dark eyes, skin, and hair a striking contrast to her stepmother's. Elsa will be a great help with children (servants getting more

‡Small town on Guimaras Strait, Negros, 23 miles northeast of Bacolod.

and more neglectful of all duties), and so nice to have someone to talk with at mealtime and to sit with in dark after blackout.

Monday, December 15, 1941. More normal life with Elsa as companion. Iloilo-Bacolod air express resumed on Saturday and people more calm.

Tuesday, December 16, 1941. President Quezon's first nationwide talk at 3:30, daylight saving time (changed clocks at midnight last night).* Everyone listening. Had told servants to come to listen to radio, thinking it might quiet their fears. Radio clear for preliminary music—"Star-Spangled Banner" and Philippine national anthem—but when Quezon began to speak there was torrential static on all stations. Frantic turning of dial produced nothing but static roars except on one pro-Japanese station (in English) which roared in clearly stating many American ships had been sunk, that U.S. was ready to give up, U.S. was suffering from shortage of rubber and other strategic materials, etc. As soon as Quezon's speech ended, reception perfectly clear again. Announced that speech would be read at 5:15. We listened, news given—including the report that conditions on land remained the same—but no mention made of President's speech. Obviously Japanese interference, which was most discouraging and disheartening, to know that they could block radio whenever they wished.

Lavendera (laundress) left this morning without touching dirty clothes of children. Girl cook played with children in afternoon while amah† washed their clothes and I thought all was well, then looked out porch and saw cook hurriedly putting big bundles and packages in caramota‡ and dressed in best clothes. Realized that she was leaving without telling me and was trying to slip away unnoticed. Had given her evening dresses and other clothes I thought I would not be needing when packing.

---

*Manuel L. Quezon, longtime Philippine leader, elected first president of the Philippine Commonwealth when it was established in 1935. Quezon served as president until his death while exiled in the United States in 1944.
† Children's nursemaid.
‡ Small horse-drawn vehicle.

Wednesday, December 17, 1941. Announced this afternoon that inter-island ship bound for Visäyas* from Manila struck mine in Manila Bay, sinking within 10 minutes. Casualties high. Was Jim on this boat? There is no news except radio, no newspapers, no telegrams, no telephone. How can I find out?

Thursday, December 18, 1941. Quezon's speech on radio—first mention of it since first blocked-out broadcast. Evidently broadcast had been blocked by American headquarters, not Japanese.

Puppy lost. Loss seemed of maximum importance due to strain. Puppy found under Jim's desk at office. Dog lonesome.

4:30 telephone call that partial list of survivors of S.S. Corregidor released, all Filipinos. Iloilo bombed in early afternoon—across bay from Bacolod, 15 minutes by plane. Three American passenger planes destroyed on ground. Oil supply of Asiatic Petroleum set on fire, smoke visible from Bacolod. Bodegas of Warner Barnes,† cadres for Filipino trainees‡ bombed.

Friday, December 19, 1941. Took children with me to see Captain Richard Jones to try to get word of Jim. Got permission for telephone call on second visit in afternoon. Spanish women back of army headquarters sitting all day in crude air raid shelter sewing and talking. Permission to put through call to Manila granted and written notice taken to manager of telephone office at home just before dark for his approval before handing notice to long-distance operator. Talked to Jim at Manila Hotel. Could not understand well but he said he was in army (quartermaster's division), had sent letter via plane (plane destroyed by Japs in Iloilo on December 18) and by boat (the Corregidor, which was sunk—now believed by sabotage bomb placed in ship), had tried to telegraph or telephone without success.

*Large island-group in the Philippine archipelago between Luzon and Mindanao. Negros is one of the Visäyan Islands.
†Bodegas—storerooms; warehouses. Warner Barnes is probably a company name.
‡From 1935 until the war began the Philippine Commonwealth, with the limited support of the United States, attempted to create an expandable army consisting of Filipinos who would be given minimal training for six months and then held in reserve until needed.

Others in distress: Mrs. Hollowell, Dutch who speaks little English, married to a Swiss who lived in Dutch East Indies many years. Mr. Hollowell in Manila and no word from him. Mrs. Hollowell and daughter 16 and son (overgrown imbecile, cannot talk, and requires semi-invalid care) living alone on hacienda.* Filipino laborers demanding pay and Mrs. Hollowell has no money. Asked Governor Lizares† for protection and he sent guards to her house.

Mrs. Jardelega, large, blonde, buxom American married to petite, pockmarked Filipino, worried about only son (dark like father) who was in school in Manila, about 12 years old. Mrs. Jardelega met Dr. Jardelega while he was studying medicine in the States—she was a nurse—but came to Philippines to nurse at Iloilo Mission Hospital before marrying him. All white friends advised her against mixed marriage, but she seems happy enough helping Dr. Jardelega with his patients (Filipino) and his relatives and Filipino friends. Nevertheless, American women married to Filipinos are generally in a social class to themselves.

Saturday, December 20, 1941. Sit in complete darkness every evening, even put papers over radio on porch so light inside will not show. All windows not yet covered with paper and cloth, and was sent message that house had been reported three times for showing light covered in heavy dark cloth. Covered lights not sufficient, windows must be closed and covered or else no lights on. In tropics this is difficult order so many sit in darkness on black porches or solas,‡ wherever breeze is strongest. With no mail service between islands or outside world we are learning to rely on inner resources for topics of conversation. The only news is on the radio and that is guarded and incomplete, as we know from eyewitness reports of Iloilo bombing, compared with single brief mention of bombing on radio. Wish had kept old magazines but these I burned when packing, or tacked over windows of nursery—only blacked-out room in house.

*Large farm.
†Simplicio Lizares, planter and politician who served as governor of Negros Occidental during the early war years.
‡Sunporches, patio-like structures.

Sunday, December 21, 1941. Shortest day in year, yet it seemed interminable. Thoughts of Jim and realization that my conversation answered none of the important questions going through mind at night. Is Jim in Manila permanently or only until securing transportation to Negros? I feel sure he is there permanently but want to hear it before I have to actually face the fact. It is dreadfully lonesome and my heart skips a beat every time there is a sound like a plane. It seems that I do not go to bed to sleep but to lie awake wondering and wondering why we have been left alone, how I can plan for future. Can I get transportation for myself and two babies to Manila when this island is under almost daily air raids? I think the government will not permit this. Also, if I go to Manila I know it would be with only one handbag, this filled with milk and other necessities for babies. Thus there would be the possible loss of household equipment, personal belongings, silver, hand-embroidered Chinese linens, and other belongings dear to every woman's heart, not to mention inability to take any of mine or husband's clothes, except what I wear. Supply of milk for children and other canned groceries would also have to be left behind (probably not to be replaced now in Manila at any cost). And the trip on the boat with two babies and perhaps having to sleep on the floor or on deck. Could the children stand it? Probably a several days' trip with unannounced landing at some point far from Manila. Can Jim support two households? Our expenses in Bacolod are no less since he left and his expenses, boarding in Manila, are high. Can we financially bear separate households? All sales cash now, many stores closed. Chinese grocery where we have had steady charge account now on cash basis.

Monday, December 22, 1941. Noon broadcast announced 80 Japanese transports sighted off northern Luzon, obviously for major offensive against Philippines. Japanese troops in Davao engaged in heavy fighting. Most serious outlook for Philippine Islands since beginning of war. Panang,* oldest British colony in Far East, abandoned to Japa-

*State of present-day Malaysia.

nese. Hong Kong (beautiful city) practically admitted lost. Where is the American fleet? Will it get here in time?

Christmas card from American friends on nearby sugar central. First indication that Christmas is near. Children will know nothing of Christmas this year. I do not expect to mention it to them. Toys from States will not arrive and cannot afford even new rubber balls at this time.

Tuesday, December 23, 1941. Called Mrs. Woods,† Hawaiian-Philippine Central, to ask about using vacant staff house after talk with Captain Jones. Captain Jones advised me chances of getting to Manila were practically nil and he suggested I leave Bacolod as I was only American there and no one could guarantee evacuation for children in case of sudden landing of Japanese troops or of air attack. Mrs. Woods offered furnished house.

Wednesday, December 24, 1941. What a Christmas Eve! Morning broadcast that Port Area, Manila, heavily bombed and civilian casualties high. No thought of Christmas. Jim's office is in heart of Port Area and bombing occurred during office hours. Packing to move, taking down blackout materials only recently taped over windows. To Hawaiian-Philippine Central with the Wileys, who advised me not to return to Bacolod for night, but to spend Christmas Eve night at their house. Two children and I slept in two single beds pushed together. No Christmas tree, toys for children, decorations, or other signs of the season. On the radio a few scattered out-of-place Christmas songs, but most stations broadcasting of the extreme suffering in Hong Kong where the civilian population as well as the army were fighting Japanese in the streets, of cut water supply but valiant effort to hold out, of reinforcements to Japanese in Philippine Islands, of bombing attacks, Manila to be declared an "open city."

---

†Mrs. A. W. Woods, wife of the manager of the Hawaiian-Philippine Sugar Central.

SILAY
1941-1942

Thursday, December 25, 1941. To Hawaiian-Philippine Central at Silay‡ in afternoon. Spent morning watching things loaded on truck and furniture stored in Bacolod. Took Jim's clothes from suitcases packed to go to Manila and stored clothes in bodega. Of course no word from Jim. Arrived at the Central in afternoon, to find flowers in house and gifts for children on hall table. Five American families and one British at Central all lovely to us—fruit cake (Mrs. Oss), homemade bread (Mrs. Woods), fresh sugar corn—in December!—artichokes, beets, spinach, bananas, eggs (Mrs. Gibbs). How nice to be among Americans again. Only other "blancos"* in Bacolod were Swiss-German Jew named Schulmann—in concentration in Bacolod public schoolhouse with the Japanese—and one Russian bachelor. Spanish of Bacolod are so intermarried with Filipinos that they are not generally included in white population. Swiss of Bacolod either fled to hacienda out of city or sat smilingly and superiorly still calling themselves "neutrals." "We're neutrals, you know," they say whenever war is discussed, and begin talking to each other in German. They take no chances while war news is bad. One actively loyal family (Mr. and Mrs. Simke) are German Jews. He is a longtime resident of Philippines and possessor

‡Port on Guimaras Strait, northwest Negros Island, 9 miles north of Bacolod.
*Literally, whites—more likely meaning here, Caucasians.

of Philippine citizenship. She is recent refugee from Germany. They met in Philippine Islands and married in Jewish temple in Manila. He taught Mrs. Simke to polish her English while she studied for medical examination in P.I. Finished medical course in Germany and Vienna and practiced in Berlin hospital, but all diplomas, licenses, and records confiscated as possession of Reich when she was forced to flee with her mother and two brothers. Mrs. Simke could not practice in P.I. as a German refugee, but as Filipino citizen (as wife of Mr. Simke) she would be permitted to take medical examination. She was preparing to take exam in Manila in the spring when war broke out in December. Immediately volunteered services to P.I. and began teaching first aid classes to Filipinos in Bacolod, organized emergency first aid groups and offered house for hospital if needed.

Friday and Saturday, December 26 and 27, 1941. Unpacking at Silay. One day without radio tantalizing but quickly installed by Central electrician—all at no cost. Salaries at Central for servants amazingly low: lavendera $5.00 per month, no chow; amah $5.00 per month, no chow; Sejio, who stuck with me and came here, $6.00 per month, with chow; cook $15.00 per month with chow, but am letting him go. (Chow = $.10 each per day plus rice, fuel, laundry, soap, water, lights.) Servants at Central live on grounds, daughters of workers here, and walk home for meals. Garden at Central provides vegetables at cost, white leghorn eggs for sale, even daily newspaper (typed) on world affairs (summary of radio for past 24 hours) sent from house to house each morning. Lights, water, and all the ice one can use for $7.00 per month. Garden kept by Central.

Sunday, December 28, 1941. Manila heavily bombed yesterday, after having been declared an open city. Santo Domingo Church in Intramuros (Walled City) destroyed by a direct hit. (Santo Domingo, virgin saint brought to Islands in 1600, elaborately jeweled later by Chinese convert, one of best dressed saints in P.I.'s, people came long distances to see her jewels.) Also two girls' schools hit, piers destroyed, at least one ship left blazing in harbor, all after Manila had withdrawn fortifications and moved all military offices and objectives. Japanese report Baguio has been taken. At news hour broadcasts there is only 15 minutes of music and then silence. This silence of radio stations and obvious avoidance of local news is ominous. On the Central, air shelters are being completed for all employees and residents, and gas masks distributed (simple gauze affairs saturated with chemical solution which would be satisfactory for one gas attack). We really know nothing of what is going on in the Islands. I cannot hope for word from Jim until this tension is eased. He does not know I have left Bacolod. A report from Chungking today announced that it would take the American fleet two to three months to be sufficiently organized to come to the Southern Pacific.

Monday, December 29, 1941. Cholera, typhoid, and dysentery shots (first of series of three) for Beth, Clay, and me. First air raid shelter completed—blocks of pressed sugar cane residue, after juice extracted, packed around stone walls of wash room and servants' room under the house.

Tuesday, December 30, 1941. Dinner at the McMasters'. A real rolled roast, drinks before dinner, Christmas pudding with whipped cream (canned Nestle's, of course). Bridge game on Central in afternoon. Effort to forget war partially successful, but conversation invariably returned to fighting in Manila.

Wednesday, December 31, 1941. Another evacuee arrived, Mrs. White from Del Monte pineapple plantation and cannery in Mindanao, expecting first baby in two months, must have Caesarean, no doctor to perform operation at Del Monte. Came to stay with the Woodses and go to Manapla Hospital for delivery.

June Conant, 20-year-old daughter of staff member here, also returned from Del Monte where she had been teaching. Told of six air attacks on the landing field at Del Monte, how Japanese missed the field repeatedly, bombs landing in woods, ditches, and on outskirts of field. Two injured planes, from which engines and all valuable parts had been removed, were placed at edge of field as decoys. Japs wasted many bombs trying to destroy dummy planes. Women from Del Monte put in houses in mountains away from company buildings and airport, but Mrs. White and June were advised to leave, June to return to family.

War news bad. Japanese advancing on Manila. General MacArthur slightly hurt by flying rock when bomb burst near him.† Flames from front line firing and tremors from guns being felt in Manila. People advised to break up stores of whiskey (Japs might get drunk?) and to stay in houses if city is occupied.

Thursday, January 1, 1942. No Happy New Year today! Manila radio stations quiet during morning. Last station (government operated) 12:45 news broadcast was heartrending. Tears in announcer's voice as he said this station must go off the air like all other Manila stations. Director of Bureau of Information and Propaganda (De Cavrila Orias) asked radio audience in the Philippines to join him in Lord's Prayer, emphasizing the part "Thy will be done." No explanation given of why station going off, of how far away the Japanese are, or whether Manila has already fallen.

Friday, January 2, 1942. No news. London broadcasts and Singapore broadcasts not clear. KGEI (General Electric, San Francisco) announces Manila still holding out.

Saturday, January 3, 1942. Manila in hands of Japanese, also Cavita‡ naval base, though ships and supplies moved. Lt. Arnold (real name Archangelski), Russian from Manapla Central, sent word he had heard Jim was all right and that I had letter salvaged from S.S. Panay which could be secured from Governor's office on Monday.

Having lawyer draw up will for me leaving everything (insurance

†There are no other records of this occurrence. It probably reveals just how inadequate news sources were in the Philippines at this time.
‡Province in southern Luzon, including Corregidor Island and the U.S. naval station at Sangley Point. The capital city, also called Cavite, is located 10 miles southwest of Manila.

policies principally) to children in event my husband's death precedes
mine, with children's grandmother, Mrs. M. C. Vaughan, Leland, Mississippi, executrix without bond.

Sunday, January 4, 1942. Dinner—delayed Christmas dinner of
"American milk-fed capon" at McMasters' house. All talk of the new
airport being built at Bacolod to accommodate large bombers. Since
Manila and most of the island of Luzon is in hands of the Japs there is
no landing field for American bombers when they come. This island
chosen for base is between Manila and Davao at the extreme south,
where Japs have also landed in great numbers. News that Sir Archibald
Wavell* has been placed in command of all Far Eastern forces is a blow
to every American here. We feel that Roosevelt has sold out to
Churchill. Evidently it was for the purpose (sole purpose) of having a
British in command in the Far East that he flew to Washington. This
means, we Americans in the P.Is. feel, that the American fleet and
planes will be called to save Singapore (and British women and children there) and pass by the Philippines and the American women and
children trapped here. Churchill stated repeatedly in his talks in the
U.S., "Singapore must be saved at any cost," and then began to apologize for British defeats in the Far East by boasting of their accomplishments in Libya. I am quite bitter about the action of Mr. Roosevelt and
toward our British allies who have led him away from what, we Americans have been made to feel, is the responsibility of our government.

Will General Brett† and Adm. Hart‡ (Americans who will be in command under "Sir Archibald," as the under has been emphasized in all
British broadcasts) bow and call him "Your Lordship," "Your honor,"
and back out of his presence? Imagine!!! Sir Archibald's appointment is
a double disappointment because of his record of defeats in Libya and
his demotion, and the wide publicity given his failure when he was

*British military leader put in command of American-British-Dutch-Australian (ABDA)
forces. Wavell later resigned and was appointed viceroy of India in June 1943.
†Lieutenant General George H. Brett, U.S. Army, deputy supreme commander in the
Far East in early 1942.
‡Rear Admiral Thomas C. Hart, U.S. Navy, commander in chief of the Asiatic fleet, 1939–
42.

sent to command the then quiet Indian forces to get him from firing lines. After admitting he is not a strategist—but of noble lineage and should not have his family's name belittled—we, the United States, become a scapegoat and let him be put in command of us to build Sir A.'s prestige again. (I read *Time* and *Life* at the time of Sir A.'s demotion and his record of military failure.) Yes, it is a bitter dose to take. The approval of this appointment by Roosevelt has caused more of a feeling of defeatism in the P.I. than the capture of Manila by the Japanese. We have kept stout hearts thinking confidently, daily, that help was on the way to us. Now we feel that while we go without food and suffer humiliation at the hands of the Japs, American aid will pass us by for British territory. How could you do this, Mr. Roosevelt? Are there no good American generals? Not one good enough to take the Far Eastern command when our great nation—the "greatest on earth," the "arsenal for all the democracies"—puts her whole weight into the fight?

Monday, January 5, 1942. On Saturday there was a call (indirectly from Lt. Arnold) that I had a letter salvaged from the S.S. Panay in Bacolod. Hoping that it might be from Jim, I sent for it. There was no letter. The army lieutenant who called me to get it is no longer here—having been transferred—so the mystery remains unsolved. A letter from Jim, even an old one, would be like a message from heaven.

Tuesday, January 6, 1942. Learning to use and to cook native vegetables. My boast always: "I shall never have to cook." Studied as many vocational subjects as possible in college—journalism, typing, shorthand, graduate work in English literature (to teach), graduate work and Ph.D. in sociology (to do social work, research, or teach), but *never* to have to cook. Always dreaded handling food, but now cooking for three, two babies and myself.

Oh for the sound of an American voice! Station after station broadcasting in Chinese, Japanese, German, French, Philippine dialects, Spanish, Siamese, Dutch, and rarely a far-off "You have been listening to London. London calling. London calling." For hours at a time there is no English (American or British) to be heard on the radio, and some of the Chinese and Japanese one-string musical instruments, and religious wails accompanying them, are frightening. It must be wonderful to turn on a radio and hear only one's own language on all nearby stations. The rarest heard and most difficult language to get here is English.

Letter from Jim today, dated December 23. Only a note brought to this island by Dr. Hallaner, who returned from Manila by devious route from island to island. Jim wrote he would call me Christmas Eve, but of course the call did not come through as Manila had heaviest bombing of all on morning of 24th and telephone and telegraph lines from city closed for all except military communications. Jim has tried to send money by telegraph but said unable to do so. Money getting scarce. Due to hoarding, there is little money in circulation, the banks trying to call cash back. Special bank notes being printed for this island from Hawaiian-Philippine letterheads due to unusual watermark on paper which cannot be duplicated here now. Haw.-Phil. paper, good brand, is imported.

Re. money: rumors are circulating that Japanese soldiers arrived in Manila with counterfeit Philippine money in pockets. Were so sure of occupation, soldiers were given counterfeit money to use as incentive to urge them on. These soldiers more successful than Hitler's, who took to Russian fronts with them medals marked for distinction in aiding in the capture of Moscow. These medals later became Russian booty.

Wednesday, January 7, 1942. Received solution to put on gauze gas masks today. As planes approach we must apply solution to masks and tie over nose and mouth. Have small pieces of wood to put in children's mouths to keep mouths open. Children wear the pieces of wood on strings around neck, like a big oblong bead. Keeping mouth open during bombing helps protect the eardrums from concussion caused by bomb. Having nothing more important to do as we await the approach of the Japanese, the women of the Central have fallen into two hostile camps concerning the best type of air raid shelter. One group—a minority, and unfortunately I expressed a preference for this type of shelter—prefers the dugout, while the majority prefer shelters above ground, seemingly suffering from claustrophobia. So most of the shelters are made of bagasse* above ground.

A censored letter from Mrs. Schulmann, German Jewess whose husband is now in concentration camp in Bacolod, thanking me for baby blanket sent to her. She expects first baby in a few months. Husband has been in concentration camp with the Japanese since outbreak of war. Mrs. Schulmann sent him a bed and sends meals daily. Mr. Schulmann has been dismissed by the Swiss company for which he was working and the Swiss have made no effort to have him released. Swiss on this island have been a disappointment to most Americans as they have given no support to civic war preparations, only taking every precaution to be sure they will be personally safe if the Japs come. Their 100 percent "neutrality" at a time like this when they (many of them) have made fortunes in the Islands under American guardianship is a bit of a setback.

The things that people throw away when they think that everything may be taken by aliens—old letters, souvenirs, pictures. There was a general burning of old love letters on Central. One lady married 32 years still had all the love letters of her husband written prior to their marriage. Destroyed all, as Japs might scatter them if they could not read them.

An Australian broadcast announces that a soldier smokes 2½ times as many cigarettes as a civilian, and that since the start of the war in the Far East, Australian consumption of tobacco has increased due to tension, as war draws nearer home.

Wednesday, January 14, 1942. An uneventful week. A game of bridge where we gave IOU's instead of money, as cash on Central is most limited. People playing for "pink elephant" ("white elephant" in States) prizes. Most people have nice things which they themselves cannot use but someone else might like. Mrs. Brown had three guests, all slim, for mah-jongg and gave the winner a pair of pink satin embroidered panties given her (too small, she is a larger woman). Going to hostess's house to play for a housecoat she does not want or need is

*Refuse products in sugar-making; husks of sugar cane after pressing.

all in fun. I have attractive smocks left from my last pregnancy but only one woman on Central could use them. What if another should win? Will have to find another elephant before I have guests.

Four o'clock in the afternoon and what a let-up of tension. Air raids in Iloilo and nearby towns have been between 12:00 noon and 3:00 P.M. This gives planes time to return to base before dark—and each day after 4:00 we all feel free to wander from home and air raid shelter—saved for another day.

Letters to Mom and Aunts Susie and Fannie† giving names of insurance companies with which we have policies. It doesn't hurt to have this in writing in as many places as possible. Of course, letters will not leave Bacolod post office, but then, if Central is destroyed with records here, the Bacolod post office may stand till conclusion of war and letters may eventually reach the States.

We are eating well. A friend with many turkeys sent a dressed one, saying she wanted to kill off surplus as she had no feed. Manager's wife killing three pigs and distributing pork (we have cold storage at Central so meat will keep indefinitely) as there is no more corn for feed. We will have a lechon (whole roast pig) on Central some Sundays.

Manapla Hospital (Dr. Davis, staff of nurses, operating tables, and many surgical supplies) suddenly moved at night to establish army hospital, destination a military secret. Dr. Davis, hospital surgeon, now Major Davis, going with the supplies on large barges by night to Mindanao‡ to treat wounded American and Philippine soldiers from heavy fighting at Davao.

On Central we gather at tennis court late in afternoon and exchange opinions. There is noticeable friction between British couple and some Americans. The English woman, at a recent Red Cross meeting on Central, said Singapore must be saved at any cost. This brought sharp retorts from American women to the effect that England could look after her own colonies, but to Americans here the P.I. seem far

---

†Jim Vaughan's aunts who lived in Mississippi. Aunt Susie, who taught school for more than fifty years, maintained a close relationship with EHV and her children after the war.
‡Second largest island in the Philippine archipelago (after Luzon) and southernmost major island.

more important than any British possession. Surely we Americans can be pardoned for preferring that our country save our lives, and save us and our husbands in the army and our children from possible torture and mutilation, than sacrifice us to save British women and children and English soldiers at Singapore. A selfish viewpoint, but when one's own life, the life of one's husband, and two small babies' lives are at stake, it is difficult to desire one's own country pass the P.I. by to protect a colony of another country. Oh well! We'll see! In a speech yesterday Sec. Knox* said that the Atlantic must be cleaned out and protected before the Pacific, that Hitler is the real U.S. enemy and not Japan. Certainly we hear enough that is discouraging so we're becoming a bit hardened—but this is good.

No more laundry starch. No more matches. The list of items no longer for sale on the island (Negros) now includes razor blades, cigarettes, potatoes, onions, butter, bacon, Carnation milk, starch, and matches. Soap supplies are being exhausted. As there are no inter-island boats now, when supplies here are exhausted there are no ways of replenishing them.

New bodega being built on Central to take care of surplus sugar. Sugar formerly sent to Iloilo (Panay)† for storage. Barges loaded with sugar are now at pier in Iloilo but workers will not unload them because: (1) Central has no money with which to pay workers. (2) Pier area at Iloilo has been bombed so many times. (3) With heavy casualties, pier workers are hard to find. Ciné‡ house at Central filled with sugar (no more films, and due to blackout also no more shows). Now Ciné is full and new bodega under construction.

Money (cash) on Negros Island has been hoarded because bank has no more, and companies that have been receiving payroll funds from Manila are now in a predicament. Bank in Bacolod to make new money from water bond letterheads of H-P Central, but the bank president is afraid to release such money. His head office is in Manila and he feels he does not have authority to manufacture and release local cur-

---

*Secretary of the Navy William Franklin (Frank) Knox.

†One of the Visäyan Islands, 10 miles northwest of Negros, across Guimaras Strait.

‡Cinema or movie theater.

rency. Many company heads are in the same predicament. Having no communication with their head offices in Manila, they do not know how much or how little authority to assume, so many of the offices have closed their doors. Of course, the local managers are receiving no funds from Manila for themselves, their salesmen, clerks, or other employees. Most household servants on the island are behind in salaries, though many are staying on because they at least have a free place to sleep and employers can still give them rice to eat.

STORY OF THE POTATO RICER

Jim, remember how you wanted a potato ricer for the kitchen, for every time we had mashed potatoes the cook, Consuela, left lumps in them? So I ordered a ricer from Sears-Roebuck to please you—and it would make Consuela happy too. The ricer arrived a few days before you left for Manila—in the rush of things I didn't tell you. We didn't have mashed potatoes while you were away, and then war came, Consuela rushed off without a word, the potatoes were exhausted, so here I am, with a shining new ricer all the way from the States to please a husband and a cook, and now there is no husband, no cook, and no potatoes.

The ricer was used for the first time yesterday to mash vegetables for soup. Instead of cutting off the tops of onions (these are only tiny native onions, almost flavorless) we put the tops in soup, also tomatoes with peelings on so as not to waste a drop of flavor. The ricer is ideal for mashing out pulp and leaving tops and skins behind. A come-down from making creamy mashed potatoes—but the ricer is serving a purpose.

Friday, January 16, 1942. Letters to Mom and Aunt Susie censored here and mailed January 14. Wonder when they will be delivered.

A letter from Dr. Hallaner on January 15 said he sheltered, during the third raid on December 24, with my husband and that after the raid Jim left for his office one-half hour from the Port Area, which received the heaviest bomb attack. This was encouraging news. Have hopes now that other news may filter through.

People here are burying silver in sealed tin boxes. Report today of "systematic looting by Japanese in occupied P.I. areas" makes this seem advisable. If we only knew if—and when— and how—and how long. Uncertainty is one of the worst miseries of war.

Thursday, January 22, 1942. First air alarm today. Twelve two-motored bombers flew directly over the Central at 2:30 P.M. Servants saw planes approaching and came running in house calling that we were being attacked. I grabbed Beth from bathroom, rushed back for sticks for children's mouths, returned second time for purse with papers and letters (Clay was in yard), and finally got out of house to see planes almost directly overhead flying very low—no bombs dropped. Later report was that bombers were U.S., but no one certain. Air raid siren blew *after* planes had passed. Watcher on lookout tower lost head at sight of planes and instead of pulling cord to blow siren left watchout tower and came running to Central.

Saturday, January 24, 1942. Second air alarm, Eleven planes flew near the Central, in clear view, at 12:30. Again report came later that they were U.S. planes looking over airfields on this island. This Central is between three landing fields.

Talked with Major Jones (Capt. Jones before) to ask whether army could help me get milk and tomato juice for children. He is sending Mr. Amechagurra to find hidden milk and other stocks of Chinese merchants, and at point of gun Mr. A.—in the name of U.S. Army— will force merchant to let me have on credit (chit to be signed by me) any supplies I need. This is kind of the army, but I don't like this way of getting supplies for the children. There is no further voluntary credit and I have no money. I need supplies and since Jim is in the army Maj. Jones thinks the above procedure permissible. I fear enmity of the merchant involved since I must sign for the goods in person after they have been confiscated by the army for me.

Friday, February 6, 1942. States mail! At least so everyone thought. Yesterday there was a rumor on Central that 2,000 bags of mail for Negros Island had arrived in Bacolod from transports bringing troops and supplies to P.I. Today when messenger of Central returned from daily trip to post office in Bacolod he brought many letters. My heart beat with joy as he handed me letters in familiar handwriting, with the censor's stamp and other postal and military markings. The familiarity of the handwriting was due to the fact that it was my own. The letters were to Jim's mother and aunts in the States which, after resting in the Bacolod P.O., had been returned to sender because there were no boats from this port. Others on the Central who had posted letters for the U.S. and Manila since the outbreak of war also had heavy mail today. Mrs. Woods had eleven such letters returned.

Monday, February 9, 1942. Sugar mill reopened after having been closed two weeks while bodega was being built to house extra sugar. All available space, including at present unused ciné, already filled with sugar as there is no chance of shipping this milling season's output.

Sunday, February 15, 1942. Mr. and Mrs. Wiley and Mr. and Mrs. George Ossorio were driving over a narrow railroad bridge to see place the Wileys had selected for evacuation house in case of invasion when car fell over side of bridge into deep ravine. Wileys both have broken collar bones and Mrs. Wiley broken ribs. Mr. Wiley black and blue with bruises. Mrs. Ossorio's back injured. Lack of drugs, opiates, X-ray plates, nurses (all commandeered by army) again felt.

Sunday, February 22, 1942. Planes—one or two at a time—several days last week. Everyone looking up but not able to distinguish whether Japanese. No doubt about lone plane yesterday which dropped leaflets addressed to the people of Southern Visäyas (word Luzon had been struck out and Visäyas substituted) telling them to "Destroy the Americans on the Islands in order that true independence might be given by the Japanese." A cartoon of a slant-eyed, knock-kneed Uncle Sam shedding copious tears as he stood looking at the islands of the Southwest Pacific occupied or attacked by the Japanese headed the pamphlet. English grammar and spelling poor. Leaflet also advised that the U.S. Pacific Fleet had been sunk and U.S. aid could not come—so surrender to Japanese and destroy Americans who had caused unhappiness and misery. Most of leaflets drifted into the ocean. Filipinos here laughed at Jap-faced Uncle Sam and at the leaflet in general.

Igorot story (over KGEI)—MacArthur's tanks had difficulty penetrating forests to attack enemy on Luzon. Igorots* volunteered to guide tanks and one, perched atop each tank, guided the driver through underbrush for attack. Successful trek through forests.

Moro story—Moros† have sought permission of the army to discard clothing so they can fight effectively. First asked permission to cut long sleeves of standardized army uniform, then asked permission to cut off collar and have it uncollared around neck. Army gave permission to discard shirt entirely and also special permission to fight according to Moro tradition, i.e., not in organized groups, but individually. Successful aid to U.S. armed forces. Moros are Mohammedans of Malayan extraction who inhabit Mindanao and are fiercest of all Filipino tribes. Other Filipinos fear an angered Moro more than Japs, as a Moro's dexterity with his curved, jagged sword will bring sure death—if unable himself, then his family will kill for him—to those who have made him an enemy.

Formerly a Filipino colonel, aided by American Maj. Jones, was highest army officer on Negros. Now new American colonel has come from Cebu.‡ At meeting in Bacolod last week all sugar mill owners were told to disable mills if Japs invaded Negros, and white women and children were advised to have a place far in the mountains to flee from invaders. Owner of this Central was gone for three days, to ends of sugar car tracks, to find location for evacuation camp for women and children. Difficulty is finding water supply and at this level, sugar cane country, woods are far away. Women and children on Negros have been asked to move to Manapla Hospital buildings where there are beds and bathrooms and a large kitchen, but each Central seems

*Proto-Malayan people of north-central Luzon, known principally for their maintenance of the centuries-old practice of rice-terrace agriculture.
†Any of the several Muslim peoples of the southern Philippines, chiefly of the Sulu archipelago and parts of Mindanao.
‡City, province, and island of the Visäyans, separated from Negros Island by Tañon Strait. Cebu City was the first permanent Spanish settlement in the Philippines.

to prefer to make its own plans. Insular Lumber Company has already built small houses far in woods for women of lumber Central. Food has been stored there, medical supplies moved, and after the women go in the blasting of one bridge over a wide and deep river will prevent Japs from reaching this outpost for a long time. Women of Iloilo (on Panay) and Cebu (on Cebu) have gone far inland, usually walking the last 12 miles. Carabao* carts bring supplies.

Thursday, February 26, 1942. Quezon (Pres.) and Osmeña† (Vice-President) arrived in Bacolod by submarine for a conference with sugar mill owners and managers. All mills must close on Saturday, February 28. Money can be borrowed from government by the mills to pay employees and cane tenant farmers, hacienderos‡ will be given money by government for cane plowed under to plant vegetables.

Sunday, March 1, 1942. Cebu and the coast of Negros (near Dumaguete)* shelled by Japanese destroyer. Cebu shelled because Japanese thought Quezon was there, but he and his party were still on Negros.

Wednesday, March 4, 1942. Puppy bit a bufo (Latin for frog and also local name for frogs imported from Hawaii) and adrenaline poisoned dog. Foaming at mouth (due to poison stinging tongue), running in circle, finally lying on ground gasping for breath—all this in two or three minutes after biting frog. Gardener said antidote is sugar, so 1-kilo sack (roughly 2 pounds) sugar poured down throat of seemingly dying animal. Sugar caused vomiting. This followed by a large dose of castor oil. In three hours dog was completely well and wagging tail again. Animals and persons eating bufos either die or recover quickly, due to short-lived effect of adrenaline. Box of frogs sent to Central from Hawaii, packed in excelsior, arrived safely here without food or

*Water buffalo.
†Sergio Osmeña, longtime Philippine political leader; vice-president of the Commonwealth; president of the Commonwealth after Quezon's death, 1944–46.
‡Owners of large farms (haciendas).
*Capital city of Negros Oriental province on southeast Negros Island. Port on Mindanao Sea, near the entrance to Tañon Strait, 95 miles southeast of Bacolod.

drink. Sent to help control insects on this Central. Now bufos cover the island. Large, warty toads with pouches of poison back of the eyes. People have tried removing these pouches and eating the frogs, but death has resulted as there are other adrenaline glands. In fact bufos are used as a source of the medicine and are being raised in some places for that purpose. Bufos eat mosquito eggs in water so there are few mosquitoes here. At dusk each day thousands of bufos come out and hop over lawns. They disappear with dawn and do not come out again until nightfall. They are harmless as long as skin is unbroken. Children love to chase them.

Friday, March 6, 1942. Mrs. White died in Manapla Hospital after giving birth to baby boy. Had come to Negros from Mindanao to have Dr. Davis deliver baby and then Dr. Davis was sent by army to Mindanao. Only white doctor, Dr. Smith, mill doctor of Insular Lumber Company, old, behind the times, uncouth. All good nurses from hospital were taken with Dr. Davis to battlefront in Mindanao. Shortage of morphine and drugs on island also. Infant son cannot be taken to Mindanao by father due to uncertainty of transportation, possibility of bombing, and likelihood of delay on trip.

Saturday, March 7, 1942. Mr. Worster (son of Dean Worster)[†] and Mr. Wilson (owner of Wilson Building, Manila) here today. Now in Marine Reserve Corps. Many prominent business men now in armed forces and in new uniforms assume new importance. Mr. Woods quite conscious of uniform when in full dress, including cap, of the "home guard."

Funeral of Mrs. White yesterday. Died at 4:00 A.M. and buried at 4:00 P.M. same day. No embalming service available now. Second funeral (white) on the Central in 20 years so all native employees (hundreds) lined road to see show, but were disappointed when there was no band, no parade of soldiers in uniform with guns and bayonets, no

---

†Dean C. Worcester (1866–1924), American colonial administrator who served on the Philippine commission, and later in the Philippine insular government. Worcester published several comprehensive studies of the Philippines.

plumes and pom-poms on horses drawing hearse, no tremendous wreathes of brilliant red, yellow, and purple paper flowers. Same afternoon a Filipino funeral from Silay Catholic Church with all the trimmings, and people quickly lost interest in our cortege. We had one delay before start of the procession, when hearse had to wait while attendant patched innertube for flat tire.

Sunday, March 8, 1942. Java‡ off the air, Batavia* has fallen. Mindora† in P.I. occupied. All are talking of fleeing to the mountains. Still no evacuation houses built, but much talk of same. "God save the Queen" the last words from Java radio. Strange that that homely, housewifely looking woman‡ should be the last thought of fighting soldiers and that she should feel the responsibility for a nation of fighting men. Such are the quirks of royalty. Strange, too, that all bad news of war has come to us on Sunday on Sunday morning broadcasts.

Visit to hospital to see the Wileys and the White baby, wee motherless mite, being cared for by sisters in Manapla Hospital. Mr. Wiley up but Mrs. Wiley still in bed from broken ribs and collar bone.

Sitting on freshly mowed grass square in center of compound—the "Plaza," we call it—about 6:30 DST when suddenly a roar and just above tops of acacia trees and coconut palms, alternately bordering Plaza, airplane appeared. Strange as it seems, low-flying planes cannot be heard as distinctly as higher ones. It may be because this was a single-motored lone plane, but we saw and heard it overhead at same time. We could almost touch it as it dipped low over the Plaza lawn. My two babies, the Osses, and their five-year-old could have been hit directly had the plane been Japanese. White star with red center on dark background plainly discernible on plane's wings. This was the first time planes had been close enough to see markings and all rushed to the bulletin board to look again at insignia posted there for

‡Principal island of Indonesia.
*Former name of Jakarta, capital city of Indonesia.
†Mindoro—island just southwest of Luzon.
‡Queen Wilhelmina, popular queen of the Netherlands from 1890 to 1948 when she abdicated in favor of her daughter Juliana.

identifying planes. We knew that the star meant either American or Russian planes—and surely the Russians are too busy at home to have observation planes flying over the P.I. (Red star on wings—Russian. We had no time to look for identifying tail marks.)

Daily sessions at tennis court in late afternoon. Those not playing discuss the war and those in the game add opinions between sets. Occasionally such irrelevant remarks as "Why is no-score in tennis called "love?" Answer (from *Reader's Digest*) giving word as *l'ouef* (French for the egg—a goose egg to us), from the French version of the game.

Monday, March 16, 1942. The first shelling of our small island. San Carlos* shelled by Japanese destroyer which drew up to pier, threw rope over bow, and towed away small inter-island ferry *Princess of Negros* docked at San Carlos pier. Such confusion and fright. All night workers from Central fled with their families to the hills. Chief cause of panic here was report of the assistant to Mr. Gibbs, in charge of outside work of mill, who was in San Carlos at time of shelling and came back here to report Japs had landed on the island—he had seen them with his own eyes. What the assistant had seen was a group of Filipino Home Guard in their uniforms and in his hysteria he imagined them to be Japs. No Jap soldiers on our island yet.

Tuesday, March 17, 1942. Saint Patrick's Day—but a big day—100th day of war and General MacArthur placed in command of all forces in Far East.† Optimism high. We've felt, like the Australians, that if we could get rid of retreating Sir Archibald the American and Australian forces might have a chance to save some of their own territory and then set in to recovering what Wavell had lost.

Cebu radio had been promising big things on the 100th day—announcement of MacArthur promotion as good as a victory. Also it was a blow to Japanese to know MacA. slipped through their fingers and was able to leave Bataan. U.S. High Commissioner Francis B. Sayre in

---

*Town on eastern Negros Island, 35 miles southeast of Bacolod.
†After his safe arrival in Australia, the announcement of MacArthur's late February appointment as commander in chief of the Allied forces in the Southwest Pacific Area (SWPA) was made public.

Hawaii also.‡ So, though we're completely blockaded, to all intents and purposes those in whose hands our destinies be can come and go above the clouds or under the sea. Quezon has gone from island to island with his wife, Maria Aurora, and his two daughters and his staff, by submarine. This is all annoying to the Japanese, who think they, not we, control the Philippines.

Reports from Manila. Dr. Jardelega has returned with his 16-year-old son who was in school in Manila when the war began. The boy looks pure Filipino (has American mother) and so Japs made no effort to prevent travel. Many other Filipino students are coming back to Negros on small sailboats, making a hop from island in the day and sleeping on land at night, as they navigate by eyesight alone in the day, seldom losing sight of land. This travel can be accomplished by small sailboat but not by larger deep-water ships.

Some bring back tales of horror: naked bodies dangling from poles on Jones Bridge in Manila near the post office—slit from throat to loins. Bodies of Filipinos who were not "loyal" to the Japanese conquerors. Feet sticking from garbage cans along beautiful Dewey Boulevard on Manila Bay every morning, sometimes Filipino, sometimes Japanese, murdered during the night hours with absolute disregard for human life. Filipinos ambush and murder every Jap they can get during the night, and Japanese on the other hand shoot for any minor discourtesy or sign of disrespect.

Starving American soldiers in the prison camp in Manila. American prisoners taken through streets of Manila in trucks amid jeers and insults of Japanese (this to impress Filipino watchers who have more or less looked up to Americans in their midst and cannot understand why Japs can do this to them unless, perhaps, the Japanese are invincible and invulnerable sons of heaven, as they say they are).

Report from three different sources so must be true: Japanese do not like women in slacks. From Iloilo, report that women in slacks get faces or buttocks slapped.

Torture stories: Mrs. Christenson, wife of U.S. Army captain, asked

‡Governor Sayre and his family accompanied President Quezon on his escape from the Philippines in late February. The party fled to Australia, then to Hawaii, and ultimately to Washington, D.C. MacArthur, who did not leave the Philippines until mid-March, remained in Australia.

by Japs to locate her husband (whose whereabouts with the army were unknown to her). Her arms were burned by glowing cigarettes held by Jap questioners until pain became so severe she lost her mind and when released committed suicide, leaving two small children. Nails driven under fingernails of personnel of radio office who refused to tell where radio equipment was hidden. Stories of rape in Manila and Hong Kong frighten us more than other incidents of brutality.

Sunday, March 22, 1942. Bacolod, our home, and La Carlota,* on this island, machine-gunned by four low-flying Japanese planes. A bus in Bacolod riddled but all passengers had fled at approach of planes. Airports at Bacolod and La Carlota evidently targets of Japs, but automobiles on highways gunned also in passing. The Japanese attacks always seem to come on Sundays. Three Sundays ago Cebu was shelled from a destroyer five miles out which indiscriminately poured heavy shells into the city, causing destruction to buildings and loss of life. We all have a fear of the weekends, this is always when people flee, and all is calm again by the middle of the week. Tension high again by Saturday.

Monday, March 23, 1942. Two cables from the States—first messages since the beginning of the war—from Ernestine,† who asked if I needed anything (nothing, not even money, can be sent by cable now) and who said, "Hurry home." Other from Aunts Susie and Fannie in Mississippi, who sent love to all four of us (Jim at front) and ended with "Mizpah."‡ Had to look in Bible concordance to trace meaning of this word and was surprised that censor let it pass since he might have thought it a code word, and no code messages allowed now. After much reading of Bible (12 references in full) found that aunts were saying in one word that if I put my trust in the Lord all would come out well. So much in one cabled word. These two cables in answer to two last week (deferred night letters) asking for reply via

*Town on western Negros Island, 17 miles south of Bacolod.
†EHV's younger sister.
‡Site in ancient Palestine where Jacob and Laban erected a heap of stones as a sign of covenant between them. Now signifies remembrance.

Cebu. Cables sent before, but no reply, probably because logical way to send cables is via Manila and of course, since Manila is occupied by Japs, this route is closed, so unless local telegraph office had instructions to route by Cebu (or sender knew this is only way open) cable might not be accepted by office.

Baby (Clay, one and a half years) has diarrhea. All thoughts of packing and evacuation out of mind for present. Only doctor near is Dr. Jardelega (Filipino married to American nurse), who is anti-American and pro-Japanese in spirit because he is not accepted by whites, but his asceite de castor followed by bismuth prescription worked after three days and baby's bowels checked. At times when children are ill I miss my husband most. Need his comfort and moral support. Japanese don't frighten me like illnesses of the children. Fear dysentery more than Japanese army, and fear coconuts falling from palms, as children play, more than bombs.

Reports over KZRH, Manila (formerly our favorite station), now Japanese voice speaking English with un-American twang. Public schools in Manila reopened with Japanese the language taught all children (to replace English). Japanese currency has replaced the P.I. peso* and U.S. dollar. Japanese stamps on letters. Railroads on Luzon functioning again—Saturday broadcast said, "All former railroad employees will report to work by Tuesday or suffer severe consequences." Everyone knows "severe consequences" means death, so doubtless many workers returned to jobs. Faced also by starvation they gladly accept pittance (Jap. money) paid them.

Friday, March 27, 1942. Trainloads of boxed goods going to the end of the sugar cane track line and thence across gulleys and mountains to our evacuation camp. A cable has been run from end of railroad line to bodega, within 9 kilometers of the camp. Goods will be stored in bodega and carried to camp by Negritoes† who sling ropes around hundred-pound boxes and trot up the mountain slopes as though the

---

*Standard currency in the Philippines. During the American era its controlled ratio to the U.S. dollar was 2:1.
†Ethnic group commonly found in mountainous areas of the Philippines, distinguished from other negroid groups by their diminutive size.

boxes contained feathers instead of canned goods. Today the "extras" went. Many boxes to remain in the bodega until the end of the war, or until the Islands are again in American hands. Carved camphor wood chests containing the beautifully hand-embroidered table linens we get here, banquet cloths with so much drawn work that the remaining cloth seems too delicate to launder. And pina luncheon sets (pineapple fiber woven under water, the most delicate, most expensive, and also the most desirable fabric of the Islands) embroidered by little orphan girls in the convents of Manila, where they sit looking through magnifying glasses to do the drawn work (threads are so fine and the demands of the work so accurate) under the supervision of European nuns. These linens, perhaps irreplaceable after the war, sterling silver, bronze work, crystal decanters, Kensington mint julep glasses which frost so deliciously—all these things one has and can do without, but would hate to see the Japs get them or have them looted from our homes when we evacuate. The Central has provided all families with boxes of uniform size (20″ × 14″ × 14″) with handles of rope on the ends, for canned goods. These will be carried in on poles slung through the rope handles, probably several boxes on a pole with a Negrito on each end. Each box should hold one or two weeks' supply of groceries, depending upon the quantity and variety of fresh vegetables and meat which may be secured in our mountain retreat. Typical box from my list #4:

2 cans prunes	1 peach preserves
12 Carnation milk (tall)	2 deviled ham
2 natural milk (large)	2 corned beef
1 toilet paper	1 large tin soda crackers
4 Lifebuoy soap	6 chicken soup
1 toothpaste	1 can butter (small)
6 Fels-naptha	1 can mince meat
1 puffed wheat	Box macaroni
2 oatmeal (small)	6 Nestle's cream (small)
1 borax	2 peaches
1 tea	6 tomato juice (large)
1 peanut butter	6 vegetable soup
2 cans beans	box salt
2 cans succotash	6 chicken gumbo soup

I have 20 boxes filled like this, with a list of contents of each. Some have Crisco, some coffee, some baking powder, and one has my last sack of flour. Some have tinned Jacob's biscuits (a Scotchman with London wife buys for the Central commissary, which accounts for the stock of Jacob's crackers to Americans—but biscuits to the British), a variety of fruits, soups, vegetables, and canned meats. But milk (Klim, Lactogen, condensed, powdered, evaporated, natural, all kinds), toilet soap, and laundry soap are in all. Then there are jams and jellies to put on crackers for the children, because crackers are beginning to have a stale taste and canned butter tastes more like cheese than butter. Strawberry preserves help kill the butter taste and do not interfere with the food value of the butter. The commissary will move with us so additional canned goods can be bought—though the desirable foods have long since been exhausted. Milk, tomato juice, coffee, tea, soap—these cannot be had at any price.

Reports from men who are supervising construction of our nipa‡ houses are that chickens can be bought (by sign language) from Negritoes in the mountains $.25 each, and eggs, corn, spinach (the local version), small tomatoes, dried fish are brought in. There are deer in the hills and in snipe season there should be more than we can eat. All the cold stores have snipe killed by hunters who find the bird more plentiful than they find shot for killing it.

The 20 boxes are packed and marked, with name, number, and contents listed in a book. A kerosene lamp, buckets for bringing water from the river, pads for cots (supplied by the Central), iron cooking utensils to use over open fire, mosquito nets, blankets, bolos* for cutting wood—these things are ready to go.

But the feminine will out. Today Dr. Jardelega came by to see the baby, whose stomach was upset (probably due to eating long beans from acacia trees, like locust trees in the States), and I asked him to remove a small mole developing on my chin. He asked why bother with such a little thing as this and I told him that I wanted my husband to think me beautiful as well as efficient when he came home. So he

‡Palm leaf commonly used for indigenous housing in the tropics.
*Long, heavy single-edged knife resembling a machete.

applied nitric acid and said he would return on Monday for a second application.

Had first official communication from army yesterday, from Maj. Richard I. Jones, Infantry, saying his office in Bacolod had confirmed my husband's enlistment in the army, with rank of 2nd Lt. QMC Reserves, and that he was now stationed on Luzon.

Saturday, March 28, 1942. Quezon has landed in Australia with his family and Cabinet. It is disheartening to have all high officials leave the Islands as a big all-out offensive of the Islands is begun by the Japanese. MacArthur is in Australia. American High Commissioner Sayre has now arrived in Washington after slipping away from the P.I. and there are only former subordinates of the political and military authorities left here. It is accepted as true that Gen. Homo,† formerly in command Jap. forces in P.I. committed suicide (harakiri) in the Manila Hotel (he occupied the suite where the MacArthurs—the General, his wife, and their four-year-old son—lived for many years) when he failed to oust MacArthur from Bataan on Luzon and take the island fortress, Corregidor, at entrance to Manila Bay. After his successful Malayan campaign and capture of Singapore, the Japanese No. 1 general, Yamashita,‡ has been given the P.I. command, to mop up the handful of American and Filipino soldiers here who refuse to surrender though greatly outnumbered and subjected to dive-bombing attack after attack with no planes in the air to defend themselves. It is reported over the radio that Yamashita has promised his Emperor complete domination of the P.I. by April 15 and he has begun his offensive by all-day raids over Corregidor and land and air attacks on the Bataan peninsula of Luzon. There is also heavy fighting to the south of us on Mindanao. So we sit between two battlefields, with

†Lieutenant General Masaharu Homma, commander of Japanese forces in the Philippines at the beginning of World War II. Homma was executed as a war criminal in 1946. This "accepted truth" is a good example of the wish-fulfilling rumors observable throughout the entire internment experience.

‡General Tomoyuki Yamashita, General Homma's replacement and in command of Japanese forces in the Philippines until their defeat in 1945. Yamashita was executed as a war criminal in 1946.

both the air above and that surrounding us dominated by Japanese. We know they can take our little island any day they wish. That's why such complete preparations have been made for the seven white women and the children on this Central to disappear as far inland as we can go to hide when the Central invasion occurs. We are sure the Japs will eventually be run from the Islands—from the South Pacific— but pending the arrival of friendly forces through the blockade the Japs have around us, we prefer a hermit's rustic existence to the horrors of a concentration camp, or whatever worse fate might be ours in the hands of the little yellow soldiers, who seem to suffer so frightfully from an inferiority complex in the presence of the larger Caucasians. For them no insult is too great to throw at the Americans, to try to compensate for this inferior feeling.

Since we must walk three hours over a narrow steep path, we think the soldiers would not risk exposing themselves in single file here to capture us. If they come to our Central it will be for: (1) food (rice) for their soldiers, (2) sugar—there are thousands of tons in the bodegas, or (3) steel—which they can secure by dismantling the sugar mills. There is such a shortage of steel in Japan that all available scrap iron is going back on empty transports which have left soldiers at the various battlefronts and occupied areas. In Davao, only a few hours after Jap soldiers had disembarked, their places in the holds were filled with scrap iron from dismantled bridges, old railroad tracks, cars, and any pieces of iron which might go into the hungry foundries of Osaka and other points.

The dry hot season is beginning after several months of rain. Avocados are ripe now. Too rich for me, but in such abundance it seems a shame to let them decay on the trees.

We wonder what is happening to our magazine subscriptions. Are the magazines accumulating on the Pacific coast, or will the publishers be wise and stop subscriptions now and extend them after the war when mail service is resumed? I ordered toys for the children from Sears-Roebuck, sent money, but they have not been received. Seventy-five dollars sent to Myron-Freeman Co. of Atlanta to buy more of wedding silver. We can only wonder if the merchants are holding the money or (more likely) the goods were already sent when war was declared. This kind of question we discuss and cannot answer.

Have you ever read the small print on the back of a steamship ticket? Most travelers never take the time. I wonder if "acts of God and of war" cause cessation of risk by other companies as well.

Sun., Mar. 29, 1942. Sunday dinner at the Yangco hacienda, "Floencia," named for Mrs. Yangco, Flora. Such quiet and peace here. None of the signs of war hysteria as on our Central. Curry dinner served by three boys, coming into dining room one behind the other, in spotless white uniforms with household "Y" embroidered on jacket pockets. Curry dinner is a popular mid-day meal. First rice, then meat deep in a curry sauce—chicken today—then grated coconut, fried shrimp, salted nuts, boiled eggs, and mango chutney sauce. This is often the complete meal, but not today. We had spaghetti with tomato sauce; a salad of pears, dates, and figs; cheeses; and ice cream and cake. Coffee and liqueurs in crystal decanters in sola on the floor below the dining room. The bar where we had drinks before dinner was also on this ground floor.

Conversation at dinner centered around the Dutch East Indies* and Java. Now we wondered if such beautiful and unusual hand-carved woodwork could be found. We also wondered about the quinine—cinchona tree—forests so zealously guarded by the Dutch as they have a world monopoly on quinine. Visitors are allowed free travel through rubber plantations, but not inside wire-fenced quinine farms for fear we might bring out a seed or a plant.

After dinner the usual bridge game for the women, poker for the men. Then a visit to the chicken farm and to the piggery. Here the swine were kept in concrete-floored stalls as clean as a house, because the floors are scrubbed daily and rinsed with a strong hose.

Strange system of ranking families on a Central causes much dissension and jealousy. Each family is numbered according to importance and salary. At the Hawaiian-Philippine Mr. Woods, the manager, is #1;

*Present-day Indonesia.

Mr. Oss, the chief engineer, is #2; Mr. Conant, the boiler engineer, is #3; Mr. McMaster, the office manager, is #4; Mr. Gibbs, outside chief, is #5; Mr. Brown, assistant engineer, is #6; and I, only a visitor, #7. There is an office, a theater (ciné), a commissary, and many bodegas. And of course there are the mill buildings.

Went to Bacolod shopping. A deserted town, store fronts boarded up, the few places open had almost no stock. There is not a spool of white thread for sale on the island. The army has bought all white thread for mosquito nets for soldiers and of course there is no more netting to be had. Even in screened houses we sleep under nets and fortunately nearly every household has an extra bed net (held high on a frame attached to bed head and foot) to be used by guests. Soldiers from the States would suffer greatly from the mosquito and other insect pests. The most tightly screened houses have numberless varieties of non-poisonous spiders, ants, moths, roaches, and lizards.

Meeting of the sugar planters at the Central to discuss plans for reopening the mill now that Quezon has left the island and gone to Australia. Planters do not want to plow under matured sugar cane, since if it is milled there is a chance of selling it at the close of the war. Feeling toward Quezon is bitter. Now that he has left P.I. the planters are openly contradicting his rulings. Hawaiian-Philippine Central cannot well reopen mill now, however, as only about 200 of the 4,000 employees still reside nearby. The barrio houses and the mill barracks have been emptied as workers fled to the hills.

Wed., Apr. 1, 1942. The air offense against Corregidor is lessening. Japanese first sent 64 planes, then 47, then groups of three. Now only two planes come at a time, due to heavy losses from anti-aircraft fire to large formations. Attack by two planes goes on steadily night and day, in an effort to exhaust the limited number of anti-aircraft gunners and use up the ammunition supplies.

The formal announcement that Canada would not send troops to Australia while Australia's very life is endangered does not make us think more of England or Canada. Canada's troops must be saved to protect England's precious population and not Australia's. It is too bad such distinctions of breeding and superiority must always be drawn by the Limeys.†

Thurs., April 2, 1942. Amah disappeared today, did not return from her breakfast. She's been singing and humming last year's love ballads all working hours and getting herself into a state for an Easter orgy. Yesterday was payday and, being Wednesday, her afternoon off. She was to return to spend the night at 7:00 P.M. But, afraid of the lovelorn look in her eyes, I asked her before her departure, in a bright green slack suit, if she planned to be back. "Yes ma'm," she replied, "at 7:00 P.M." She appeared at 8:00 o'clock this morning, saying she had had an attack of appendicitis yesterday during her time off and could not return. She said also that she thought she could not sleep upstairs with the children and me any longer. It was no surprise when she failed to reappear after breakfast. Some servants here are undependable and not worth even the small salaries paid. Whether we'd get better service and more honesty with higher wages, I don't know. But people who have been here many years say that these people do not comprehend our ideas of loyalty, integrity, and dependability.

Due to a shortage of diesel fuel the motor running the electric plant for the Central is cut off from 10:00 P.M. to 6:00 A.M. So there are no electric lights after 10:00 P.M. At least once each night, often three times, it is necessary to get up with Clay to take him to the bathroom, and sometimes to change his bed. The flashlight is dim but I will not change batteries until the light goes out. There have been no batteries on the island—in the commissary—for many months. I have six, enough for three changes, that I have to keep locked up as if they were pure gold.

Wed., Apr. 8, 1942. Easter has passed. It was another stretch of daylight in our unending series of lightness and darkness. Except for the calendar and a few hastily colored eggs for the children (with

†Slang term originally referring to British sailors and derived from use of lime juice to prevent scurvy on early sea voyages. Later the term often referred to all the British.

water colors) the day would have passed, like all others, in hopeful waiting. Went to Bacolod to look for table salt. Am using large, yellowish crystals ordinarily used for making ice cream. All glass shop windows are covered with heavy boards, and entrances to the few stores that are open are so barred that only one person may enter at a time. This would prevent rush of pedestrians into store during air raid and stealing from shelves which might result during or after the raid. The air raid alarm sounded while I was in the drug store. There were several other customers. My heart skipped a beat. I started to cross the street to join friends from the Central who were on the other side. A calm, elderly Philippine clerk in the drug store said, "Be not afraid. Stay where you are. The law forbids anyone going out of building after the alarm has sounded. All cars must stop where they are. There must be no motion and no confusion until the air raid is over or the 'all clear' is sounded."

The "all clear" sounded soon. No bombs dropped. A single Jap bomber overhead, evidently on patrol flight or reconnaissance.

Bad news: Maj. Richard I. Jones, who has been trying to get a definite agreement from Jim for an army allowance for me, has been transferred suddenly to Iloilo. Afraid this means further delay. Am anxious also for Jim to know we are safe. If he was told the request came from me to fill out allotment forms, he would know I was fine and in normal circumstances, i.e. needing money.

War news bad also. Troops on Bataan retreating. Base hospital back of the lines bombed for second time. Casualties heavy. Always after reports like that, I wonder ? ? ? If only we were not cut off from all communications.

Thurs., Apr. 9, 1942. "The Voice of Freedom" from somewhere in the Philippines, broadcast last night at 7:30, and news from KGEI, San Francisco, at 8:00 were both gloomy and contained chilling reports of fighting on Bataan. "Jap dive bombers and fighter planes are bombing and machine gunning our front lines, causing heavy losses. Bombing attacks on our rear are with greatest intensity since the beginning of the war. Attempts are being made to land Jap troops in our rear. A crisis should be reached soon. Attacking Japanese troops in superior numbers are using tanks against our center. The Japs are constantly receiving reinforcements." Our troops are thin, hemmed in on a small peninsula where the only retreat is into the sea and they are subjected to merciless, continuous, withering overhead machine-gunning and bombing without a plane of their own for protection or defense. It is ghastly. In the same broadcast: "And American planes are being ferried daily to England without let-up. The pilots who take the bombers and fighters are also returning by plane. Many pilots make three round trips a month to see that this flow of aid is not interrupted."

The Central mill will not reopen this season. Nearly all workers have been dismissed with two months' pay. Some of them have been here over twenty years and were told to leave the Central grounds and depart from Central-owned houses. Many came here as youths, married, raised families, and have sons working. The only home some have had. A sad plight, but a necessary war economy. There is enough fuel to run the electric light plant for 60 days only. After that we must use candles. There will be no kerosene for lamps. There has been a rush to buy candles and there are now none for sale. I have some dinner tapers, some Christmas gifts from Sacony (Standard Oil Co.), and others bought for ornamental use. Those special hand-dipped and hand-painted Christmas candles will doubtless serve a more utilitarian purpose than that for which they were designed.

BATAAN HAS FALLEN! Just announced, no details. Jim a prisoner-of-war! Horrible! Dear God, if Jim has to die let his death be a quick one. Let him not be left wounded on the battlefield, to be kicked and laughed at and passed by, by the victorious Japs. And let him not meet slow death in filth, hunger, and disease in a Japanese prison camp. Dear God, please!

American troops were outnumbered more than 10 to 1. 200,000 Japanese to less than 20,000 Philamericans.‡

Fri., Apr. 10, 1942. The things that go through one's mind in a crisis. During the long hours of last night, I recalled standing on the deck of

‡Phrase favored in the Philippines to describe joint efforts of Philippine and American forces.

the Greystone Castle, Junior, dressed in navy blue with crisp pique piping, a cocky white felt hat with 3" navy band and streamers down the back. That was the style then. Ship pulled to the pier in Shanghai about 7:00 A.M. With pounding heart I stood on the bridge with the captain, who knew I was coming to be married. You had on a white tie with colored embroidered dots.* When I first spotted you and pointed you out to the captain, he exclaimed, "He has on no tie, probably drunk, probably been up on a spree all night." Teasing of course.

We went to see the clerk of the court. To Mr. Jorge Bacolio (best man). Called the newspaper, and when the reporter asked, "What kind of flowers will you have?" turned quickly to a blinking Jim who admitted he had forgotten to order flowers. Thirty minutes before the wedding got a lovely white orchid shoulder corsage in time to wear with cool white short dress and large afternoon hat.

That night top floor Bayview Hotel, so high we did not need mosquito nets. Our first married dinner together in our room. Jim undressed in bathroom, asking me to let him know when I was ready to be tucked in. Lights out. Jim's voice, "We have forgotten something, *Darling of My Heart*. Let's kneel together and thank God for bringing us together." In the darkness I bit my lips to hold back tears and thanked God for sending men like Jim into the world. The next day both of us back on the Greystone Castle, Junior, to Hong Kong for honeymoon.

Saturday, April 11, 1942. Sent letter to Captain Leonard Cairns asking about Jim. Asked him to telephone me as I could not call him. Letter to him by messenger. Mail now takes a week for 50 kilometers, and then uncertain.

Tried to send cable to Jim's mother but Cebu radio dead. We shall go to the hills Tuesday. Recommended by Col. McClellan, new officer in charge of Negros.† We expect invasion soon of all Visäyan Islands. KGEI announcer mispronounces this, calling it Visaiyan, which is the central group of the Philippine Islands.

---

*As earlier indicated, EHV originally meant this diary to serve as an extended letter to her husband, hence the use of "you."
†EHV may be referring to Colonel Carter R. McLennan, executive officer of the island of Negros in 1942.

Sunday, April 12, 1942. Formation of eleven bombers flew directly over the Central. We are having at least two air alarms daily now. Five towns have been occupied by Japs on Cebu Island, which is very close by. One town, Toledo, across strait from San Carlos, Negros. Only reason to occupy Toledo would be in preparation for occupation of Negros.

CAMP IN THE HILLS
1942

Tuesday, April 14, 1942. Left Central at 7:00 A.M. for evacuation to camp in the hills. In the group: six women—Mdmes. Woods, Conant, Brown, Gibbs, McMaster, Vaughan; five children—June (age 21), Charlene (7), Beth (3), Clay (2), Douglas (6 weeks); three men—Mr. White, Mr. Conant, Mr. Brown. The animals included six dogs, four cats, 75 chickens. There were twelve servants—four women, eight boys. Forty cargodores,‡ with bamboo poles, carried our belongings. There were thirty carpenters and helpers already at camp. Not a house on the trail, but occasionally a bush-headed Negrito peered through underbrush at us. Many kilometers of the trail so steep that steps had been carved in mountain side and bamboo railing attached to poles erected to aid women and children, as well as men with burdens. Tiny baby went in an open-weave clothes basket, with securely fastened top, rope handles on each end, through which pole passed, carried by two cargodores.

First night seven people in my one-room house. For supper prepared cereal and canned fruit, with milk for children. First night no one slept, though all had thought we would. Too tired!

First night drinks in glasses or cups by candlelight, in celebration. No chairs. Sat on beds and served from two bridge tables. Most too

‡kargador [Tagalog]—porter, baggage carrier, stevedore.

tired to go to river for bathing so, like Mrs. Brown, had a "Russian" bath—perfume without benefit of water.

Workers who are brought in from outside will sleep in the least finished houses. Must keep fire burning at all times for food as no matches for starting new fire each meal. No mosquitoes! Houses of local materials cut from woods, except for flooring, with nipa roof. Houses six or seven feet off ground with tiny room for servants underneath. Outhouse a tiny duplicate of house. Kerosene lamps. Drinking water, from 5-gallon tins, is brought from spring two kilometers away.

John Cowper Paney, professor when I was student, said, "Culture is determined by extent of inner resources." Now we must draw on our inner resources. No reading material, no radios.

Thurs., Apr. 16, 1942. Report Japanese have landed on Negros. Someone suggested we go still farther into the hills. If we do we'll be out of hiding and back near the coast.

Combination amah and lavendera fled, also one of the carpenters left, to go back to the Central, when news was out that Japs were on Negros.

Stove is a work of art. A table about 30" high, 3 feet by 5 feet with an 8" layer of sand on top. On the sand are nine large rounded stones, approximately the same in size, grouped in threes. Three separate small wood fires can be built at one time between the stones of each group and a pot placed over each fire, stones being arranged close together or farther apart according to size of cooking utensil. Kitchen separated from main room by tiny 5-foot porch to allow smoke to escape instead of entering house. No flue to kitchen.

Fri., Apr. 17, 1942. Wife of one of carpenters came to wash children's clothes today. Surprised to find she spoke a little English. She set own wage, 6 pesos monthly, about $3.00. Hours 7:00–11:00 and 1:00–5:00. When not washing or ironing she will look after the children. Applied in native sarong which mountain women wear. Said she could not begin work now because had no clothes to work for Americano. Told her her clothes made no difference to me, but if she wanted an American dress I was sure I could find one to give her when I unpacked.

Before I could do that she came to work today in a brilliant rose-pink nightgown, which she said she had borrowed from a neighbor, proud as a peacock because she was "dressed like Americanos."

News that was brought in by cargodores, still bringing chow boxes and clothing from the Central, is that Cebu has fallen and Iloilo has been invaded. Negros may as well be in Japanese hands as approaches to the only two harbors of the island are in territory they now control. There is not even a battery radio set in our camp, so what news comes in comes by letter from husbands still at the Central.

Another group came in yesterday, Filipino members of camp to fill the last of the incomplete houses. Mr. and Mrs. Diaz; three children (ages 11, 10, and 7); two girl servants and one houseboy; Miss Ganahan, R.N., formerly with Dr. Jardelega, who will live in our hospital house and who has her sister to be her companion; and a girl servant who will cook and clean for the hospital. Nurse busy first morning treating children's mosquito bites (mosquitoes have found us) which had been scratched and had begun to be infected. Also dressed an infected cut on Mrs. McMaster's arm and bandaged foot of a workman who had a deep wound where tree fell on it. Though some members of camp wondered if we needed a hospital or a nurse, wisdom of having them already clear.

Mr. Thompson has not come in yet. He is a bachelor to all intents and purposes, though he's been mated for years to a native woman who lives in Manila with their mestizo children.

A peddler was just in with two bolos for sale, holding them out in front of him and calling out in Visäyan dialect. Sejio has been asking for a new bolo. I gave him one when he first came to us. Every Filipino now carries a bolo attached to his belt. Used for cutting cane, scaling fish, eating at table, and for many other uses. Peddler's cheaper bolo was $1.50, its wooden sheath flashily decorated in strips of polished brass and handle carved into a dog's head, but Sejio advised against getting as he said price was too high. No matter how far one penetrates into forest, peddlers follow the trail.

Our houses still have no doors nor windows and until these can be built we put some of our boxes of food across top of the front and back steps each night to keep stray dogs out. Doors and windows will be the last things added to houses as this is dry season now and we would probably leave houses open for ventilation anyway. But, we have heard, rainy season is severe here. Rains for weeks without a let-up. I would like a floor under the house for playroom for children, if possible. Boxes of food are brought in as the men may come to them. They were stored in boxcars at the Central. I have asked cargodore many times to bring up suitcases with our clothes. I have only one change and the children barely enough to see them through one day. To one who has had no small children, toys and personal belongings, such as unbreakable cups and plates, rounded spoons, blunted forks, may seem non-essential and the last thing to be brought in, but to me they seem far more necessary than the ornamental rugs I saw freshly unpacked and airing.

Sun., Apr. 19, 1942. I am drunk today, as drunk as one can be and still be aware of the world about me. Beth and Clay need their faces washed and I don't care. Sejio is already complaining at having to bring water so far for drinking and bathing, and anyway why do children's dirty faces matter now?

Two men came from Central this morning and Nora asked the five other white women in for pre-lunch drinks to hear the news of the outside world. The news is that the Japs are ten minutes away, by plane, having occupied Iloilo airport, or one and a half hours away by boat. Our American friends in Cebu and in Iloilo have suffered the cruelest torture at hands of Japanese soldiers who are turned loose on small islands with no one to check their sadistic pleasures. White women are a prize. The army advises us that if a message comes to our camp from Japanese to come to headquarters to register to pay no attention to the summons—though there is threat of death if we do not come. A handful of women who answered the summons in Hong Kong and in our neighbor city, Cebu, were put in a brothel for use of Japanese soldiers. So the U.S. Army advises white women not to be captured alive. There are two or three guns in camp for hunting. How we are to end our lives was not explained. We giddily took a second and a third drink.

I would kill Beth and Clay before destroying myself. These tiny bits of blond humanity who crave and expect constant sympathy and affection, whose every scratch and "tumble down" calls for immediate attention, they could not be left to cry to unresponsive ears nor to hold out their tiny arms to a scornful rebuff. So, because it's our first Sunday in camp and the war has closed in around us, we drank too much in our tiny mountain hideout. We are aware that a white woman cannot hide in a brown population, that any one of hundreds of Filipinos would bring Japanese soldiers here for as little as 10 cents.

Some unpacked toys came today by cargodore. Eugene Field's touching poem "Little Boy Blue" ran through my head as I put Clay's toy dog and soldier side by side on the newly constructed shelf. More suitcases of clothes arrived also.

Took children to river for all to have baths since writing first part of today's notes. Stream clear and swift, had difficulty holding Clay and the soap. Sejio helped, gave Clay a good scrubbing and brought him back to the house over stony pathway.

Saw three monkeys, one very large, two smaller ones, playing in the trees near the houses. So now we are afraid monkeys will come in our windowless, doorless houses tonight. This fear of monkeys at least diverted our minds from fear of torture by the Japs and so ended a most unhappy day.

Mon., Apr. 20, 1942. Motherhood is a strange phenomenon. Today I gave myself entirely to my children, responding to their every whim and wish. In the afternoon I gasped for breath after having chased Georgia Miss* with them. Back in the house I let them ride my back, glanced in the mirror expecting to see my face aglow with heavenly love and beauty. Not so! Instead my hair was stringy, my skin parched from overexposure to sun, nails dirty and cracked, and instead of a look of beneficence I looked a hag. Neither Jim nor the children would want me as unkempt as I was and I suddenly recalled having heard a father say it was too bad children had any of the parental attentions showered upon them before the age of three and that such

---

*Vaughan family pet, a dog named after the home states of EHV and her husband.

attentions, in many ways, were a waste of time. So ideas of motherhood are in confusion. I love the children, but feel that to neglect myself too much for them is an unrecoverable waste of time. There was no time to think of Japs. News came in by carrier that Tokyo had been bombed.† Maybe our end is not so near.

Jealousy of the women here is so apparent and so petty at a time like this. Some of them spend day in and day out with no other thoughts than to see that no one else gets more than they. Also some women forget that while their husbands discussed what might or might not be wise to bring, there was no man in my family to bring fresh fruits, so I brought what seemed reasonable and logical and an imposition on no one. Phooey to jealousy!

Tues., Apr. 21, 1942. Negrito women in camp to sell vegetables today, dressed in rags resembling American dresses, necks open to waist, revealing with unconcern large drooping breasts. In native dialect they told Miss Ganahan they would fight to protect Americanos if Japanese came to camp, if we treat Negritoes right. (By "right" they meant pay good price for produce.) To help Americanos they will dig holes covered with brush on mountain pathway to trap soldiers who will fall in, also will shoot the soldiers from ambush with homemade bows and arrows. But if we don't treat the Negritoes right they might do the same to Americanos instead of Japanese. So went a very serious conversation in strange babbles. When it was over and interpreted in English we assured the Negrito women by nods and smiles that we would treat them right and they could kill Japs and not Americanos.

Thurs., Apr. 23, 1942. Letter by messenger from Mr. Woods that Japs are on Guimeras Island‡ scouring each inch for food for army. Japa-

---

†On April 18, 1942, sixteen USAAF bombers commanded by Army Air Force officer James H. Doolittle attacked Tokyo from the carrier *Hornet*. After dropping their cargo of bombs, the planes flew on to airfields in China, where fifteen planes were ultimately recovered. Of the 80 crewmen, 71 survived, one was killed during a parachute jump, and eight were captured by the Japanese in China and court-martialed. Five were given life sentences, and three were executed.

‡Small island at the southern end of Guimaras Strait between Negros and Panay islands.

nese women are fighting along with men in Iloilo and some Jap soldiers are mere boys, evidently boys and their mothers shooting and killing, living like wild animals and as ferocious.

Nauseating smell and taste of cold-storage chicken and beef. Had chicken from the ice plant at Central today and simply cannot swallow it, though Sejio and I spent a long time preparing it. Due to shortage of fuel for running the engines the cold-storage temperature in the ice plant has been raised and the meat is slightly "high." Some people here like the taste but I shall go meatless before trying to eat it again. However, I shall cook it for the children as the spoiled taste does not bother them, and can only hope the extra cooking will destroy germs.

Fri., Apr. 24, 1942. Mr. Thompson came today with much news. Only two white families were caught in Iloilo, Mr. and Mrs. Kerr, with two small children, and Mr. and Mrs. McCreary, whose children are in the hills with other American and British families of Iloilo.

Mr. Woods, according to Mr. Thompson, had heard that Col. H. B. Carlton of Cebu had seen Jim on Bataan and knew him and he is one who said Jim was a 2nd lieut. I shall get in touch with Col. Carlton as soon as the war is over as I think he will be a good man to help find Jim if he is sick or wounded.

Twice fresh vegetables have come up from Central. We gather at one of the nipa huts to divide them, sitting on the floor. There were four bundles of beets, three bunches of bananas, five packages shelled lima beans, three bunches parsley, four bunches white turnips, three bunches asparagus, twenty peppers, four cucumbers, and five bunches spinach. Divided between eight households. Those who got lima beans and no spinach last week got the reverse this time. It is a great help to get these. Also, in an effort to dispose of commissary goods, a list of cases was sent from house to house and we could buy, cases only. An assortment of commodities in each case. In case 51, which I took: 17 cans fruit cocktail, 5 cans cherries, 1 niblet corn, 3 cans pineapple juice, 4 cans sliced peaches, 1 can without label. Am glad there was no bird-seed in this case. One case 14 packages bird-seed and 10 quarts dill pickles. One member took an astounding amount of mustard and apple sauce. There were 29 cases of Campbell soup, a few cases of fruit juices (one kind), and a few cases of vegetables (one kind). All went quickly. The unlabeled can did not bother me, for our first day in camp I unpacked the first chow box with two-weeks' supply of assorted canned goods and then during my first trip to the outhouse Beth and Clay removed labels from all cans. Since then we have no menu for a meal and when a can is opened for supper it may be pepper-pot soup, evaporated milk, or crushed pineapple. Having no refrigerator we eat at once whatever is opened.

Huge ants are lurking around opened food, one-inch black fellows with legs so long they walk high off ground. Ants evidently do not sting as children have picked them up with no ill effect. Beth is happy with the unending variety of large bugs, worms, and other live creatures infesting camp.

Sat., Apr. 25, 1942. Mr. Woods came to camp today and named it "No Belly Ache." Its real name is Binagsukan, or, The End of the Road. Sejio returned from trip to the Central. He left yesterday. He brought back new two-toned yellow and brown shoes in his hands. Also brought children's tub, serving cabinet, and clay water jug.

Sun., Apr. 26, 1942. Curtains put up today. Two old scalloped blue bedspreads which, when split down middle, make curtains already edged and hemmed at bottom. Also, with material from local bodega, made curtain to tie to cross beam of roof to cut off a part of bedroom for bathing. Cloth like heavy white canvas, filter cloth used in sugar mill, is the same material supplied each person for sending bedroll to camp.

Windows put up today. Squares of nipa tied to tree branches. No hinges. Windows tied to house with heavy wire. A long pole stuck in hole in base of window and another hole cut in window sill holds window propped open. To close we simply remove stick, or pole. For half-open window will have to cut other poles to desired lengths.

A tri-motored Jap bomber flew low over camp this morning and few people even glanced up. We have become reconciled to the fact that we shall probably lose our lifetime collections of household effects in this country occupied by enemy troops. We can do nothing in the face of thousands, possibly hundreds of thousands, of armed hordes. Sometimes I feel equally as helpless to prevent the destructive playfulness of my two rip-roaring, orphaned offspring.

When the children are most annoying I wonder if Pearl Buck might not have been right when she said, in effect, that housekeeping is deadening for a woman. Then I recall how Jim and I, while engaged, sat in darkness watching the lights on Manila Bay and timidly agreed that we'd like a family someday. And I remember, too, the morning in Iloilo, at Letty Tyron's house, and how the three visitors admired Letty's layette on which she was working. Doug, her husband, was decorating nursery furniture with pink and blue bears, ducks, and rabbits.

At lunch that day I told Jim my mind was made up, I wanted a family at once, for I wanted to be making pretty baby things like the ones I had seen and I wanted Jim to be painting little pink and blue animals on tiny white furniture. How Jim laughed. But he said, "You are the one to say when you want a family. I think we can afford a baby now. Are you sure you want what might be a little duplicate of me?"

We anxiously and happily waited for Beth—named by Jim over my protest at having two by the same name. Before leaving Mission Hospital I asked Dr. Waters how soon I could safely have the second baby as one was not a family. How friends laughed at Jim because he had to go to bed for 24 hours after the strain of my having Beth. Clay was as eagerly awaited as Beth. Jim knew the second would be a boy and he wanted to name him after Jim's father, who died of cancer when Jim was about twelve. Jim's happiest memories of childhood were of his father. We were shocked to learn that Dr. Waters was going back to the States, on vacation, but were relieved to have the woman missionary doctor take over his duties at the hospital. Dr. Dorothy Chambers had coffee brought to the delivery room early on Sunday morning and she, Jim, and I drank to the new one not yet arrived. Then I went under ether and Jim went to corridor-tramping again.

Tues., Apr. 28, 1942. A whole pig cooked over charcoal here at camp, was delicious. Pig raised off ground in a floored pen. Each household paid one peso, as pig cost eight pesos.

Wed., Apr. 29, 1942. To the river for a cold bath and a hair wash. Sitting on rock, in red bathing suit, drying hair, when Jap plane flew low overhead. Rushing water had prevented my hearing it sooner. Ducked into water, then laughed at my own action.

Returned to house to have old Filipino woman, wife of one of carpenters, rush toward me explaining in her limited English, "Your husband come! See!" My heart jumped. A man in khaki shorts and shirt, wearing a tropical helmet, knapsack on back, water jug at side, coming down our hidden trail. There were carriers behind him bringing wooden cases, suitcases, bedroll, and bundles of all sizes. He was tall and slim like Jim but I knew at a second glance that it was not he.

It was Mr. Brown, whose wife was my next-door neighbor. The Filipino woman had heard a name which she confused with Vaughan. The momentary shock completely unnerved me.

There is no news at all of conditions of thousands of American prisoners from Bataan, but since it is known that there is insufficient food for the Japanese soldiers, conditions of their prisoners must be horrible. I cannot let my mind dwell on this.

Mr. Brown brought war news of lull on all fronts except Russian, where the Russians continue to advance. Corregidor still subjected to heavy raids and still holds out. Saravia airport, in sight of Hawaiian-Philippine Central and built partially by Central labor, was bombed three times today by a group of twelve Jap planes. Near enough to shake Central buildings.

Thurs., Apr. 30, 1942. The things Mr. Woods thinks of! First we had a supply of kerosene tins waiting for us for holding water. A few days later larger covered garbage cans (new) were delivered to each house to replace these. And today mud scrapers were attached to both our front and back steps in preparation for the rainy season which is ahead for us. An incinerator has been built for camp garbage.

Venison today. Deer killed by one of the laborers at camp. We had all we could eat which, seasoned with bay leaves and cloves, was cooked in Dutch oven and was delicious.

Clay has had bad cold for several days. At 2:00 A.M. and again at 4:00 had coughing spells and began to strangle on discharge in throat. Carried him to nurse's house to have throat swabbed. Nurse cleaned throat with swab, but scolded me for bringing him out without covering. Said I should have left him in bed and come over alone. Couldn't do this with him gasping.

Onions and avocados. There is a bumper crop of these two commodities and each family is sent an allotment from the Central twice a week. As other vegetables and fruits are short, we are glad to have these, but I never want to see another avocado. We get the fruit green, ten large ones today, but all ripen at the same time so we eat them three times a day to keep from having them go to waste. Beth has learned to eat a small amount but Clay will not touch except to play with a whole one as a ball. Had native large leaf spinach today and Sejio added nice variety by putting tiny green tomatoes in with the greens. A nice flavor.

Yesterday Japs dropped leaflets over Bacolod telling civilians not to fear the Japanese army, that when they came they would only fight soldiers. Civilians should go ahead calmly planting and harvesting their crops and go ahead with their fishing as usual. (For whom?) Bombs previously dropped on Bacolod and the machine-gunning of the town by Japs did not make the civilians believe these leaflets.

When at 3:00 A.M. had to go out with Georgia Miss, the full moon caused me to remember reading that the Dutch East Indies could not be defended against night-bombing due to brilliance of the tropical moon. Bright nights mean greater chance of invasion and attack.

Sat., May 2, 1942. My sewing machine was brought in tied to a long bamboo pole carried by two men. Machine and men covered with dust. Several new and expensive electric machines were at the Central. No good here. This treadle machine was given me by a family moving to the States two years ago. Little sale value then and now. But after the war its price will doubtless be high. Sejio will build a floor under part of the house and the machine will be placed there for anyone at camp.

Sejio cutting pingas* today of different lengths, shorter ones for less

*Poles for carrying weight across the shoulder.

heavy cargo and longer for two full cans of water. Strange as it seems, it is easier for boys to bring two 5-gallon cans of water balanced on ends of pinga than one tin alone on shoulder.

Shortage of calendars in camp and those who have them tear off sheets at end of month and pass on to those without calendars who are happy to have them. There's been no mail since last Dec. 8. Most stores had not received theirs, so the calendar shortage can be understood.

Mon., May 4, 1942. Heavy trees being felled on mountain side to build another bodega for camp. First bodega built already full of unshelled rice, unrefined sugar, unrefined salt—which is very necessary in tropics where people lose body salt in perspiration. These are all products of this island, Negros. Flour, milk, and other imported products are not available.

All work on houses stopped until bodega is finished. Houses still need kitchen window, back door or gate, servants' room floor, and other finishing touches. Want to get additional supplies in before Japs strip the island. Drying meat. Have a piece of beef—whacked off carcass with bolo—cut in thin strips, salted with sea salt, drying under mosquito net, to keep off flies. Bring the meat in at night and put in covered pan to keep monkeys from stealing. Dried skin and remnants of baked pig very tasty with native greens and sweet potato leaves.

Nights cold up here. Children not accustomed to sleeping under cover. Had to sew tapes to sides of blankets to tie them to beds and now children cannot pull loose.

Tues., May 5, 1942. Venison again today for camp. All eat the same thing the same day due to jealousy. Each houseboy was going into hills to bargain with Negritoes. Some houseboys were more successful in bringing back supplies than others, so due to complaints this practice stopped. Now boys who find anything for sale must report it to Mr. Diaz, who speaks Visäyan, who then buys supplies and prorates to households on basis of members in family. Beth and Clay, together, count as one, so my allotment of eggs yesterday was four, compared to two eggs to a woman who is alone. This woman complained loudly to me at this, saying her dog requires an egg every day and she saw no reason why I should get twice the number allotted her. This comparison of dog care with child care makes my temperature rise!

Wed., May 6, 1942. Visitors at camp today. A patrol of eight Filipino armed soldiers just "looking around" and refusing to tell from whence they came or where they were headed, spent an hour chatting with Filipinos in camp and finding some were from provinces on the other islands. Said they left their headquarters early this morning and had eaten only one cookie each and a coconut apiece today. Also Mr. L. D. Robinson, manager of San Carlos Sugar Milling Co., came in today, dripping in perspiration, panting, and limping. He will have a grass shack built in our camp to which he can flee when San Carlos is invaded. There is a mountain trail leading to San Carlos from our camp, to the south to the Hawaiian-Philippine Central, to the north to San Carlos. Mr. Robinson said of today's hike to the camp that the next time he came it would be to stay—that no one would torture himself with that grueling walk for pleasure.

Beautifying of the grounds has begun in earnest. Began when the houseboys came back from long trek to the spring with orchids as well as cans of drinking water. Each houseboy refused to be outdone by the others so large "air plants," a parasitic, non-flowering, long-leafed plant, began to appear in hastily constructed bamboo baskets on the corners of rock walls for which all the boys are gathering uniform-sized stones which they suspend from the house floor with a strip of rattan.

Thurs., May 7, 1942. Corregidor has fallen! America's last stronghold in the P. Islands has had to surrender due to exhaustion of food and ammunition supplies and a complete blockade by Jap. forces. In the same news brought in, in typed form from KGEI broadcast taken down in shorthand by Central office stenographer, was a lengthy report of increased strength of U.S. bomber units attacking occupied Europe and Germany from English bases. Yet there is not one American bomber on this greater American soil to protect American-born and bred loyal citizens. It is difficult to understand—repeated reports of our efforts to save English homes and English lives—but American lives in the P.I.—what is the U.S. attitude? Jim, my husband, who, typical of many young Americans in the P.I., came here in adult life because business opportunities beckoned, always was proud of his U.S. citizenship. Every centavo we put aside was for our permanent home—a farm in Mississippi—at a not too far distant date. And the children, we have already discussed what U.S. college they should attend from reading U.S. newspapers and magazines (of course a little late). There were times an air-mail edition for foreign subscribers took up this lag in our lives. Also we listened to Charlie McCarthy, Ben Bernie, and other typical American broadcasters on shortwave. We are still as American as though our residence were on American soil. So why have we been left to such mental torture? Why has not aid come to us in the face of invasion by the cruelest, most sadistic of peoples? All of America knows of the rape of Nanking. Why let the rape of the P.I. take place without opposition?

Jim, I now know, is either dead or a Jap prisoner, which is worse than death. As long as Corregidor stood I could ease my aching heart with hope, however distant, that he had escaped with the handful of soldiers who arrived safely on Corregidor before Bataan fell. It must be necessary and good military strategy to let the Philippines go to the Japanese without assistance to American civilians while the aid we feel a right to expect goes to other, to non-American parts of the world. But the wound inflicted upon us is deep. We wonder if people at home know there is an American civilian population, like themselves in every respect, living in the P.I., Americans who were never warned of impending danger from the war and who have been seemingly forgotten while their personal property was destroyed, their health undermined by food deficiencies, and their lives taken by murderers from a land at war with the U.S. The Japanese are not at war with the P.I. and we suffer solely because of our race and citizenship. Perhaps events will change their course soon. We can only say, like dear old Aunt Susie in Ocean Springs, "Mizpah!" And "Remember us, Uncle Sam. We trust you with all our hearts. We know we're really not forgotten."

Fri., May 8, 1942. Two loaves of bread today, two chickens from cold storage at the Central, two kilos (four pounds) roast, two kilos of liver, and sixteen eggs. This was first chicken and first liver in a month at camp. Cooked it all today. We have no ice and extremely warm daytime temperature. Chicken goes into soup, roast for tomorrow and succeeding days, and the liver for one week, probably. No bread since entering camp 'til yesterday when we received not one but two loaves, and two more today. All from bakery in Bacolod, rushing to use up flour before the Japs arrive. We had to pay the human carriers who brought it up.

Sat., May 9, 1942. "And so it goes ad infinitum. Even fleas have small fleas to bite 'em." Though Pope in the eighteenth century wasn't literally thinking of fleas when this was written, we are in constant worry from fleas. Where do so many fleas come from? Monkeys have fleas. Dogs simply can't make any headway scratching. Today, sweeping leaves from the yard with a bunch of sticks tied together, I noticed fleas hopping from the ground to my ankles.

Had a fire in camp at 4:00 A.M. Fire burned through bottom of McM.'s stove, fell to the floor, burned hole in floor and caught nipa side of the kitchen. Perhaps a monkey spread embers left on sand. This seems possible. Fortunately a late afternoon rain had left the nipa damp, so fire was extinguished with a few kerosene tins of water from McM.'s. and other houses. Fear of fire has been in minds of all of us. Dry bark shavings left from trees used in houses, nipa rubbish, dry leaves, all make fire hazard imminent. Having seen such evidence of fire destruction, crossing the burned area coming into camp, we know how widespread and uncontrolled fires can be in forest areas. We are in the midst of a forest, the plan being to leave all trees overhanging and overhead vines uncut to protect us from sight by enemy planes. But we have cleaned, to some extent, the ground immediately surrounding homes as forest fire could consume us in a few grisly moments. The river is near and is wide, clear, and shallow with many rocks protruding from its surface, so if necessity forces it one might sit atop a stone in comparative safety with feet in freezing water while woodland around turned to ashes. It was a joyous sight a few days ago to see fire extinguishers from the Central coming into camp. Each house at the Central is supplied with a large extinguisher and the buildings likewise protected. These will do no good if the Japs set fire to the Central as there will at that time be no one at the Central to use them. So they are in the bodega for the time being.

Sejio brought in more orchids and some ground palms and flowering bushes when he returned from the spring with water today. Now decorating a plot around Beth's and Clay's swings and will then beautify walk to children's reading room.

Due to the situation of camp on a steeply sloping mountain side, occupants on one side climb to reach their nipa "telephone booth," or antipolos† as they are called locally. Occupants in the five houses in the upper half of camp go down. As someone remarked, the round trip entails some amount of climbing and slipping no matter where you are located. My walk begins with a steep decline and we will cut steps in the stony earth and pack solidly with stones of almost uniform size. Large rocks for a walk border are already being accumulated in piles before being fitted together in the border. It is difficult to keep the grounds clean now as this month here corresponds to October back in the U.S. The slightest breeze brings showers of yellow, brown, and red leaves. After three months of drought, foliage of all kinds shows an end-of-the-season look. The dry season is the colorful time in P.I.

We had three varieties of bananas come in today. The sweetest variety here is those that are green when ripe. Then there are those that are yellow when ready to eat, and the red banana, red of skin and meat.

Have come to realize how necessary a father is for the children. Discipline seems hard here because dangers faced by the children are so numerous. There is no auto traffic to fear, no shocks from touching open sockets (this happened to Beth), but there are falls from rocks, walking too near the swift river, picking up refuse around camp, and putting poisonous berries or herbs in their mouths. (Beth cried two

---

†The opposite pole; the direct opposite (strictly defined). Here, a euphemism for outhouse.

hours because her tongue burned when she consumed beans from a
favorite flowering plant of Mrs. B.) Clay had already humiliated me by
pulling leaves from the same lady's garden. It seems a warning word
from Jim was worth a dozen from me. The children see too much of
me. I'm taken for granted and big "don'ts" and little "don'ts" all assume equal importance.

I remember the first morning after the first night in camp. We had all
been tired, very tired, after the long walk the day before. Not only
were most of us not accustomed to climbing up sides of ravines, pulling ourselves by vines and underbrush, tortuously and precariously
picking a footing down steep inclines, but this attended by constant
fear men carrying our children might lose their footing. Trying also to
keep in sight of long lines of human beasts of burden. We arrived in
camp dead tired but spent the rest of the day checking our luggage,
unpacking bedrolls, putting up children's beds, and trying to get ready
for a night's rest in this quiet, peaceful spot. Next morning we peeped
from windowless, doorless houses across to neighbors trying to make
sufficient privacy to dress and ask, "How did you sleep?" "Not so well
as I had expected" was the reply, and a similar answer came to the
same query at all other houses.

Each day I had said, "Tomorrow will be different." Then I recalled a
story of an unhappy stepfather who tried to keep to himself the cruel-
ties of his wife to her son by another marriage. The husband kept
repeating to himself after every unpleasant episode, "Tomorrow will
be different," but it never was. So I have come to with a jolt. How
stupid I have been, thinking tomorrow would be an easier day, that
tomorrow would be different.

Tues., May 12, 1942. Four weeks in camp today. But my mind is on
the past, not camp. Two other wars have touched my life, but strangely
my memories of those other wars are mainly pleasant. First, the Civil
War, or as Grandfather always said, "The War Between the States,"
going passionately into the distinction between the two terms. "This,"
he said, "was not war between fellow nationals, friends, relatives, and
countrymen. No, it was a war between separate states. The autono-
mous political decision of each state was agreed to by its citizens. This

was a war of conflicting states, not of citizens of one federal state," he contended. Men followed the will of the state in this time of state crises and dissensions as men follow the laws of the nation in times of international conflict. Grandfather saw active service on the Confederate side during the whole of the war, coming through unscathed but with a devotion to the Southland needing to be salved of her wounds, in need of caressing understanding like a sick mother who has lost her sons and is near death herself. Grandfather knew pain from enduring it, he knew heartbreak from experiencing defeat of his noblest ideals of statehood because of the might of gunpowder. Grandfather did not bury his defeat in solitude. After darkest days he became mayor of our town to hold out a guiding hand to its populace in a united struggle to establish new foundations on ash-blackened ground. And Grandfather carried his sympathetic ideals to the State Legislature. He died from an attack suffered at a reunion of the Confederate soldiers. (How he loved and looked forward to these reunions.)

My home town declared a legal holiday for the funeral of Cap'n. Mac,‡ as he was lovingly called by university officials of this small college town and by Negro garbage collectors alike. This is among my earliest memories. The tangible part of Grandfather's war experience to me is in the collection of pre-war and War Between the States literature he left to me. Rare books, some passionately prejudiced, some more liberal, a few illustrated ones with sketches of the horrors of war—more frightening than serpentine drawings for a copy of Milton's *Paradise Lost*. A part of Grandfather's library was my most concrete heritage from him. My grandmother talked mostly of her romance with Grandfather during the war. When Grandmother's father, brothers, and all male relations had gone to the battlefront as it slowly pushed farther South, closer to her own doorstep, her mother became sick and was afraid she was dying. Grandmother was sixteen years old. Her mother asked Grandfather, a slip of a boy not much older than sixteen himself, to marry Grandmother then and there. (He was from a family of life-long friends.) Great-grandmother wanted to be assured

‡EHV's grandfather, John James Crittenden McMahan, was at one time mayor of Athens, Georgia. A bank president in Athens, McMahan later joined his daughter Leila Mae's husband, Van Head (EHV's father), in a men's clothing store, Head & McMahan.

that when she died her daughter had someone to look after her. So a marriage service between two frightened youths occurred and Grandfather returned to the front. Years later he returned a sad, matured man to find his bride waiting. A strange love story, yet theirs was one of the happiest marriages I have known.

That's the War Between the States as I heard it first-hand, told with twinkling eyes by Grandmother, who long outlived Grandfather. Grandmother smiled even as she described the days when there was no food in her house and Great-grandmother kept her in bed all day, saying if she stayed still she wouldn't have quite such a big appetite nor miss her meals so much if she should happen to sleep through one.

The next war I recall is World War I. Too young to realize the horrors of war. My father too old for service, three brothers too youthful, but the oldest son of the family was a student at Annapolis at the time the U.S. entered the war. His class was rushed through the four-year course in three, the first class to finish in the shortened period. (Was it the only one ever?) As he was slightly under age when he entered the Naval Academy he had the distinction of being one of the youngest ever to receive a navy commission. His service consisted of going on an almost uneventful transport escort. The Armistice was signed soon after he arrived in France. My personal memory of World War I is limited to the sight of khaki-clad troop-laden cars passing through my home town. On one occasion I stood near one of these trains as its uniformed occupants whirred past. A small white card fluttered from one window and fell at my feet. When I picked it up it had a printed name, address, and a note at the bottom—"I'm a lonely soldier. Please write. Pvt.——." My mother forbade my writing, though I was sure at the time that some heart-torn soldier was waiting for my letter.

Today, May 12, word came to camp by messenger that we, the island of Negros, had surrendered with the other Visäyan Islands, to the Japanese. Terms are being arranged. Our fate will be known soon! For the first time my fears have become a realization.

Now we will come face-to-face with our conquerors, that is inevitable. Perhaps my training in racial differences and work with blacks of the American South and with other racially different groups may make for tolerance. I hope my captors are tolerant, but that they also be ardent students of sociology is too much to hope for!

It comes back clearly, an interest in people, all peoples, has really led me here—a prisoner of war, with a mere handful of other white people—in the heart of the Philippines. A dear old soul, perhaps dead now, Dr. T. J. Woofter, an old-timer of the oldest chartered state university in the U.S.,* first awakened my interest in sociology. I wanted to study what he taught. When there were many in my family in college at the same time and others nearing college age, I asked Dr. Woofter if he knew how I might relieve the financial burden on my family. My senior year I worked in his office four hours a day and worth far more than I received each month for services were the daily contacts with this tired teacher and administrator who the next year was added to the emeritus list, due to ill health. The day will always stand out when Dr. Woofter's car drove up to our house and he called me from a lawn croquet game with my younger brother and sister to ask me if I should like to go to Vanderbilt University to study for a Ph.D. in sociology. I tensed, waiting for his next sentence. "I have received a letter from Vanderbilt," he said, "offering me a student fellowship for next year. I am to pick the student to go. I am offering you this fellowship if you want it. Talk it over with your family and then come see me." Then came the year in Nashville. One rainy, dreary day Dr. Will W. Alexander came to lecture on race relations in the South. I had heard of Dr. Alexander and the Rosenwald Foundation's Commission on Interracial Cooperation, of which he was director.† When I spoke to Dr. Alexander later he told me to come to see him in Atlanta during vacation. I went and stayed to work for the Commission.

Dr. Howard W. Odum walked into the Commission office one day. When we were introduced Dr. Odum's eyes twinkled and instead of "How are you?" he began, "A fire mist and a planet, a crystal and a cell."

*The University of Georgia at Athens, Georgia.
†Established by Julius Rosenwald (1862–1932), the Rosenwald Fund had as its chief purpose the improvement of education for black Americans.

Amazed when he hesitated, I added the next line, "A jelly fish and a saurian, and caves where cavemen dwell."

Then he added, "Then a sense of law and order, and a face turned from the clod." To which I concluded, "Some call it evolution, but others call it God."‡

So began a friendship which took me to the University of North Carolina, where Dr. Odum headed the School of Social Science, in which I spent twelve months in research and study. When I had covered the catalogue's offerings of the university I felt ready to contribute to the problems of the society which I had so thoroughly picked apart. I did work in the office of the Resettlement Administration in Raleigh, N.C., then to Washington to serve in a study of living standards, called the Consumer Purchases Study.

But a simple verse tormented me which said in effect:

There was this little boy who lived in Italy,
. . . . (Can't remember)
There came a letter from this boy across the sea.
"Dear Little Foreign Friend," it said plainly as could be,
Now I wonder who is foreign—that other boy or me

I wanted to see other people, other races, Orientals especially. So I decided to accept the invitation of a former college roommate to visit her in Shanghai. She had married the Yale suitor who had courted her even when she visited in my home in Georgia.

So a round-the-world ticket resulted. The unloading of scrap iron at Kobe and Yamata now assumes new significance. Passengers could go ashore only with Japanese guards. The ship's captain stated, "It isn't that the Japanese have anything to hide that they are so strict in censorship, it's that they don't want the world to know how little they have." He was a nice captain but I think he was mistaken then.

War threatened China. My friends returned to the U.S. I visited Manila, sojourned there to teach at the Filipino State University in Manila. Then I met Jim.

‡From "Each in His Own Tongue" by W. H. Carruth (1859–1924).

Wed., May 13, 1942. Last night all this went through my mind again. How many years can be covered in a second's dreaming time?

Almost six years have passed since I returned to the States to make preparations for marrying Jim. I would come back to live among the Filipino people.

I was in Davison-Paxon Co. on Peachtree Street in Atlanta ordering calling cards. When the clerk asked where to send the cards when the engraving was finished, I hesitated to answer—being 12,000 miles from Manila, and a month away from marrying. So, giving her a number to call, I said that I (really a member of the family) would pick them up. Bought a new suitcase also, having initials (not yet mine) stamped on the leather. It amused me wondering whether Jim would notice that I already had his initials on the luggage when I should get off the ship to marry him.

This went through my mind last night as the Japanese were planning how to dispose of us, our property, and perhaps our lives, in conference with our surrendered leaders, leaders who had had no ammunition, few soldiers, and now no food. Will our captors leave us alone here? What future is ahead for Jim, for Beth, Clay, and me?

A feast for supper. Midget peas, tenderloin roast, spiced pears, canned Irish potatoes, avocado salad, Jacob's cookies (biscuits), prune whip, and coffee with cream. The peas, pears, and potatoes were being hoarded as gold. Now that we've surrendered they are not going into Japanese stomachs. (Is this the way a death-sentenced prisoner feels when a sumptuous meal is laid before him after months of prison fare?) The children were surprised this afternoon when called in from play and given a large glass each of precious tomato juice, and even an extra glass of milk for supper.

Someone—probably Sejio, who knows everything as soon as it happens—told Beth about the Japanese because she surprised me tonight by crying and saying that the Japanese were going to get her and she was afraid to go to bed. Beth has no idea what a Jap is, but if she did I do not like her discovering such fear at so tender an age. I have made a special effort to keep the children from being afraid.

A disturbance in the night (screeching of owls and birds, shrieking of monkeys, lowing of carabao) made me sure someone from a camp household was burying personal belongings. Things and food—these are constantly in our thoughts. Will the Japs confiscate the few months' supply of canned milk so necessary for Beth and Clay?

Today we expect the terms of our surrender to the Japanese. General Sharp* in Mindanao is sending representatives to discuss and to accept Jap terms. Word has come from Iloilo of the shooting of Mr. Garrett, 60-year-old dignified English president of the Hong Kong–Shanghai Banking Co., and three or four of our other friends and acquaintances in Iloilo. Captain Paul Ming, a young pilot who flew the plane Jim and I used many times to go from island to island, also has been shot. Possibly it was the actions of the Japanese in destroying the very small white business population in isolated communities which led to our surrender.

I told Sejio last night we must begin to repack to return to the Central at once under Jap guard if called upon to do so. Tears came to his eyes. He is trying to show his loyalty and sympathy by extra services. How the glassware shone today.

Social life was not my chief interest before my marriage. My closest friends were those with whom friendship had blossomed in the intimacy of research together, or undertaking of a common task to be accomplished, contingencies of one office, or the give and take of a classroom. Card playing I simply had no time for. A lively discussion was much more entertaining than a ciné. I gasped with pity for a woman who said she and her husband went to a different ciné every single evening. But now I'm acknowledged a "good enough" bridge player and I have learned to talk cinés with enthusiasm. Not that I love bridge, but that I don't dislike it and one simply must play here. The men usually play poker when the women gather for bridge after dinner in the P.I. But gambling for high stakes is a thing Jim cannot bring himself to do. He abhors it. Mr. Harblentzel, the Swiss patriarch of Bacolod, felt the same and he and Jim have had many long conversations I wanted to hear instead of listening to bridge partners bidding.

*Brigadier General William F. Sharp, U.S. Army, in charge of Philamerican forces in Mindanao until their surrender.

Sejio is a marvel to me. He came as a garden boy in Bacolod who weeded and worked yard and garden. A carabao-pulled plow and wheelbarrow prepared the way for a lawn. The part-time gardener we had was not dependable nor interested when Sejio came asking for work and a place to live. At that time we had a chauffeur, a cook, a nurse (amah) for the children, a houseboy, lavendera (laundress), and part-time gardener—not many servants as households go in the East, but I hesitated about Sejio. He was young, inexperienced, and another one to provide a bed for in the servants' quarters, another one to buy "chow" for, to provide with white uniforms, to provide with soap and water, to let entertain his relatives below-stairs when they came to visit him, and to pay doctor bills for if he became sick. All these things he had a right to expect if I employed him. So is the code here and servants know all Americans abide by it. So he came "on trial." He began to come into the house to help. He always "just happened" to be on hand when Jim's bags were to be taken to the car for Jim to catch a plane or boat for one of the many trips business required of him. After Jim's return, Sejio had hands on the bags first to help unpack. Jim thought him clever, honest, and appreciative.

I liked the girl servants—the cook, amah, and lavendera. All were high school graduates and friends who had come with us by boat when we moved to Bacolod. That was a memorable day. We had gone aboard, Clay sleeping in his basket, Beth in Juanita's arms, and Georgia Miss (Miss for Mississippi) on leash, servants, boxes, bags, and a refrigerator. When I saw the big white GE refrigerator hoisted aboard by ropes, we knew we were ready to pull out. (Some people paint refrigerators black out here because rust comes through enamel easily due to salty atmosphere.) The two babies required milk almost until the hour of departure, so we had emptied the refrigerator just in time to get it (uncrated) to the pier. I prayed for a smooth trip so its motor wouldn't be too shaken for use.

This started out to be about Sejio. The other servants fled when war fear swept the Islands. I begged them not to become panicky and told them each day of the news. When I realized Jim could not get back and I should have to see things through without him I still prided myself in the girls, in their neat white dresses which I had designed and had made for them. These had button openings down the side instead of the front, as front buttons might hurt the children. But the girls left without a word. Only Sejio remained. His home is on the island of Leyte.† He had never worked in a white person's home when he came to us, he could not turn on electric lights, he had never seen on a door a lock with a key. He knew nothing of cooking American food, but now he does.

When Nueva, Teresita, and Edgardo Diaz, neighbors across the way, came galloping on horses (long wooden poles) that have wooden blocks for noses, Beth and Clay cried for horses too. Next morning Beth and Clay had horses which made the other children's eyes "green with envy," for they had green steeds to ride. The horses' heads were made of fish heads which Sejio had dried (his food) with their eyes still staring and teeth showing.

Fri., May 15, 1942. Animal voices were raised in ever increasing crescendo before dawn. They began with a wildcat caught in a trap near the chicken houses on the river's edge. Chickens are kept away from the houses because snakes are attracted by chicken waste. The cat trap was baited with the head of a chicken killed and eaten the night before. Cat had all feline facial characteristics except a longer fox-like nose. It also had a trailing bushy tail, a civet cat, grey and black, a lot of ferocity in its 15″ body. Sejio tells me it's only a kitten (singarong in Visäyan), not yet a real cat. We should add Osa Johnson to the list of women invited here.‡ She could inform us on animal lore.

Ours is a women's camp. My next-door neighbor's husband is a civilian employee of the army, stationed at La Carlota, on this island. The manager and his assistant (my neighbor's husband) are still on the grounds. They send notes in by runners who bring in limited vegetables and meat twice a week.

We have waited for our fate since the surrender of the P.I. Today a messenger brought a three-page typed copy of a news report from KGEI in San Francisco. This report dealt with MacArthur in Australia,

---

†Large island of the Visäyans east of Negros.
‡Osa Helen (Leighty) Johnson with her husband Martin Elmer Johnson wrote accounts of their expeditions to the South Pacific, Borneo, and Africa.

the Burma and South China fighting, the Germans, the Russians, reports from Cairo, the British Air Ministry, U.S. batteries in Iceland, and finally Secretary of War Stimson's* report from Washington. The Philippine Islands were never mentioned.

Sat., May 16, 1942. Still awaiting terms of the surrender. General Sharp, commander of Visäyan and Mindanaon forces,† is sending a representative to Negros Island to discuss surrender terms. His emissary has not yet arrived at Fabrica Occidental,‡ on Negros, for the conference.

Miss Ganahan, nurse, walked two hours over the trail toward the Central to a grass house hidden in the woods which Mr. Woods arranged for her mother and father before Miss G. would consent to come to camp with us. The hidden house serves a double purpose. The Woods' silver, linens, and some of the office records are stored there and the occupants have a secluded living spot and act as caretakers at the same time. Since they are Filipinos there is little danger of the house being searched or noticed by passing Japanese patrols. Miss G. walked two hours alone through woody twilight (an unheard of action in pre-war days in P.I.). Here girls lead chaperoned lives of old Spain, from whence the social and religious foundations of life have come. The reason for Miss G.'s nonconformity is probably that she is a product of the Mission Hospital of Iloilo, trained and educated by Protestants in a Catholic world. Though religion has not been mentioned here, she and Miss Bayona, wee Douglas White's nurse, were singing "Nearer My God to Thee" and "The Old Rugged Cross" the evening the news came that the white flag was flying from the Occidental Provincial Building in Bacolod. These are not the songs of Catholics.

Miss G. went to spend the night with her parents because her brother was home from the army to bid farewell to his relatives. He is in the

---

*Henry L. Stimson, longtime U.S. statesman, secretary of state in the Hoover administration, secretary of war during World War II.

†Although General Sharp had originally been given this joint command, in March the Visäyan command had been transferred to Brigadier General Bradford G. Chynoweth, who surrendered the Visäyans from Cebu on May 16.

‡Town on Negros Island, 32 miles northeast of Bacolod.

Philamerican Army and when surrender became necessary, before terms were agreed upon, soldiers were released for farewell visits to their relatives. It is certain the soldiers will go into concentration camps, guarded perhaps by some of the same Japs who are now in Bacolod. It is also certain the Philamericans will be hungry in the camp and they will not receive proper medical attention if they become sick. After five and a half months of complete blockade there is insufficient food on our sugar cane island for the normal population. We cannot expect Japanese conquerors to deprive themselves of food and our exhausted medical supplies so that their conquered victims might not suffer. That isn't the way in war. So Miss G.'s brother knows what is ahead of him. Yet he returned to his post promptly at the expiration of 24-hour leave. He could have hidden in the hills and not returned. But in surrender there are codes. His company would present themselves whole, in order that they might not be punished by more severe cruelty because some of the number failed to present themselves to the Japanese. Josi also said in the event Allied soldiers landed in the Philippines in an effort to retake the Islands, it is sure the Japanese would place the Philamerican forces they had conquered here in the front line of battle against their countrymen that they might be slaughtered from guns of their kin. This has happened in China where Chinese prisoners-of-war (Japanese) were made to march in the front line of the Chinese army, against the advancing Japanese.

President Quezon is in the U.S. now with his family, Vice-President Osmeña, and members of the Cabinet. One of our group, when told this news, said, "President Quezon is not a Filipino. Had he been he would not have deserted his country and his people. He is only a mestizo of mixed blood whose chief interests have been financial and his money has been safely taken from the P.I. to U.S. banks before the outbreak of war. He has no further interest in us or the Islands." This was surprising from a quiet, unobtrusive, and (I had thought) unopinionated Filipino. Copies of President Quezon's speech, broadcast over KGEI (San Francisco), were brought into camp by paqueros* bringing wood.

*Carriers.

We had a delicacy sent today by Miss G. Made from camote,† cabay (starch root of small tree), coconut milk, grated coconut, and sugar. A small dish came, still warm, just before bedtime. The children's share I thought I would save till the morrow and I ravenously ate half. Asked Sejio if the other would keep safely till morning. He shook his head and said it would not, that nothing with coconut milk would keep, but would spoil overnight. So I said, "All right, you may eat this half now." How Miss G. laughed at my ignorance. The candy is better after several days' standing. As this is one of the commonest and choicest of Filipino sweets, Sejio knew. He is a little minx sometimes, but then he probably was hungry for a change of diet himself.

What a welcome for Quezon in Washington. With his wife, two daughters, one son, he was met personally at the station by President Roosevelt, Sec. Ickes,‡ Com. Sayre,* Paul McNutt,† and Frank Murphy,‡ and Gen. George Marshall.* (This from KGEI broadcast.) Heard in the same broadcast: "Though communications have been severed between the United Nations headquarters and the Philippines, it is believed in Washington that Philamerican heroes are striking effectively from jungle and mountain fastnesses in the islands of Mindanao, Panay, Cebu, and even the principal island of Luzon."

So all communications between the P.I. and our homeland have been severed and no one outside knows that the white flag flies here. Perhaps it was original with Quezon to request that the national flag in the P.I. be flown upside down after the first attack by the Japanese. In his broadcast President Quezon asked that the flag in all public places

---

†Sweet potato.

‡Harold L. Ickes, U.S. secretary of interior from 1933 to 1946, and therefore in charge of the Bureau of Insular Affairs, the governing body for the Philippines until independence.

*Francis B. Sayre, high commissioner of the Philippines at the beginning of World War II.

†Former high commissioner of the Philippines. McNutt later served as head of the War Manpower Commission during World War II.

‡Former high commissioner of the Philippines, later associate justice of the U.S. Supreme Court.

*General of the Army George C. Marshall, chief of staff of the U.S. Army during World War II. Marshall later served as secretary of state and secretary of defense in the Truman administration and was instrumental in developing the European Recovery Program for which he was awarded the Nobel Peace Prize in 1953.

be flown in this manner to indicate a state of invasion and not to right the flag until invaders were driven out.

Mon., May 18, 1942. Remarks on the report from KGEI, San Francisco, May 18:

This report told how MacArthur, with American and Australian bombers, is hitting the Japanese in New Guinea. The Russians are attacking German defenses at Kharkov. Told of Japanese losses in the Hunan province of China. The British R.A.F. planes were over France and Belgium. Cairo reported activity over the Libyan front. A U.S. official statement revealed for the first time that 600,000 U.S. troops were moved to battle stations, many of them far distant from home, during the first three weeks of the war. Following is a direct quote from this broadcast: "The U.S. Navy revealed last night that in February an American submarine successfully visited the island fortress of Corregidor and executed an important mission under the very noses of the Japanese siege forces. The undersea boat delivered a vital cargo of anti-aircraft ammunition to the Philamericans at Corregidor, ammunition with which they so effectively shot down several dozen Japanese planes. Then the submarine was loaded with an immensely valuable store of gold, silver, and other precious things which the Japanese had hoped to seize with the fall of Corregidor and Bataan. The submarine lay alongside Corregidor for 48 hours, discharging and loading cargo, then safely left Manila Bay, and Japan knew nothing of the visit until yesterday's announcement. The fortune in gold and other valuables is now in a safe place, to be held in trust for the Philippines until it can be returned when the Islands are liberated."

Tues., May 19, 1942. Bright clothes line at camp! Brightly colored red, orange, pink, and yellow cotton underpants of the Filipino servants—men and women—are on lines strung between trees beside the paler hued clothes of the foreign occupants. White or flesh underthings have no appeal to native women. Brassieres are an unknown article of dress. Slips or petticoats (chemises, my lavendera insists upon calling them) are lavishly embroidered in colors. Rounded neck and wide shoulder straps, cut in one with the petticoats, are always scalloped.

The native woman's canusa (or blouse) is of stiff, loosely woven net, exposing to full view the undergarment beneath. This accounts for the fussiness of the slip. With the popularity of American outer dress the change from native underthings has been slow. Sejio's bright red drawers and orange knitted undershirts in a far corner of our garden in Bacolod gave me a shock when they first appeared to view.

Also hanging from each improvised woodland clothes line at camp is a net meat-drying bag. Meat-drying, begun as a curiosity, and the attitude that if the meat isn't good then the pets can have it, has changed. There is a determination to dry meat sufficiently successfully for our own consumption. That we shall soon be without fresh meat is a known fact. Whether our last fresh roast will be this week or next is uncertain. Meat is only "meat," not tenderloin, T-bone, porterhouse, round, chuck, rump, or other cuts. These words mean nothing to animal slaughterers here. We buy by the kilo and get a hunk of flesh, bone, skin, and hair from the part of the carcass adjoining the last piece severed. Each household is taking all that's available and putting it, covered with coarse-grained salt, in direct sun each day. Correctly dried meat has no odor and often the meat (cut in small pieces) is hung on rattan strings in the kitchens of houses like pepper strings in American Southern homes. Our first experiments in meat-drying did not all meet with success. Camp reeked with decaying meat scent. Houseboys exchanged suggestions and experiences. By trial and error we have learned a process known to our forefathers in the wilderness of America, long before refrigeration was even a dream in the minds of men.

No mention of the Philippines in the news today except the story of the submarine that came to Corregidor in February.† (The full story is given in the report from KGEI on May 18.) We are, like Guam, Hong Kong, and Singapore, lost and of no present interest or news value.

A sack of onions came to camp today. Later I saw only a few in the basket where Sejio has kept only onions since our arrival here. To my query as to whereabouts of the onions Sejio replied, "The onions

---

†Here EHV is referring to the submarine by which the Quezon and Sayre families were evacuated to Australia in the third week of February 1942.

were too small to eat yet. I planted them so they would grow bigger."
Perhaps he's wise. He has also planted papaya seed and avocado seed.
He evidently thinks we'll be here a long time.

Wed., May 20, 1942. No war news in the P.I. White flag still flies on
Negros. It is supposed that Gen. Sharp, commander of Visäyan and
Mindanao forces, is a Japanese prisoner. His representative to a conference with the Japanese has not arrived. The army has no instructions from the commanding officer, Gen. Wainwright,‡ on Corregidor.
A supposedly official release from his post as commander-in-chief of
forces in the P.I. aroused doubt of a radio broadcast from Manila.
From records made of the speech and replayed before audiences in
America who knew Gen. Wainwright's speech phraseology and pronunciation of Philippine names, it has been proved conclusively that
the surrender speech supposedly addressed by the General to the rest
of the U.S. and Filipino forces in the Islands was a forgery of the Japanese. This is a deceitful practice of the Japs. Soon after the fall of Wake
Island, prisoners taken to Japan were "permitted" by Radio Tokyo to
broadcast to their families in the U.S. Once a week, after the 8:00 A.M.
news was completed, one, two, or three prisoners-of-war told
through the Tokyo microphone of the fair treatment in Japan. Names
of the prisoners, addresses in the States, and names of those to whom
broadcasts were addressed sounded convincing. But close examination and checking in the U.S. showed the voices not to be those of the
persons supposed to be speaking. Mothers and wives listening in the
U.S. failed to be reassured by this shoddy propaganda scheme. We
soon caught on here that this was an effort to draw us to Japanese
broadcasting stations so that we might hear Japan's version of the
news. The faked Wainwright broadcast was not Japan's first of this
kind.

We have no paper for starting fires for cooking. We tear the wrapper
from each tin can now as the can is opened and save the paper for fire

‡Lieutenant General Jonathan M. Wainwright, U.S. Army, in charge of Philamerican
forces in the Philippines after MacArthur's departure. There is no reason to believe that
his surrender speech of May 7 was a forgery, although MacArthur and others originally
maintained that it was.

making. More paper, naturally, is needed in the rainy season when the wood is damp, hard to light.

Information is seeping in concerning Cebu and Iloilo. All the American and European evacuees to the hills above Cebu City were ordered by the Japanese to return to Cebu City. A few came from their hiding places to the Japanese headquarters to register as ordered. These were put into concentration camp in Cebu City and are now being given a daily ration of rice and an edible but not palatable variety of seaweed. No other food. White women have been assaulted. We plan to stay here until forced to leave.

I put the children's oilcloth table cover, with bibs to match, in a handy place for quick wrapping of a strongbox if the Japanese come here. The box contains items wrapped in plio-film to make it waterproof, and will be wrapped in the oilcloth and placed in a hole in the ground at the moment we are sure the Japanese are coming. It has been their custom in other conquered areas to destroy and burn all that they could not read nor understand. Destruction is their byword.

A brief review of the news broadcast from KGEI in San Francisco:

The front pages of American newspapers reported that the largest convoy sent anywhere during the war had landed in Ireland. Reinforcements continued to flow into Australia also. In the Far East the Japanese have been unable to consolidate their gains. The Soviets announced advances in their offensive against Kharkov. New evidence was seen of the Allied fleet's dominance of North Atlantic waters. Announcement was made of the signing of a treaty between the U.S. and the Republic of Panama for their mutual protection.

Thurs., May 21, 1942. There are many stray dogs around camp. One of my first comments about the Philippines was that in the barrios I visited there seemed to be more dogs than children—and children swarmed the roads. Dogs breed in endless repetition and no one takes the lives of pups, however unwanted. Underfed, mangy, diseased dogs are everywhere. But the poorest families share their food with animal pets. These dogs are friends and protectors, barking loudly at the approach of a stranger. On the gates of wealthier Spanish and Filipino homes there are often signs in English, Spanish, and Visäyan,

"Beware of the dog," and the warning is wisely heeded. People pride themselves on the ferocity of pets. We had been in Iloilo but a short time when I met a Mrs. Greenfield. She is a grey-haired matron from the States, visiting her married daughter. She had a bandaged ear. She and her daughter were visiting a Swiss family, the Harblentzels, in Bacolod, having tea on the porch. Mrs. Greenfield put down her hand to pet the German police dog which stood by her chair. As she leaned over the animal he sprang at her face, catching her ear between his teeth and ripping it. An apology and an offer to take her to hospital for treatment. No scolding of the dog. This same dog nearly caused me to fall down the front steps of the Harblentzel house backwards on my first return call in Bacolod. Had my hand on gate at top of the steps to push the bell beside the house door. Dog leaped from behind a corner of the verandah and his teeth were almost on my hand before I withdrew it—and myself. Mrs. H. came in answer to the loud barking and said I should not have attempted to come on the porch but should have pushed the bell on the steps to the verandah. I had not even seen the bell concealed in some vines. The dog was tied up while I visited.

A few months later Mrs. H.'s sister-in-law was in a hospital with permanently scarring facial abrasions caused by this dog jumping in her face while she stooped to feed him. A ripped lip, a deep gash on forehead extending almost to eye, bruises, and swelling on her face were being treated in Manapla Hospital. The patient was suffering also from severe shock. Today this dog, which to my knowledge has drawn blood from three women, is still a family "pet" and the pride of the family. "There was never a better watchdog," they say.

Negritoes have an unusual interest to me. My romance with Jim had its beginning on a trip to visit a Negrito nomadic tribe north of Fort Stotsenberg* on Luzon Island. It was July 5, 1937. July 4 fell on Sunday and the next day, Monday, July 5, was the official holiday.

A month before I had arrived in Manila from visiting my former college roommate in Shanghai. She and her ten-year-old son were packing to return to the States for home leave and were speaking con-

*American military base near Clark Field in central Luzon.

tinually of the coming war with Japan. Her husband pointed out to me land given by the Shanghai government to the Japanese at their (Japs) request for a golf course. The land was leveled and fairways laid off. These fairways proved to be runways for Japanese planes landing in Shanghai before and after bombing the Chinese people and their homes. The "golf course" was between the Shanghai Bund and Shanghai College where he (Saxon's husband) was in the English Department. (Interruption here.)

(Later, same day.) At 2:00 P.M. Mr. Woods walked into camp in the first heavy rain of the beginning rainy season. We were smiling through the downpour from house to house as we all stood at windows to watch the rain put out forest fires which have been raging on two sides of camp. Then in walked Mr. Woods, the Central manager, giving news as he passed the lane of huts, "Negros has been invaded and occupied. Bacolod is taken by the Japanese."

The post office telephoned Mr. Woods at 6:00 A.M. that two Japanese transports were at Bacolod pier. The Central called Mr. Simke at Bacolod to tell him of the danger. "The Japanese are here now," Mr. Simke replied, and the receiver clicked. The two transports were accompanied by a torpedo boat, a cruiser, and six Q boats. The Banago pier and oil storage tank nearby were in flames. The people at the Central were told by Mr. Woods to leave at once. Mr. MacW. left the house door unlocked, sheets on the bed, the breakfast table set, fuel beside the kitchen stove, and the refrigerator stocked. The engine running the cold-storage plant and the separate household electric generator were stopped. There was much food in cold storage which would spoil.

There were only two frozen chickens of mine left at the Central. Some had sheep, some had young beeves. All gone now! To the few laborers and gardeners left at the Central, the Commissary doors were opened and they were told to take free of charge all they could carry. All stock was soon gone from the greatly thinned shelves.

It is reported that Col. McClelland of Iloilo was standing on the bridge of the first transport, a prisoner-of-war put in a conspicuous place to insure no resistance. Surrender terms had been discussed in Iloilo and no resistance and *no sabotage* were agreed to by the American officers. Lt. Col. Richard I. Jones, who had been staying at the Central, was prepared to meet the Japanese and accept their terms. Col. Hillsman,† who is in charge of Negros Island, had given orders to all Negros forces.

In the afternoon a rumor came that a Central's newly completed bodega was set afire by frightened Filipinos wishing to keep sugar from the Japanese.

Sejio was to have gone to the Central today for an oil stove oven (one burner) left in my home. We have round clay jug ovens up here. Sejio would have filled light-weight oven with freshly cut camote stems with leaves, peanuts, corn, and onions from the Central garden—these to be planted here, not eaten. But the Japanese came too soon. Another houseboy was going on the long walk with Sejio with three pairs of shoes to be half-soled. Rocky terrain of mountain camp is hard on shoe soles and heels.

Fri., May 22, 1942. "I dreamed about a crocodile last night," said Mr. Thompson, as I gave him a half-filled spool of thread needed for mending his clothes in exchange for three Bantam eggs. "And at home in Scotland that means bad news. Wherever a Scotsman dreams it, the same is true."

No news today of activities on Negros. Day is cloudy and rainy, visibility with field glasses poor. No messenger from the outside world to camp.

Bartering is a common practice. Exchanged canned niblet corn for fruit cocktail. Have been exchanging Carnation milk with Mr. Thompson. I have one case of small tins and he has only tall cans. As he uses milk only for coffee, a tall can spoils before it is finished. But two small tins are not quite equal to one large so a bit of arithmetic is necessary.

The Japs landed at Bacolod on Thursday, a propitious day for Japanese people. Former Thursday successes have led them to believe in this day for advance and attack.

---

†Colonel Roger B. Hillsman, U.S. Army, commander of USAFFE (United States Army Forces in the Far East) on Negros.

(Later, same day.) At 3:30 P.M. a messenger came in to say that at 9:20 this morning nine truckloads of Japanese arrived at Central to take over. Japanese will probably sleep in the houses (including mine) at Central tonight. I hope they sleep on beds and not on sola cushions, take care of the stove, and keep the toilet bowl clean!

Alice has been telling me of "suspiciousness" of Japs—that they doubt all they do not understand and that they may burn our valuable (to us only) papers because they do not know what insurance receipts, stock certificates, and savings account books are.

On her first trip to Japan she had, under "occupation" on the passport, "dietitian," and took much time explaining. "Teacher" they understood. "Of home economics" they understood. "Then take off the word 'dietitian,' they said, not realizing that we cannot alter or mutilate legal documents such as passports.

Similar experience of mine: my occupation on passport "research worker." Asked by Jap official to explain the meaning of "research," Capt. Edwards said, "To secure information." He might just as well have said I was a spy. Hours after other passengers were ashore I was still trying to explain why I wanted information about Japan and what information I wanted. The fact that I had been engaged in research in the U.S. and was now on vacation got only a doubtful grunt in response. I was shadowed during the entire stay in one small port, Yawata, even to having a police guard squat behind us when another passenger and I squatted on the floor, Jap fashion, in a small ciné which had no seats nor benches and was showing a ten-year-old U.S. movie with the dialogue in Japanese. There was reason to be suspicious of strangers at Yawata. A large steel factory belched fire and molten metal day and night. Our ship unloaded scrap iron to feed this hungry giant. It was not a tourist spot. There was none of the beauty here that is shown on cherry blossom posters. To reach Yawata we went through a narrow bay separating Mogi and Shimenosaki.‡

(Still on Fri., May 22.) At 5:00 P.M. an exhausted, sweat and mud covered patrol of twelve Filipino soldiers walked into camp. They had as a guide through the mountains a three-and-a-half-foot Negrito, car-

‡Moji and Shimonoseki—ports on Shimonoseki Strait, Kyushu, southwest Japan.

rying a seven-foot spear with a nasty pointed poisoned spearhead. The soldiers had been patrolling outside Bacolod when the Japs arrived. They had orders to join their commanding officers at Victorias,* but Japanese were there also. So they were hiking through the woods with a guide to try to join other parties before surrendering. They had not eaten all day. We fed them rice, fish, and camotes. Very poorly dressed, shirts and trousers not matched, assorted headgear. Had no supplies except gun and ammunition in belt, no food, no provision for sleeping, no protection from rain. They started out again in drizzling rain near twilight with a box of rice (gift of Mr. Woods). They smilingly waved good-bye to us all as we stood in our doorways. All were young and alert, but all looked unhappy and uncertain. Surely a home would be preferable to the future that faces them.

Sat., May 23, 1942. Three and one-half years of saving for, choosing, and buying sola, dining room, and porch furniture to harmonize and today it all disappeared at the hands of vandals, the civilian population gone wild with looting. (Must stop and hide diary.)

Wed., May 27, 1942. Gov. Lizares of Occidental Negros gave a dinner last Sunday and is assisting the Japanese to restore order. A message has gone out to Filipinos asking them to return to their homes and go ahead with their crops. Rice must be planted now to take full advantage of the rainy season. If people fail to plant now, there will be starvation soon.

Japanese patrolling the Central are under command of a German officer who has a duplicate of Hitler's mustache. The distillery at Talisay-Silay Milling Company was started yesterday under Jap supervision. Jap officers are living in Mr. Wiley's house and other staff houses are occupied by soldiers.

Perhaps it is true of human nature in times of great stress (I do not know) but there is great secrecy among families in camp. Some are burying foodstuffs at night, others are building grass huts farther back into the hills and caching supplies there with paid watchmen. Every

*Town on northwest Negros Island, 18 miles northeast of Bacolod.

method kept secret and each effort to save supplies by any method is condemned by the others in camp.

A second report that Japs were on the way to camp was traced down to group of hoodlums trying to frighten us into fleeing and leaving our supplies. Besides a month's supplies in each house, there are coveted sacks of rice, sugar, and salt in the bodegas at camp.

Thurs., May 28, 1942. Reports continue coming in concerning the burning of Central houses, sabotage of the mill, looting of the bodegas, and destruction of workshops by disgruntled planters with a grudge against the Central. Eleven years ago there was a strike there. Striking workers were given forty-eight hours to return to work. Some returned, others followed the strike leader and refused work on the basis offered. New men were employed. The strikers, hungry, disillusioned, asked for old jobs back on old basis. Refused by Central. Strike leader abandoned followers. Hatred for the Central and for each other resulted. After eleven years, hatred for the Central has a chance of expression in burning, looting, and sabotage.

Most serious sabotage was in harm to mill machinery itself. The mill is the heart of the Central. It is feared that destruction is so great and the cost of repair and replacement so high it would not be profitable for the company to reopen after the war.

So far as is known there has been no destruction of importance at other centrals. Some tanks holding oil for mill have been burned, but this is relatively unimportant. Mills have not been burned, nor mill-site residences touched. Talisay-Silay Milling Company already reopened by Japs in perfect order and organization. Insular Lumber Company, at Fabrica, also reopened by Japs, who are continuing to cut and prepare lumber for export to occupied areas or to Japan. No word of looting or sabotage at Victorias or Manoa sugar centrals. Our Central is the only one American owned. Others have Filipino, Spanish, or mestizo managers. The hatred seems to be against American managers, with American ownership and profit.

Mr. White was with the Del Monte Pineapple Central on Mindanao. He was assistant manager of the cannery there. This Central is also American owned and American staffed. It has been a wonderful agricultural experiment and development. Mr. White thinks this Central has probably suffered a terrible fate.

Reports from Bacolod and Silay (post office for the Central) that the Jap army is calling in all Philippine currency and replacing with yen— one yen for one peso.

Miss Ganahan has located an old Negrito who will let her use his house (formerly hers) to hide hospital supplies, also hide her sister and herself if Japs send Americans to concentration camp. The old man had on but two garments, a man's cast-off sleeveless knit undershirt and a dirty G-string. He wore nothing else, yet there was a dignity in his five feet which commanded respect.

The thing that has impressed me most about Negritoes (besides surprise at beards—Filipino men do not shave) is the majestic way they carry their small, slight bodies. They are proud and they are sensitive.

For breakfast today five precious Bantam eggs scrambled, which were brought in by a Negrito, for sale, yesterday. Children were hungry but would not eat because the eggs tasted like smoke. Smoke from wet wood used in cooking them had gone through and through the eggs. We had no fruit, bread, or cereal. Eggs were breakfast.

Lunch was rice cooked with tiny native tomatoes and green papaya. Children refused again. Food tasted again of smoke. Sejio is taking advantage of the smoke by hanging drying meat across the rafters above the stove.

For supper I made a blanc mange pudding with flour instead of cornstarch. The small amount of flour left is heavily infested with bugs (larger ones can be sifted out), but also many tiny worms which go through sifter into any dish being prepared. Of course, flour should be thrown away but we throw away nothing now. Made pudding with heavily watered milk, a little chocolate, some sugar. Knew the children would eat it if sweet and thought flour in pudding might be of same benefit as flour in bread. Sweetness counteracted smoke taste, in part. Smoke we will continue to have, Sejio says, until the wood dries or we can put a flue in the kitchen. The latter is impossible with the open fire we use and also there is no tin for a flue.

Careful check of canned goods reveals enough evaporated milk for one can each day for four months, one can of fruit or vegetable (never both on same day) per day for ninety days, one small can sausages or canned beef twice a week for ninety days, cereals for about seventy-five days. Strongest optimist here cannot expect liberation of the Islands and arrival and distribution of new food supplies by that time. So I decided to stop using canned goods if possible. This is mango season in the Philippines. A messenger from the Central recently brought each family in camp four of them. The coconut is a fruit common in towns because the coconut plantations are established near towns. Dried coconut meat, copra, has always been a leading export of the Islands.

Sat., May 30, 1942. The end is near at hand. Yesterday as I planted some ferns on a rocky incline between my house and Miss Ganahan's, Mr. Woods had a summons to report to Japanese in Bacolod for instructions for our entering concentration camp. We think and hope that we will be put in schoolhouses. This means we will have no beds and no chairs—but what are they compared to food for hungry children?

Perhaps this is punishment due us all—God's way of bringing us back from a sense of false values. Probably I have been intolerant of what seemed to me stupidity, when it may not have been stupidity at all. I have not intentionally hurt the feelings of another human being. I do not gossip. (I feel that I must list my one *good point*.) Loyalty to friends does not permit malicious talk. And gossip, to me, is uninteresting when there are so many beautiful and more interesting matters to fill the mind and consume one's time. Remember this, Beth! The children will both go with me. I cannot be separated indefinitely from them. Perhaps the Japanese will permit me to take them to the home of a Filipino near the site of the concentration camp. Dr. Jardelega's farm, where he, his wife, and his son are now living, is not far from Bogo.† Perhaps, I hope and pray, I can get Beth and Clay to him. Dr. Jardelega offered his home to all children at the Central at the beginning of the war.

My personal belongings—a few linens, initialed silver flatware (gift

---

†Town on northern Cebu Island on an inlet of the Visäyan Sea, 50 miles north of Cebu City.

from my parents, both of whom have died since I left them four years ago), a cabinet of articles of Jim's, Jim's picture, marriage license, birth certificates, passports, insurance papers, stock certificates, and bank accounts—will go to Miss Ganahan or Mr. Diaz. Mr. Diaz will stay here. Other friendly Filipino families will be invited to live in our nipa houses to protect the houses and the remainder of our supplies from vandalism or arson.

"Deborah danced when she was two, as buttercups and daffodils do." From Aline Kilmer, widow of Joyce Kilmer. In this little poem Deborah might be Beth. Beth is lively, cunning and coy, with her little secrets and plans. With eyes glistening but little lips trying to conceal her merriment, makes such observations as, "Mommee, I think I had better eat your dessert today, because there is spinach left on your plate." Or, "Mommee, I think I'll make a cake today, you can help me, because Clay likes cake very much," not saying what Beth thinks of cake.

Then chubby, red-lipped Clay. A Filipino bachelor told me when he first saw Clay that he was healthy because red lips were a sure sign of vitality in a baby. Clay is a lovable ball of perpetual motion. He is more active than Beth, running around and around the single table in our nipa hut on rainy days where Beth is happiest with Eva, her nine-inch doll she dresses, undresses, and redresses hour after hour with continued interest.

Sun., May 31, 1942. Mr. Woods and Mr. Robinson walked back into camp at 5:20 P.M., tired but with grins on their faces which set all at ease. Two Filipino lookouts had been stationed on a mountain peak two miles from camp to run in to tell us if Japanese were accompanying Mr. Woods. This would give us a few minutes in which to hide diaries, money, rings, and watches, and to get changed from slacks to skirts. It would also give Mr. Diaz time to send his two girls, nine and ten years old, to Miss Ganahan's house. Time too for the Filipino lavenderas, amahs, and housegirls to leave camp, as they all fear rape. However, nearly all of them are over thirty, which is old in the P.I. where girls usually marry before twenty and are soon worn out with childbearing—thinking of the rape of the Sabines.

But no runners preceded the returning emissaries to the Japanese headquarters. The men had found two old-time friends, one an employee of the Central, who were waiting as interpreters. This one, Yasamori, had been a carpenter at Hawaiian-Philippine Central and on his last visit to Japan had been arrested as a Korean spy. Mr. Woods had tried to get him released without success. Yasamori had been living in the Philippines 22 years and was married to a Filipino woman. The Central had paid his wife and children one-half of Yasamori's salary during his confinement. This generosity was repaid by the friendliness of Yasamori now that Mr. Woods is to go to concentration camp.

The other interpreter encountered, Ishawata, a former Bacolod contractor and scrap iron dealer, now an advisor in Japanese headquarters, also asked leniency for Mr. Woods. The fact that Mr. Woods reported promptly as requested also helped.

There are three concentration camps for Americans, British, Dutch, and other United Nations nationals on Negros Island. Mr. Woods was given his choice of camps for all people (men, women, and children) from Hawaiian-Philippine Central to be in the same location, an unusual consideration for prisoners. He chose Fabrica. We have ten days to report there. We may send clothes and foodstuffs ahead. No supplies will be molested, so the Japs promised. We may take anything except firearms and whiskey (to be decided definitely later). Mr. Woods goes back to Bacolod in three days to discuss other details of transporting our supplies and ourselves to Fabrica. The news seems too good to be true. American officers are in a camp near Fabrica at Cadiz.‡

The Japanese commanding officer on the island is Col. Ohta. One hundred twenty-six Japanese men were interned and cared for by the Philippine government officials at the start of the war. All are now released, of course. Mrs. Woods made several visits to Yasamori during the time he was there. This kindness is now being repaid.

Mr. and Mrs. Wiley were called back from their hideout and returned to Talisay-Silay Milling Company. They are living in a house formerly occupied by a subordinate because Mr. Wiley's house is now

‡Town on northern Negros Island, 31 miles northeast of Bacolod.

headquarters for the Japanese running parts of the Central. Mrs. Wiley came from the hideout with only one change of clothes, was not permitted to get another. Mr. and Mrs. Wiley are not permitted to leave house, no one is allowed to enter except with Japanese pass. Guards at the entrance to house.

Our Central is a nightmare—blackened embers where office, houses, ciné, and bodegas stood. Springs from the beds, now contorted coils, only faintly resemble their original forms. There are holes in the ground where our houses formerly stood. A few people had buried boxes of canned goods and silver here. Even septic tanks were opened in the search for hidden goods. All plants and trees are scorched and seared by heat from the flames. Japanese are no longer guarding the Hawaiian-Philippine Central as it is given up as a total loss. Mr. Woods felt uneasy as he inspected the damage to his Central. It hurts him that no other Central has been harmed.

The tropical climate sometimes sours the milk of human kindness. Mr. Woods is a wonderful placater of ruffled dispositions in our mountain camp. Some feelings have been so ruffled (like a broody hen's) that they have hatched eggs of jealousy, greed, and discontent. Some of the women have always frightened me. I never know how to answer their malicious talk.

The following is a copy of a letter that I wrote to my mother-in-law on this date:

Dearest Mom,

Late in November Jim went to Manila on business with a reservation to return to Bacolod on Tuesday, Dec. 9. War started so unexpectedly on Dec. 8 and immediately all boat service, all plane service between the Islands was stopped. Also telephone and telegraphic connections curtailed and then discontinued. Jim tried to return to us. He could not. He joined the army—2nd Lieutenant, Quartermaster Corps—and was last heard of the latter part of December in the midst of the fighting in Bataan. I have had no message from (nor of) him in five months. When the Bataan forces surrendered he must have been taken prisoner.

The children and I left Bacolod, where I was the only American woman, and the town was wild with hysteria. I had no money for rent, lights, water, etc., not to mention groceries with prices that had skyrocketed. All credit was stopped. We'd left our surplus money in Manila bank that had no branch in Bacolod. Through the courtesy of Mrs. A. W. Woods, wife of the manager of Hawaiian-Philippine Sugar Milling Co., at Silay, we moved into an unoccupied staff house on the sugar Central grounds. There was no rent and we were permitted to buy supplies from a commissary run by the company for their own employees only. Then Bataan fell, Corregidor fell, and we knew we were not safe in Silay. The manager, Mr. Woods, built nipa (grass) huts far in the hills in virgin forests inhabited by Negritoes for a hideout. Along with houses for other white families (including his own) he built one for the children and me. We hiked into the hills with minimum belongings. We have been here now almost two months, living primitive lives, but we have felt our security was uncertain. When the Japanese landed at Bacolod our Central, Hawaiian-Philippine, was looted by angry Filipinos—not the Japanese—and our houses burned. I have lost every piece of furniture Jim and I had collected. The loss hurt momentarily, but material things do not matter much when the children's lives are in danger.

Yesterday Mr. Woods was summoned by messenger to report to the Japanese at Bacolod for the purpose of deciding where our "mountain" families shall be imprisoned. We have heard the men will go to one place, the women and children to another. What we shall find or what we will be fed, we do not know, but there is a dreadful shortage of food here and it is becoming more acute each month. The Japanese hate us Americans. They will do all they can to humiliate us and make us suffer. So we won't have much to eat as prisoners-of-war.

I think only of Beth and Clay now. If they come through this alone there is insurance for them. Jim has two policies with the Sun Life Assurance Company of Canada (one policy straight life for $5,000, the other an educational policy for Beth and Clay which begins when Beth is sixteen). I have a policy for $2,000 with New England Mutual and $500 in a savings account at First National Bank of Atlanta. This will help you in locating the children after the war and in taking care of them if you do not hear from Jim or me. I shall try to get the children out of concentration camp and into hands of Dr. Jardelega, a Filipino doctor of Silay who has offered to take them if the Japanese will permit it. The Japanese are not so hard on Filipinos, trying to win their support in annihilating the white population. Dr. Jardelega has a farm and can feed the children. He is married to an American woman, formerly a trained nurse.

I hope I have painted a picture more dark than it turns out to be, but it is in the hands of God alone. I am leaving this hastily written letter and a diary I started keeping as a letter to Jim, to be sent to you. If the diary is typed, some parts edited or deleted, it may be sold for Beth and Clay. This was in my mind in the last part of the diary.

I hope this reaches you. There are two camphor chests of linens hidden in the house of a Filipino, and two suitcases of silver and papers left here at camp that I hope can be salvaged. I have left a will in one of the suitcases making you guardian for the children. That is why I am writing you. You, Aunts Susie and Fannie, and other of his relatives, as well as my own have been in my mind constantly during our trials. I know you have been worried. There has been no communication from the States to us since Dec. 8 except a cable from Susie and Fannie and one from Ernestine. You probably know my father died last November, following Mother after such a short time. Please let Ernestine (E. Jernigan, Greensboro, Ga.) know of this letter.

I must stop and give this letter to Mr. Diaz, a Filipino living here at camp with us whom we think the Japanese will not molest. Mr. Diaz has been employed for years by the Hawaiian-Philippine Company. You should get in touch with Mrs. A. W. Woods of this company if you hear nothing further from me or from Jim. There should be army compensation for the children if Jim has suffered death or injury. I want the children to live with you and spend their lives in the United States.

With a heart full of love and sorrow,

Your daughter,
Elizabeth

Tuesday, June 2, 1942. Unsettled days, sleepless nights spent in planning packing schedule for the next day. Must retuft Clay's mattress, wash bedroll covers, put in aprons for children, oil the children's shoes (leather is stiff from repeated wetting), don't forget tea and a pan for heating water, leave recipe for fudge with Sejio so he can make some and bring to camp if he can secure Japanese pass.

So my mind runs. But I know full well that if Clay starts the day in a fretful mood and rain makes our one room the children's only playground, I'll get not one of these things accomplished.

Since leaving Bacolod I have been unable to find amahs, since they and their families are in hiding. Also I cannot pay the salary of an amah. I have only borrowed money and now there will be no more of that.

How much help was my husband! One word of discipline from him was worth ten from me. Probably my upset mind, indecision, and worries are reflected in my treatment of the children. The move to concentration camp, on my fourth wedding anniversary, June 10, will be our third move in three months, and this move, we know, will not be our last. We have no home to go to after we are released from internment. There is a box of clothes for the trip home to the U.S. I am leaving with Sejio. Dresses and shoes for myself, brother and sister suits (pants, skirts, blouses) for Beth and Clay in which they look like twins. Someone has said philosophically but not very comfortingly, "If everything is lost, perhaps the Red Cross will send you home." Our relatives in the States have never seen the children, nor have most of Jim's relatives met me. I don't like the idea of appearing in Red Cross gift apparel, though it may be necessary.

We can take two "chow" boxes per family (of uniform size), filled with canned foods, and two suitcases per person to the concentration camp. If the Japanese are still in a good humor, we may take bedroll (with mosquito net), cot and mattress, sheets and cotton blankets. My goal was to have chow boxes and suitcases packed today to give re-maining few days to putting food and clothes to be left here in boxes to be moved somewhere later—though I have no idea where. The packing goal was in sight but I've been thrown for a twenty-four-hour loss. A torrential rain set in. Two boxes of clothes and bedding neatly packed were drenched through the packing case before I noticed rain coming in through the window.

We hear there is a sign across the highway at Talisay in huge capital letters: BOW THE GUARD. Filipinos and Americans alike must bow. As Mr. Woods commented, "The Jap guard doesn't bow in return."

Thirty Japs entered the Harblentzel home. No one spoke nor gave any explanation. Went to the refrigerator and looked in. Mrs. Harblentzel, big buxom Swiss, twice the size of a Jap soldier, said, "Nein," and closed it quickly. They opened the pantry filled with food supplies. She pushed the door shut and said, "Nein." They entered the bathroom and opened the medicine cabinet. Again she pushed ahead of them, shut the door, and said, "Nein." One soldier washed his hands in the bathroom and after drying them on a towel, walked out with the towel across his shoulder. They searched clothes closets, looked under beds, and, contented that whatever they might be looking for was not there, departed by front steps. Japanese sergeant waiting at foot of steps immediately spotted the white towel and after a point of his gun at the soldier and a few commands in Japanese, soldier hastily returned towel to its bathroom rack. Mrs. Harblentzel was given a pass by the Japanese to permit her to leave her house, as a native of a neutral country, but she prefers to stay within.

The Tribune, Manila newspaper, reported a staff officer of the Japanese Expeditionary Forces in the P.I. who had just returned from the Bataan front declared that more Filipino officers and men have died from the bullets of the American surveillance corps and from slow starvation than from Japanese guns.

In the same paper a headline: "Aid to P.I. Impossible—F.D.R." The article stated that the north and east islands are shielded by Japanese mandated islands while the southern and western parts are bounded by Java, Borneo, and New Guinea, which areas Japan controls. All Japanese propaganda!

Am preparing to part with Georgia Miss. Sejio will keep her. Mr. Diaz will buy deer or carabao meat and bones for both Sejio and Georgia when the Negritoes bring in their kill. There was one delicate matter to be attended to. "Sejio, I do not want puppies when I come back from concentration camp. Please see that Georgia is kept indoors during a part of June. Do you understand?"

A perplexed expression was on his face. "No, ma'm, I do not know what are puppies—like fleas?"

I explained that puppies are what we called baby dogs. Then this was understood, but I think I'll ask Miss Ganahan to watch Georgia also. I don't want her pure strain mixed and a litter of "wonks" or half-breeds.

Wed., June 3, 1942. Packing, packing, packing. What shall I put in suitcases which may be our only belongings for one month, six months or a year? What will be most hardy, long lasting, and easily laundered clothes for growing children and for myself? There must be room for a tiny sewing kit, with extra buttons for sunsuits and changes of shoes for the children, for during rainy season shoes dry so slowly. Put in a dozen nails and told Sejio I wanted a small hammer he always keeps handy for odd jobs.

"Why nails and hammer?" he asked, worried and disapproving.

"The Japanese will not permit us servant help of any kind, and I must put nails in wall of camp to support mosquito nets, if we are permitted to take them in." Sejio was embarrassed and turned away.

I tore July and October pages from wall calendar and put in suitcase. Each page had three months, two in small type. If we aren't out by December, too bad.

Mr. Woods and Mr. Robinson back in camp at 5:30, wet to their skin. We go to Bacolod for concentration to the same elementary school where Japs. before were housed forty persons to a room. Col. Ohta put his hand to heart and said his code was to consider the welfare of every *civilian*, he hated only enemy *soldiers*. Col. Ohta asked Mr. Woods why I was at the Hawaiian-Philippine Central evacuation camp when my husband did not work for the Central. Mr. Woods told him that my husband went to Manila in November on business, was caught there by the war and I had not heard from him since.

"And you gave Mrs. Vaughan a house, food on credit, and spending money?" he asked, astounded.

"Yes, for five months," Mr. Woods replied and he said Col. Ohta was impressed.

Col. Ohta pointed to Mr. Robinson, who expected to be questioned about personnel at his Central. But Col. Ohta wanted to know how many tons of molasses were at San Carlos when he left.

"Two thousand tons," Mr. Robinson replied.

"Do you have distillery?" Col. Ohta asked.

"No."

"Where do you ship your molasses?"

"To Japan and Siam" was Mr. Robinson's reply.

The mention of Japan caused Col. Ohta to smile. Then the two men were dismissed.

The best news the two men brought back was that they heard of

American broadcasts of the bombing of Cologne and Essen with great success.

Thurs., June 4, 1942. Packing in pouring rain. With shutters closed, made it dark. Window is heavy when dry, weighs "tons" when wet. To close it requires Herculean muscle plus bravery. Have told Beth we are taking a "trip." The new word intrigues her. She has chattered all day about the "trip" they are to take. She has chosen suits and socks they are to wear and has helped me pack her clothes.

I have some money in my possession and do not know whether it is better to take it to the new camp or leave it here. Col. Ohta told Mr. Woods to tell us to bring all our money to concentration camp and if it is *acceptable* we will be given yen in exchange. (It is all paper money of new issue in Bacolod since the war started.) We know we shall need cash for fresh foodstuffs, if they are permitted to be sold to us, and for tips, tips, tips—if water goes off, lights fail to burn, and other necessities need attention. So we have been told.

I wonder if the boxes we're sending ahead tomorrow with our choicest groceries will ever reach us and if they do, what about those left behind? Where are things safe? Whom can we trust? Sejio tells me looters will be here as soon as white people leave. Worrying does not help.

Packed my clothes in leather suitcase to which I have lost key. Will tie it with rope. Some people taking nicest clothes in hope of saving them. I am leaving mine here in the hope of saving them. Will see who is right later. Perhaps we are both losers!

Mr. Woods gave us passes (in Japanese) to go to concentration camp on or before June 10 which are void after that date. Would like to have the Japanese translated. Japanese writing includes the English numbers, written in vertical columns, 965, 966, and 967. Passes are 4″ × 6″ white slips of paper. We go on Saturday morning, June 6, if the rain is not too heavy. At best it will be muddy and a dark, slippery mountain descent which we hope does not end in colds for us, especially the children. If it is pouring on Saturday there will still be Sunday, Monday, and Tuesday to try to find a few clear hours for walking.

Sat., June 6, 1942. Left Camp Binagsukan at 7:00 A.M. after paqueros
had taken bedrolls and food boxes ahead of us. Up at 5:00 A.M. in early
moonlight to have bedrolls and two children's beds packed and down
in time. Two and one-half hour pull up mountain side and down
other to wagon train line. Mountain trail bordered with fresh green
rice that had sprung up after rains from seeds spilled from sacks
brought into camp. Beth and Clay had great fun riding astride the
backs of paqueros and walking for a rest in a few level places. There
was a decided change in temperature as the day progressed and we
descended from hills. Fifteen or so looted boxcars stood amidst rubbish scattered by robbers at the end of the line. Half-empty food
cans—anchovies, olives, asparagus which had been opened, tasted,
and discarded with part of contents still in cans—littered the ground.
Hawaiian Philippine Co. papers (office records) blowing in the wind,
yellow paint poured on the ground, oil which had been discarded in
order to empty drums, and empty house (former house for guard at
end of line) told the story of theft and destruction. Our group coming
out was the same as going in except for pets—all animals left behind—and most houseboys who had accompanied "masters" before,
carrying lunch baskets. Sejio had a heavily loaded basket of peanut
butter sandwiches, hard-boiled eggs, bananas, scones, fudge, and
filled water bottles. Said good-bye at track line, gave him $16.00 to
keep for me, or use for food for me—paid him salary to the 15th and
told him to charge to my account rice, fish, sugar, mangoes, and salt,
and other supplies needed at camp. Left $10.00 with Mr. Diaz for meat
for Sejio and Georgia (Georgia left chained in house with a last farewell pat).

Two trips of Kolomigos (?) hand car carried us down the track to
hacienda of Ciro (pronounced "zero") Locsin, manager of Bacolod-
Murira Central, where we were to leave the line and go into Bacolod
by truck. At Mr. Locsin's we drank our fill from our hoarded water
bottles, refilled them, and sat down to wait for bedrolls to catch up
with us. At lunch time Mr. and Mrs. Locsin brought out hot rolls (what
a treat!), butter, jam, cold sliced meat, and ice cold Coca-Cola and
beer—the first sign of ice since leaving the Central. No bedrolls until

4:30 P.M. We decided to spend night at hacienda rather than arrive unwelcomed, and perhaps unprepared for, at concentration camp at night. Spread mattresses on floor with nets. Men slept inside garden house (summer house) on concrete floor (with mattresses) at end of concrete tennis court (too bad if it had rained!).

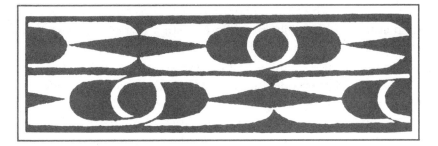

BACOLOD CAMP
1942-1943

Sunday, June 7, 1942. Up early again Sunday morning and feasted on breakfast of hot coffee, ham, eggs, sliced pineapple, hot muffins. The Locsins had left Bacolod-Murira Central feeling safer at hacienda and at the hacienda had large rattan basket packed for each member of family ready to flee, on a moment's notice, farther away from town. Mrs. L. apologized for towels and table linens, saying she had at beginning of war packed away her good linens and hidden them.

Miss Bernos, nurse for three Locsin children, helped me first day with mine alone. Missed Sejio!

Our party left in three trucks for Bacolod after breakfast with good wishes (Locsins') and our passes in our hands. Arrived at Central, could see blackened smokestacks, collapsed concrete ends of burned bodega, skeleton frame of new bodega taken to pieces bit by bit for tin and nipa. Cars for hauling sugar cane overturned on tracks approaching the mill. Tons of sugar (200,000 to 250,000) destroyed, sometimes only for the bags, worth $.25 each. Houses near the Central stacked beneath with sheaths of nipa and looked closely for stray pieces of my white wicker furniture, which would be conspicuous, but did not find any. Shirted Central Filipinos looked at so many "blancos" curiously but without malice, though posters on all schoolhouses, telephone poles, and even houses told of brutalities of Americans to Filipinos and urged "Let's work together for peace—Japan and the Philippine

Islands." Also, "The New Philippines," with a picture of school children at their desks—Filipino children with a strange, Japanese look on their faces. No cars on highway—though usually on Sunday morning traffic is heavy—families visiting relatives, to and from mass, etc. An abandoned late-model Packard on the side of road, an abandoned truck, with two tires removed, pulled off into a side road. Closed houses on both sides of road. A quiet, deserted and desolate country. Cut and unmoved sugar cane soured in the rain and now steaming in the sun with a putrid odor. Rice planted here and there between long stretches of untouched cane fields. Everywhere neglect. In Silay stores were burned, a few people around a pork vendor with his cooked pig (lechon?) for sale in tiny pieces. Apparently more onlookers than buyers—few Filipinos of working class have money now. First Japanese soldier at Talisay—where we showed our passes after "bowing the guard" as per sign—and on to Bacolod after a flat tire which held up all three vehicles. Passed other highway guards with unsmiling faces on the way to our destination on the outskirts of Bacolod, Bacolod North Elementary School. Did not go through town nor see destruction there we had heard about—burned stores, burned market place. After a hot wait at the entrance to the school grounds we were let in the fenced grounds and instructed to go to the home economics building to await orders. A few chairs, an old stove, water faucets which did not run, and a toilet which did not flush. From 11:00 A.M. till 2:00 P.M. we sat, stood, and fumed, waiting for someone to tell us what to do. We ate from baskets amidst thousands of flies. Children hot and crying. At 2:00 o'clock inspector arrived and told us to go to north wing of classroom building and arrange ourselves in three classrooms—men and women to room separately. There were 21 in our party, with the Oss family (H.-P. Co. engineer and wife and 5-year-old child) to join us from their hideout near Bacolod the next day. Of these 24, ten were men. The ten men took the room between the women's room and the nursery where Douglas White (3 months) and his Filipino amah (only Filipino in camp), Beth, Clay and I, Mrs. Oss, and Thora Ann had been placed. Our rooms were filthy, cockroaches on floor, heavy cobwebs on wall. But we had companions ahead of us! The Fabrica group had come in the day before us and had already established themselves. What a reunion! There were no cooking facilities when they came in, but they had built a wood stove similar to ours in the mountains. The first night each person in the group ate alone. I found that the two fried chickens I had brought had spoiled in the heat. Drinking water out and afraid to drink from faucets here. Bacolod water engineer left when Japs arrived and water impurities are no longer counteracted by chemical treatment. The children were hungry and cried all night, intermittently. Up early to fix oatmeal for the children, took one hour to get water to boil with our own fire, no breakfast for self. Roll call at 8:00 A.M. and then meeting of the Fabrica and Hawaiian-Philippine (or H-P) groups to decide about cooking, drinking water, etc. Japanese decided the problem for us. "All people in concentration camp must pool their food. Otherwise some would have more to eat than others and there would be complaints from those with less," is the way the order was interpreted to us. Fourteen Fabrica people came to concentration camp without food, they had had two hours in which to get out of their houses and Japanese guards stood over them as they packed suitcases and forbade their taking food. We had much food in our group and left orders for more to come next day.

June 8, 1942. Five inspections while in bed last night. At 10:00 o'clock two guards accompanied by Mr. West, who said as light was turned on, "Ladies, keep to your beds," and two guards looked into each bed. At 12:00, 2:00, 3:00, and 4:00 A.M. guards returned alone, turning on lights and shining flashlights in faces of bed occupants. No explanation. No one slept.

June 11, 1942. Order of the day:

7:00 A.M.	Breakfast
8:00	Roll call on front steps
9:00–11:30	Housekeeping (scrub floors, do laundry)
11:30	Lunch
12:00–2:30	Siesta—quiet
3:00–5:00	Sewing, cleaning, laundry, bath
5:00	Tea
6:00	Roll call on front steps
9:00 P.M.	Lights out

Men were assigned duties: clearing and planting garden, cutting grass with blades, raking, digging incinerator pit, cleaning toilets, building showers for men and women, scrubbing porch floors. Four men each day on kitchen police duty—cleaning chickens or fish, making fires and washing dishes for entire camp. Four women each day do cooking under supervision of Mrs. Harbart, who has had years of experience cooking for large numbers of men in lumber camp and who knows how to cook cheaply, appetizingly and appropriately for seventy people. The Japanese will provide us no food. To date our commissary of canned goods brought with us is almost untouched (June 11) as fresh meat, fish, vegetables, fruit, and bread have been sent us by friendly Filipinos and bought for us by our servants outside. We cannot communicate with anyone outside by writing, nor receive written messages, but visitors (one at a time) are allowed in presence of Japanese Commandant and an interpreter.

Pictures taken at 8:00 A.M. roll call. Lt. Nagasi took one (moving picture Kodak) and then picked up Sylvia Aucoin (4 years) in arms and smilingly held her in front of group while Mr. West took another moving picture of us all, Lt. Nagasi and Sylvia included. Good publicity to use in Japan, showing kindness of the Japanese to prisoners of war.

When we came to concentration camp men brought guns to turn in as these were registered, but ammunition each brought in his belt did not necessarily fit weapons turned in and chambers were emptied before arrival here. Permission to wear guns into Bacolod was given when requested by Mr. West in order to protect food supplies accompanying us.

"May driver of truck keep his gun to guard other food supplies coming from the hills?" Mr. West asked.

"To protect your food from whom?" asked the Commandant, wondering if we thought Jap soldiers might accost caravan of foodstuffs.

"To protect from Filipino thieves." Mr. West replied.

"And who is guarding your food in the hills for you?"

"Filipinos," replied Mr. West. The Commandant was really perplexed.

June 16, 1942. Today Poldo, caravan leader, brought word that six boxes of food (at least *one* was mine) were stolen on trip down from mountains—at end of train line—by same looters (former employees of H.-P. Central) who looted and burned homes.

2nd Lt. Nagasi, 29 years old, unmarried, five years of military training including study of English. Soldiers, to have his rank were required to learn German, Italian, or English, and to serve a 5-year training period before the war. Lt. Nagasi has charge of our lives, he says, to guard and protect us, and for this purpose soldiers are housed all around us, in private homes around the school grounds and in barrio nipa huts between the school and the beach. Lt. Urabi has charge of the garden, whose produce we share with Japanese soldiers.

Five serious cases of diarrhea with fever. Dr. Smith was furious because he had no medicines. He was given one-half hour's notice to leave his hospital in Fabrica and was not permitted to bring any medical supplies with him. All supplies confiscated for the Japanese army. Dr. Smith attempted to enter hospital against orders and bring out supplies. Has large bruise on loin to show where he was kicked by a soldier. Needs bismuth, other medicines, and bedpans. We have pooled medical supplies but there is little here. Man with toe amputated shortly before sent to camp in danger of death from further spread of infection. No anesthesia of any kind in camp. Dr. Smith wishes to amputate part of abcessed foot to try to stop infection, but cannot without anesthesia. When he told the Japanese that the patient's life is in danger, the guards replied, "Do not worry, if man dies we will bury him." Dr. Smith swore, which only angered the Japanese and got us no anesthesia. Dr. Smith served in Turkey during the last war and he says no cruelty of Turks equalled the smiling refusal of Japs to answer his humane requests. At roll call today Lt. Nagasi asked why so many people were absent and said through an interpreter (although he understands and speaks almost perfect English), "Take precaution to safeguard your health. I do not want you to be sick." We bowed and smiled at his interest and concern. "The lieutenant regrets, however, that the permission granted yesterday to keep a light burning in the toilets used by the patients, and in some patients' rooms, at night, must be withdrawn. Patients who must go to toilets after nine o'clock must do so with flashlights or in the darkness." Dr. Smith's face grew livid and he began to sputter, but we have agreement in camp not to speak to the lieutenant individually—all questions and statements given to Mr. Pope, our elected spokesman, so Dr. Smith will have to tell Mr. Pope and he will pass complaints on to the lieutenant.

Yesterday we had visitors from Manila and today a reprimand. "The lieutenant wishes to say that the officers here yesterday said the attitude of this concentration camp compares badly with ones of the camps for Americans in Manila and other places. The lieutenant wishes to say that the visiting officers were amazed at disrespect shown them by failure of those in camp to bow when in the presence of officers, by their failure to greet all officers with appropriate salutation, 'Good morning' or 'Good afternoon.' The lieutenant wishes to say that in future all persons in camp will please bow whenever a Japanese officer approaches and will please be more courteous to these officers. Discourtesy is a serious offense and must not be repeated."

A Japanese carpenter, Yasamori, for twenty-two years a laborer on the Hawaiian-Philippine Sugar Central, has become our camp warden—from workshop to administrator's polished desk by the chances of war. Yasamori's former employer has become one of his prisoners and now sweeps Yasamori's floor each morning. The smile never leaves Yasamori's face. He has risen to heights of which he never dared dream. He is fed in camp and sleeps on a cot in his office at night. We ask him for little items like more light bulbs and tell him about a broken faucet. These things he reports to his superior in the downtown Bacolod Japanese headquarters. We think the former carpenter, well known on Negros, was placed here to humiliate us.

Yesterday the wife of Yasamori's former boss at the Central was trying to move the baby bed of little Douglas White when one of the casters caught. Yasamori was passing and as he went by she said abruptly, as she had done for years, "Mori, move this bed for me," and he moved it—both forgetting for the moment that order-giving and order-taking were reversed.

Lt. Nagasi, sitting on the porch talking to people today, brought out of his pocket a watch—a lady's wrist watch from Entreken del Nort* of

*Probably the name of a jewelry shop.

Bacolod. "A gift for my girl friend in Japan," he said. "It is a Swiss movement. Is it a good watch?" They assured him it was, but nothing was said about how he paid for it, etc.

June 17, 1942. The hot, humid days are enervating. Flies are thick in the bedrooms, the toilets, and on the food at mealtimes. There seems no way of controlling the flies as Japanese army horses are kept in fields adjoining the concentration camp grounds, and the doctor says flies probably come from there.

The nights are too hot to sleep—mosquitoes terrific—and we are forced to come indoors at dusk. We fight them until bedtime and even then they sometimes come through the nets. We are anxiously awaiting the heavy rains which had already started in the mountains, though do not know yet how we will eat—there is no dining room, the kitchen is out of doors, there are no covered walks. We eat on small children's desks scattered around the yard.

Toilets are huge concrete affairs on which the students climbed and stood with feet apart after removing inner underwear. The custom here is not to sit on the toilet but climb up on it. More sanitary than our custom but inconvenient for those accustomed to American plumbing fixtures.

"Men must sleep in one room together and women in other rooms," the Commandant instructed us upon arriving and so instructed seven newcomers today. "But you may live freely," he concluded. Husbands are assigned yard duty during the day, women to kitchen and housecleaning tasks, or laundry. Wives and husbands see little of each other except at meals and after 10:00 in the evening. Couples, all married, are seen strolling about the building hand in hand between 6:30 (after roll call) and 8:30 P.M. (Everyone in rooms ready for lights out at 9:00). Husbands and wives kiss each other goodnight on verandah, before eyes of others crowded in this narrow space before bedtime to get what breeze there is. The bedrooms are stuffy hot with many beds, each with its mosquito net hanging from wire near ceiling—cutting the breeze, if any. A strangely isolated family life: seven wives in one room, their seven husbands in the next, and so on down the long corridor: men, women, men, women, in alternate rooms.

Thursday, June 19, 1942. A Japanese doctor visited our five very sick diarrhea patients today. Dr. Smith's repeated requests for medicines from his own hospital at Fabrica finally brought a small supply of medicines—Japanese ones—which Dr. Smith refused to administer. The Japanese are becoming really worried about the fever and sickness in our camp. Mrs. Wiley has a temperature of 104 degrees. A Catholic nun is equally sick. Miss Bayona, the only Filipino in camp, nurse of Douglas White, is in desperately weakened condition from diarrhea, which seemingly cannot be checked without medicines not in camp. Dr. Smith will not administer Japanese medicines with which he is not familiar. The situation is becoming critical.

Five additional persons were interned yesterday: a Dutch priest and two American-Filipino mestizo families consisting of mother, father, and child each. These are the first mixed bloods to be brought in by the Japanese, though we have been told that anyone on Negros holding enemy alien "citizenship" should register for possible imprisonment.

July 1, 1942. Isolated Americans and British on small sugar centrals and haciendas have been brought in, one or two at the time. Most of them were glad of the protection of camp, for living is difficult outside and food is hard to secure. There are now 95 internees in Bacolod, 22 of them children.

Permanent fatigue overtaking me. Constant, unending care of Beth and Clay. Take them to outhouse toilet with me when I go because there is no place to leave them, no one to leave them with. There are now in our one small room Mrs. Oss, Thora Ann (5 years), Mrs. Mac-Williams (Scotch) with 2-month-old baby, Douglas White, 3 months, his amah who lives in room. Beth and Clay cannot be left alone in room for one minute because they touch babies' things or the babies themselves. To take a bath in outdoor shower in rain yesterday Beth and Clay sat on wet bench in partially enclosed, open-top shower in rain while I bathed. Both children coughed in the night as a result. No one offered to look after them for one minute. So they must go everywhere I go, their little feet worn out trying to keep up with me as I go from washtub to clothes line, to mop floors then wash mop at distant water supply, to kitchen for food, up and down stairs all day.

Old Bacolod incinerator for city garbage blazed all night. Fire, not far from camp, lighted it. Hearse at the incinerator in afternoon with the body of a dead Japanese—ambushed or diseased.

July 3, 1942. At roll call this morning we were told that we might celebrate July 4 if we wished to do so without violating the rules of camp. Facetiously we asked each other how we could celebrate with rooms to be swept, mopped, dusted, clothes to be washed, children to be bathed, fed, taken to toilet, watched at play, meals to be cooked, dishes to be washed, and the endless round of daily duties which completely consume our time and make us welcome—no longer dread—the "Lights out" which is shrieked at us each evening by guards living across street from camp.

Mr. Pine was brought in. Stooped, bearded, long-haired "old-time" American, former bartender in Bacolod. He came to Philippine Islands in Spanish-American War, 1898, and has never left. Married twice to Filipino women and has truly "gone native" in sense of being careless about dress and cleanliness. Other Spanish-American War veterans are here. Mr. McIntosh is one, 89 years old, who trots around camp barefooted like a youth and talks about his mestizo grandchildren.

Box of fudge and scones from Miss Ganahan at Camp Binagsukan. No notes are permitted but she had written my name on outside box and underneath, "Regards to all." Yasamori opened box for inspection, liked fudge, took out double fist full and crammed in mouth, gave another fist full to five Porter children (mestizos) standing in office, took another bunch for himself and then sent me, crushed, the remaining one-fourth box. Nothing was said. He was showing his authority. I had no comment. Yasamori's shirt open to low hanging trousers, bare breast and navel exposed. Why does navel look so repulsive? And we must bow twice daily to him, in morning and evening when he comes out, as we are lined up for roll call.

July 4, 1942. Breakfast—scrambled eggs and red rice, oatmeal for children. Dinner—boiled ham slices in hot biscuits, two per person, potato salad, rice Valenciano (rice, green pepper, pimento, chicken, sausage), iced tea (ice from one of centrals reopened by Japs), spiced cake and candy. Everyone dressed in red, white, and blue. Japs took moving and candid camera shots of us all day as we went about duties as usual. Began at roll call with picture of prisoners taking picture of Lt. Nagasi, and one of the 98 prisoners, as he called the roll.

Yesterday a large Jap boat was at pier, could see only masts of winches for lifting cargo from holds. Steady stream of trucks down roadway by camp to the pier—we can see water but not pier itself or boats, which are hidden from us by coconut grove and nipa houses used as barracks. Truckloads of fully equipped soldiers brought to Bacolod, truckloads of supplies in large wooden cases. Truckloads of bags (rice and sugar, perhaps) going from Bacolod. All trucks bearing names of Negros firms—three with Hawaiian-Philippine plainly written on them—a bright yellow truck with Pacific Commercial Company still in bold black letters, a Caterpillar Tractor Co. service car, Insular Lumber Company trucks, etc. The Japanese brought no trucks with them but have almost endless streams of cars and trucks confiscated for their use. Buses are running again on the highways, but have few passengers, whereas before they were always overcrowded at reasonable fare—one centavo† per kilometer. Where a fifteen kilometer ride was formerly fifteen centavos, now $2.00 in old currency only.

New soldiers who came in yesterday lined up before the camp this morning for rising sun greeting. Impressive. They chant together before sunrise, and as the sun appears peeping over mountains they turn in unison to face it, chant again, turn sharply to original position, chant, and then solemnly break ranks.

Filipino dentist here today. Went in office where he was working to have back filling, which broke in half in mountains, replaced. We were told by Mr. Pope and Japanese that only old currency can be used. I told dentist I had no old currency but if he would fill on credit I wanted work done. He said I could pay later and seemed uninterested in money when I further apologized. Said gruffly, "Next time." Electric drill not attached (had only hand implements), Jap standing by chair (ordinary chair, no head rest) as dentist scraped tooth for minute gently with small scalpel and then put filling in. Whole operation not more than five minutes and he was ready for next patient—there

†1/100 of one peso.

were many. I asked cost of filling when work was over and dentist dismissed question and said again only, "Next time." We were told the dentist would be allowed in for one day only and am perplexed about "Next time." Dentist knows also that if I have no old currency today I cannot likely have any at later date in camp.

Latest arrivals are from San Carlos Sugar Milling Co. on the opposite side of Negros. They were told by Japanese officer there not to bring food with them to Bacolod as Japanese were providing camp with food. Strange!

July 6, 1942. Visitors found in camp today—bed bugs. Teehera family (Mom, Pop, Tony, and three children) put their beds out in sun and passerby noticed crawling bugs. Investigation proved mattresses so inhabited as to be almost able to walk. Mosquito nets, pillows, pillow cases found bordered in black where bugs had lived, excreted, mated, laid eggs and died. Evidences of generations of bugs. Mrs. MacW. of my room had 3-months-old baby on small pad on school bench near where beds were sunning and found three bugs on pad when she was advised to look. (This after pad and baby returned to room.) Wonder if other bugs escaped and we've started something. Very little disinfectant in camp to fight bugs if they get in floor and wall cracks as well as beds. Teeheras immensely unpopular, not American in any sense of word. He, an Italian born in Philippine Islands, served in U.S. Navy during W.W.I but not an American citizen. Wife a low-class Filipino. She and children have to be reported daily for failure to flush toilets after use or after emptying foul smelling chamber mug each morning. Mr. Teehera could not prove he was not American and the fact he had served in the navy was sufficient to send him and his family to camp (Tony is tattooed from shoulders to wrists). They love it here—plenty of rice and little to do. They are not like the rest of us who, when not on kitchen duty, spend much time scrubbing to keep clean. They don't bother.

"Camp experience will be something to tell our grandchildren," one inmate said lately.

"If the celibate lives we have had continue, there'll be no grandchildren!" was reply.

Col. Ohta, who has recently been promoted from Commanding

Officer Occidental Negros to C.O. (all) Negros, visited us yesterday, smiling under his drooping mustache. At Mrs. Amechagurra's room he stopped and singled her out to come to him. Frances, a beautiful American-Spanish girl, black eyes and hair and whitest skin, not more than twenty-five years old, is married to a Spaniard fifty-one. Col. Ohta pointed to Frances' breasts and asked her a question through the interpreter, "Are you nursing a baby?"

"No, my youngest child is two years old."

"Then I should warn you to beware of undressing, even during the rainy season which is approaching."

The blush on Frances' face was no greater than that on Mr. Pope's, who was present. Persons in room with Frances have complained that soldiers in house directly opposite their room sit on porch all day with field glasses looking into bedrooms. Of course we have no curtains and with women crowded together in small rooms there's hardly space to curtain off one tiny corner for dressing. In mornings we dress quickly beside our own beds. We have several times found a Jap guard standing by our windows looking in. We can only duck low beneath window sill and wait until he has decided to go on, before standing again. This morning I sat on floor to pull dress over head as guard was outside looking in again. This kind of thing is annoying.

At 5:00 this morning Mr. White's baby in our room (now five children and five adults) was crying loudly and Filipino nurse got up in nightgown, with hair in long braids, to see what was the matter. Lit candle (no flashlight bulb and cannot turn on light during night). Yasamori was up and came in to chat with nurse. She was horrified in her undressed state and asked him to leave. She said she had to blow out candle before he would go from room. I slept through this, having been up till midnight with Clay, trying to coax him to silence as he did not want to go to sleep—too excited from the screaming and shouting of older children who tear in and out of rooms and wear to a frazzle the nerves of younger children and adults. (Yesterday heavy rain and children could not go out of doors.)

Japanese soldiers have shaved heads, faded khaki uniforms, trousers usually darker than shirts (fewer washings?), teeth that appear white (against dark skin) like American Negroes seem to have white teeth.

Reason American women use such heavy lipstick (for contrast) is to make yellowish teeth look lighter.

Col. Ohta, on visit, praised camp for improvement to grounds—grass cut, garden cleaned of weeds, onions, beans, corn, eggplants growing. Also threatened us that if anyone questioned visitors in camp about business, meaning what is going on at the prisoner's central—most of people here are from sugar or lumber centrals—visitors would cease to be allowed and person or persons inquiring after forbidden information would be severely punished. We are also forbidden to ask war news, but we already knew this.

Col. Griffin, father-in-law of Mr. Pope, arrived on Negros from Manila with a pass from the Japanese there. Colonel, about 70, retired officer, U.S. Army, was in Manila in December to see about army pension when war began. Left Manila on ship sunk in Manila Bay, Dec. 22 (?), was rescued from the water, and put in concentration camp there. He became ill and was removed to hospital and after dismissal there was permitted to stay out of camp, due to age and health condition. Visited here and then returned to Manila. Strange!

Colonel said there were over 3,000 civilians in the camp in Manila,‡ only 26 let out permanently and a few more out on temporary passes requiring continuous re-approval. Feeding of prisoners had been by Red Cross but Japanese were to take over this week. Friends and relatives in Manila permitted to take food (left at camp gate) for those inside.

New nurse for Douglas White—fourth in four weeks. Before assuming duties she had to sign an agreement with Japanese to stay in camp, without permission to leave under any circumstances, for five months. Japanese peeved at continuous change of nurses, who do not like being lone Filipino here. Why five months? Strange. We all say we'll be here till Christmas, six more months. Do Japanese think war will be over about that time, too?

More mestizos with native wives and Americans with native families coming in. Mr. Grant, a 1900 relic with 20-year-old native of lowest

‡EHV is referring here to the Santo Tomás Internment Camp, to which the internees in Bacolod will later be moved.

class (lace dress at breakfast and barefooted), and Mr. Pauli (suspected of being strongly pro-German) with his native family.

July 15, 1942. Two planes circled overhead before landing at Bacolod field, red rising sun plainly discernible under each wing. Also a Japanese flag is plainly seen from camp as it flies over a nearby provincial building.

Latest news: Moscow surrounded by Germans, Sebastopol taken by Germans.

Saturday, July 19, 1942. The Harblentzels—Mrs. Nena and Marlene—tried before to get a pass to visit camp but were denied. Moving from Bacolod to hacienda next week. Mr. Miller (Swiss) of Manila, business partner of Mr. Harblentzel, to bring family (wife and 2 children) from Manila to live in Bacolod in the Harblentzels' house. Living conditions are cheaper in Bacolod. Swiss can get permits for inter-island travel. Any Swiss of Manila offered passage to Santiago, Chile, by Japanese if they cared to take it. Most Swiss prefer to stay in P.I. because business interests are here.

Sunday, July 20, 1942. Visitors in morning. Lt. Nagasi and some friends. The children and I were eating alone near the wash room in a spot of shade. Lieutenant stopped to admire blonde hair of children, to ask age and whether they could talk, to say hair was not color of mine, etc., etc. Guests were served ice cold native lime juice, cake, and candy from our Sunday lunch.

Afternoon Col. Ohta visited camp and asked for all women to meet him at 2:15. Began (Yasamori as interpreter) by asking how many women present smoked. Twelve out of thirty-three raised hands. Colonel reached in pockets and brought out two packages Camel cigarettes, two packages Philip Morris cigarettes, and four packages "Cherry" brand Japanese cigarettes, asking that smokers divide these and sample Japanese brand. Packages opened and passed, 26 of 33 women took cigarettes. Japanese brand was their preference. In haze of smoke, conference continued. (Smokers carry empty tin cans around with them for ashtrays.) He said, "Life is like an ocean of waves, sometimes we are on the crest of a wave, sometimes in the hollow. When down we must keep up our spirit (tapping his head) and our health. We must keep busy and keep happy. I hope the war will soon be over so you can go to your homes." Applause from all the women.

Then Colonel told us about himself and his family. He studied English four years as a child. Father of three sons and two daughters, oldest daughter 20 years old, oldest son 18. Has not been home for six years, has been fighting in China. Bald, mustached, one side front tooth missing. Colonel had a good time. His cousin was in the attack on Pearl Harbor. Colonel had not been to U.S. "yet." In answer to a question he said very few women in Japan smoke. Meeting was like that of a group of little children—our best stage smiles on. Colonel had a broad grin. Commented on cake and said he would visit us again if we fed him so well. All women rose and bowed as he entered room, and rose and bowed again as he left.

Mr. Wiley commented that camp was like the Mexican army, where every soldier is a general. True. Everyone here trying to tell others what to do, and especially what not to do. Everyone spying on everyone else, especially kitchen workers to see if food is taken from kitchen, trying to see what is going on in rooms, peeking to see what is in packages delivered from outside by families and relatives, and the unending gossip about people who do not wash floor-mop clean after using, who "flit" through mosquito net in face of nearby bed occupant, who get extra service from kitchen, who take up too much room on clothes line, etc., etc., etc.

July 21, 1942. Letter to Mr. Pope: "In the conference of women called yesterday by Col. Ohta, the Colonel asked if he could be of service to us. I have a favor to ask of the Colonel, through you. I wish to locate my husband who is, I believe, on the Island of Luzon . . . etc."

The horrible monotony of living. To bed each night with back aching, arms sore, legs tortuous to move, a dull headache, and the prospect of another day the same. Standing in blazing sun for roll call after a hurriedly swallowed breakfast and no time to go to toilet. After roll call a rush to overcrowded, dirty room where women push and jostle each other at one faucet used for filling buckets to flush toilets and for washing and rinsing clothes. Water splashing as one container after another is pushed under the faucet, feet and ankles soaking, water all over floor of toilet room, mud outside around tables for washing clothes, and all in glaring blinding sun. My face has burned. It is hot both day and night, indoors and out. I feel in a continual fever. Even Beth tells me so, in mornings when I pick her up.

Each morning the guards quartered across the roadway from us are out at dawn to give the rising sun salute. A soldier who speaks English told me that when in Japan the soldiers always face the east when giving the daily salute. If stationed in foreign countries the soldiers face Japan. As the Philippine Islands have become a part of Japan, the soldiers here look directly at the rising sun itself. The daily salutation is chanted—of five distinct and separate verses, with each verse a pledge: 1. Life dedicated to the Emperor, 2. To be courteous, 3. To have strong, healthy bodies—to be good fighters, 4. To be frugal, 5. To be truthful. In rainy weather or in dry, the Japanese soldier's day begins with this "pledge."

Wednesday, July 22, 1942. Five more priests (now seven in all in camp), including three Dutch and one English. Short, round, popeyed padre from Holland sat behind me on steps after 6:00 P.M. roll call, as I watched the children at play.

"Vant to hear the latest radio news?" he whispered. "Ve had de radio on 'till late last night," he said. I nodded. We are forbidden to discuss war news but news comes in whenever there are new arrivals. "De Germans are within one hundred miles of Moscow but have been stopped for three days now. Heavy fighting in the Celebes.* Fighting on Negros—" and as he began the details Yasamori came and sat on my unoccupied side. This, of course, stopped the priest's conversation. He rose hastily, said, "Good-night," and left us. Yasamori then departed also, he had done his duty. But later that night no less than six inmates asked me if I wanted to hear news brought in by the priests. Trying to control conversation among a large group of people

*One of the islands making up modern Indonesia, 90 miles east of Borneo.

is like blocking a bubbling spring by putting pebbles in it. There may be temporary apparent cessation of flow but water will bubble underneath for a while and spring out somewhere else. The flow is changed but not halted.

Flash! Was stopped by two soldiers while writing the last word.

Was sitting out of doors with children. Had put clothes on line and taken children to hospital—for Clay's nose (he fell on paved walk and wore off end of his nose), and for infected mosquito bites where both Beth and Clay have scratched their legs, and also for prickly heat (spreading watery blisters) on Clay's neck. Was also given lime juice in Clay's little silver baby cup which I had along for that purpose. Two soldiers found my sitting place—one had three front teeth covered with tin, side teeth gold, second soldier had three gold teeth. I had knitting bag with Red Cross on it, in which I carried a notebook, change of clothes for children, book, cup, and bottle of drinking water. Soldier pointed to Red Cross and asked a question in Japanese, presumably, "Why?"

"American Red Cross," I answered, "used for knitting."

"What in bottle, whiskey?"

"No, lemon juice."

"See," the Jap replied, and put it to his lips, unsweetened pure lime juice. He spat it forcibly as the bitter juice bit his palate. I refrained from laughing as soldiers passed on.

July 25, 1942. Priest told me of dinner given him by Bishop back in Holland when he was home on leave. Bishop's housekeeper wanted to be especially pleasing and planned a curry dinner. Boiled meat served and can of curry powder put nobly by visitor's place. He did not let on that this was not the proper way to serve curry. Priests tried to bring wine into camp. Got only three bottles under pretense of using it for "sprinkling heads, this way"—as he went through motions to Japanese guard, who may have known something of our religious customs. Guard let three bottles pass but admonished him he must not drink it. Others in camp tried to get in whiskey disguised in vinegar bottles, in old dirty containers of one kind or another, but guards have keen noses and but little of forbidden drinks have seeped in.

Wed., July 29, 1942. First of weekly sing-songs led by Catholic priest. Opened with "God Bless America," some standing, most sitting, then some W.W.I songs—typed words, no accompaniment—"Smiles," "Keep the Homefires Burning," and others. A Scotch ditty solo, with his own piano accompaniment, by Sandy Baigre, a solo by Jean Mac-Williams, and last a recitation and an imitation of camp snores by Ar-nell (the only American Negro in camp), which brought down the house.

Young Mr. Jones, whom I had met in Bacolod back in February, joined concentration camp today. Had been hiding with a Filipino family until apprehended.

New dining room opened—old manual training building. Men in camp connected water for the kitchen, built sinks from pieces of tin roofing; building is large, barn-like, with concrete floor. We eat on benches in three long rows, low desks serving as tables, cramping for tall people. Beth and Clay too excited by the crowd—over 120 people here now—to eat first two meals indoors. We had been eating alone— the three of us—in a corner of camp yard or in our room on rainy days, until now.

How expensive are Clay's feet! His last pair of shoes is wearing out and I have been letting him go barefooted on rainy days to save this pair of shoes. He is enjoying it. Sits contentedly on the top of verandah steps, waiting for some kind passing adult to hold his hand so he can get down, or to take him down, his chubby feet crossed and relaxed. I should never have known how beautiful and full of life his feet are had he continued to wear shoes as he should. There is hookworm in the tropics and white children are never allowed out without shoes. Clay and Beth have had no new shoes in months. The shoes worn in the mountains have come apart from hard wear. I have no old currency with which to buy them—if shoes could be had even at exorbitant prices, which is doubtful.

Clay's name in camp is Wah Wah, because he cried so often for water (wah wah) the first few days of camp. Though he has learned to say *water*, the nickname sticks.

Before roll call this morning I left Clay on the top step while I took Beth to the toilet. Returned to find roll call started, so rushed to place in line. (We stand in two long lines with toes at trench dug to keep lines straight.) Took Beth to the line but left Clay on steps. Roll call half over when Clay decided to join us, managing to get down steps and sauntering between the two lines as the guard called roll. Clay's pants had come unfastened from his shirt and he held them on with his hand. Giggles on all sides as Clay unconcernedly walked full length of lines to the place where I stood. Guard was amazed, but Clay and I went unpunished.

Wish I did not feel a compulsion to read, but cannot "amah" the children continuously without a book under my arm, in case a free moment should arrive. Cannot take diary as it may be taken away by passing guard. It is all right to read, but dangerous to be seen writing. There has been little choice from the library. Have had to read fiction or nothing, and though writers are good—as reviews and reputations go—some have left a bad taste in my mouth.

July 30, 1942. What a difference a cool day makes! New energy, new hopes, a feeling that all may not be hopeless. New arrival today, Mrs. Mercado from New York, married to a Filipino on Negros, came crying with three-months-old baby, leaving other child, 8 years old, with her husband. Her husband had been slapped on face and head and hit severely in mouth by Japanese who brought her to camp. Mrs. Mercado registered as an American, as requested, immediately after Japanese occupation of Negros and carried out all instructions—was told to stay at home until sent for. She was sent for today and told to go to camp at once, without explanation.

Had been listening to radio, Quezon and MacArthur both speech-making again, saying, "Have patience in the Philippines," but we took this with smiles and not disgust as before. Maybe help is coming. Russia is holding again, New Guinea has been freed of Japanese, Japan has been bombed (this really makes us feel good), and Rommel is on the run in Libya. Maybe we shall be out by Christmas.

Monday, August 3, 1942. Yasamori away on short vacation. Had on new shoes before his departure to meet daughter returning from Iloilo. He said these shoes and one pair of shorts were only salary he had received for two months he has been at concentration camp. Rather difficult as he has a wife and children to support. Japanese general arrived by plane yesterday from Cebu. He will inspect our camp today. A civilian Japanese employee is taking Yasamori's place and strangely he is a Christian. He stood at the door last evening at Reverend Monger's (?) 6:15 church service. Full Sunday yesterday: 7:15 special mass for Catholics, 9:00 baseball game of six innings (fast and exciting playing). Several Britishers in game had never played before, adding to confusion and joy of spectators, many of whom likewise knew nothing of game. One Dutch padre running from third base to home plate saw he could not make home before arrival of ball from field, so returned to first base from which he had originally run to third. Could not understand why he was not allowed to return safely there (crossing field from third to first base). The seven padres here are much fun and well liked, as are the two sisters.

One room—called "children's playroom," but which children enter only on rainy days—is used for mass, Protestant services, for bridge, mah-jongg and poker games in evenings, for reading room in afternoons, and for dancing on the sly (forbidden). This is also Wednesday night sing-along room.

The confidence we put in these Japanese! Mary Davis just stopped me to ask if I had received a reply from my letter to Col. Ohta about Jim. She has written a letter to her husband, Major Davis, in medical corps, former staff director at Manapla Central Hospital, and asked Col. Ohta to see that it is delivered. Major Davis was with American forces on Mindanao, and whether these forces have surrendered or are still resisting is unknown.

Saturday, August 8, 1942. A table with a white cloth placed in the road in front of camp. Japanese flags flying from each house, used by soldiers, surrounding camp. Lt. Nagasi, with white gloves and full-dress uniform, read to soldiers from scroll taken from table. Doubble salute to early morning sun. Celebration because 8th day of 8th month of war—double 8th—just as China has her double 10th celebration each year. Cavalry parade in the afternoon—five saddle horses and some native caramota ponies, horses taken from stables of the centrals and from wealthy hacienderos.

Mrs. Harblentzel visited camp again. Brought live sheep and live rabbits. She is moving back to her home in Bacolod. Says we are fortunate to be in camp. The husband in the family nearest to the Harblentzel hacienda had his head severed (cousin of Aquinaldo Gamboa) by armed Filipinos who entered his house to steal. Mrs. H.'s farm home was robbed of curtains and all materials of any kind while she was last in Bacolod. She is afraid to leave the hacienda and afraid to stay there. Stories of activities by the Filipinos against wealthy land owners pour in. In Icabella† a wealthy Spanish family (son last year married daughter of comptroller of Notre Dame University) was burned out. Boy had been a student at university. Beautiful girl—came to P.I. to be married. She was not visited by the white community on Negros nor asked to white parties—must have been a shock to her, not what she expected. The son is refined but his mother still eats with her fingers. An example of the social lag of the older generation of the newly "arrived" nation—Philippine Islands. As workers made threats all the family moved into the mother's house for protection. In the middle of the night the house, in which all close relatives slept with all joint possessions, was set afire by disgruntled laborers. Family escaped with lives only, all possessions lost and one Filipino maid burned to death in the flames.

Sunday, August 9, 1942. To outdoor shower at 11:15 as usual to bathe Beth, Clay and myself before 11:45 lunch. Shower not so popular in morning, most people prefer it after siesta and after heat of day, so I go in morning with children. Bathed Beth and Clay and sat them on bench just outside shower room while I stood under open faucet which spattered in all directions on already soaked floor and walls. Scream from Clay. I rushed out half clothed. He had a nail completely through his foot. Had picked up stick, nail protruding from end, used for piercing leaves, papers, and other rubbish for garbage can—and pierced instep from top to sole of foot. No anti-tetanus serum in hospital here or in Bacolod. Yasamori called Dr. Jara‡—called Mansion House to have someone there locate Dr. Jara as Dr. J. must go by Man-

---

†Isabela—town on western Negros Island, south of Bacolod.
‡Dr. Jara, apparently a new physician appointed by the Japanese, is not to be confused with the earlier mentioned Dr. Jardelega.

sion House twice daily to receive orders from the Japanese army, if any. Dr. Jara has no phone in his home or private hospital. Dr. Jara came. (Sister Luciosa had squirted iodine with eyedropper, sticking point of dropper into hole in Clay's foot and forcing iodine through to the bottom opening.) Dr. Jara looked at Clay's foot and said Clay must have tetanus injections and he would make an effort to secure serum from a private source.

Monday, August 10, 1942. Dr. Jara gave Clay 1,500 units tetanus serum. Found vial of 5,000 units at home of Mr. Jose Caraminas near Bacolod and said I could buy serum for $25.00, but I must buy the entire vial. Price is nothing if Clay's foot or life is involved, but the price is preposterous. I have no old money. Hospital here not interested in buying remaining 3,500 units. Mr. Pope suggested I borrow $25.00 from Mr. Van Kaufman as Mr. Van K. and Mr. Nolen (Bacolod attorney who married a Filipino) have the most old currency in camp. Mr. Van K. gladly loaned money which I shall repay with emergency currency.

Wednesday, August 12, 1942. Clay given hot foot baths in a very hot solution of epsom salts twice daily since Sunday. His screams when foot put in hot solution heart-rending, even when foot placed in tepid solution. Pus in both punctures in foot, though bottom hole is healing. No fever. Dr. Jara gave second tetanus injection today. First injection was in arm. This injection beside wound, in the instep.

News has seeped into camp that Hong Kong has been retaken by the Chinese.* We hope this is true. No news from Russian front.

Sunday, August 16, 1942. Clay's foot healed on bottom opening and doctor advises his walking—to force pus out hole on top. I am happy Clay can walk again, for his sake and mine. His thirty-pound weight seemed sixty before as I had to carry him everywhere. Mrs. Canova and Mr. Thompson helped carry Clay to and from meals, and Clay

---

*Hong Kong was not removed from Japanese control until the end of the war. This is another example of the internees' desperate need for hope.

thoroughly enjoyed this part of sickness. Thought Mr. Thompson must be his "daddy" as other children's daddies often carry children on their shoulders in play. Must remember date of tetanus injections as a later shot might prove fatal.

Cinema tonight—compliments of Japanese—(1) Felix the Cat (2) Yale-Army football game, Oct. 30, 1930, score 7–7 (3) Charlie Chaplin (4) Bill Tilden in How to Play Tennis (5) silent Laurel and Hardy (6) a travelogue showing an American family visiting New York City, government buildings in Washington, a boat trip on a N.Y.C. liner, a visit to Tokyo business centers and shrines, another boat trip via N.Y.C. to Hong Kong and then the picture suddenly stopped as the boat pulled into Hong Kong harbor. With a kind "Good Morning" we were dismissed by the ciné operator. Beth's first ciné. When Felix began moving, Beth shouted in surprise.

Monday, August 17, 1942. The camp population is steadily growing. Another American Negro has been interned with us, and four more American and British priests have been rounded up by the Japanese.

Ferdinand the Bull also joined camp today. This young carabao bull, nine sheep, ten rabbits, twelve ducks, and thirty chickens were brought in to begin a camp livestock and poultry farm. Ferdinand is to stay with us until we can get no food from outside, a time we all feel sure will come in the near future.

Thursday, August 20, 1942. Clay spent a sleepless night, complaining of neck and refusing to lie down in bed, crying continuously, only comforted when sitting upright in my arms in a chair so I moved bed from under mosquito net and put Mrs. Oss's rocking chair under net and rocked Clay from 10:00 to 2:00 A.M. He still cried so I called Dr. Smith of camp. (Dr. Smith has been replaced as camp doctor by the Japanese, who selected Dr. Jara as our camp doctor). Dr. Smith could find nothing wrong with Clay except swollen neck glands. Continued rocking till morning as Clay refused to put head on bed in a sleeping position. Morning showed greatly swollen gland, fever of 102 degrees, throat too swollen to swallow. During the day the fever increased and

Clay was sent to the hospital by Dr. Jara, who made a call during the morning. Diagnosis, abcessed gland. Treatment, hot compresses, with ichthyol.

Friday, August 21, 1942. Bad case of hives on Clay's body. Face swollen till eyes almost closed. A few adrenalin injections available in hospital. Serum used for Clay with almost immediate results, though hives returned after effect of adrenalin wore off. Paregoric to make him sleep, also ¼ aspirin crushed in water. He woke and cried during the night to the dismay of other patients in the single hospital room, eight patients and myself—nine people (2 men, 4 women, 2 small babies, and Clay).

Saturday, August 22, 1942. Hives better but Clay's genital glands swollen. Swelling continued rapidly. Clay unable to urinate due to swelling. Dr. Jara could not be obtained and Clay in danger of rupture. Dr. Smith punctured swollen and swelling parts many times to prevent rupture. Clay in great pain. Neck no better, so sleep lying down impossible. Short naps only in my arms or on my lap. Another night spent holding him. No nurse on duty during night. Two Catholic sisters sleep in an adjoining room but have so many duties with patients during the day they have asked to be called at night only in greatest emergency. Cannot serve night and day efficiently as they have only inexperienced helpers with a makeshift, but rather complete, hospital under their care.

Sunday, August 23, 1942. Clay better. Illness due to reaction from tetanus injection. Severe reaction, but Clay is now throwing off poison. Still not eating due to swollen throat. Hives inside body as well as out, but he is recovering. Will move him to Room 7 again where his crying will not disturb so many people. Completely exhausted—Clay and I—from lack of sleep. My back aching from sitting in wooden-bottomed chair and carrying Clay continuously. Second tetanus injection often makes patient ill with "serum sickness," but this was Clay's first. I had the injection myself when pregnant with Clay. Wonder if this may have acted upon Clay as a first injection. Will ask doctor about this. I sat on scissors, which entered my hip and broke off in hip bone. Had tetanus injection, especially necessary since scissors' point could not be removed due to depth of wound (4 inches). Clay is afraid of the Sister who had injected him with adrenalin in both arms, both legs many times.

Tuesday, August 25, 1942. Planes, in groups of three, and dull thuds, like bombs, in distance.

Visit from Alunan,† who is in the Japanese puppet government in Manila, Gov. Lizares, Col. Ohta, and their staffs. Officials in shining boots, guards, and secretaries with leather portfolios arrived by plane from Manila. Filipinos (Alunan and Lizares) all smiles but had worried looks on their faces. Arrived and left camp in cars, preceded and followed by a truckload of armed Japanese soldiers. Loyal Filipinos have sworn to kill "betrayers" like Alunan and Lizares. So these men fear their own people—not the Japanese.

Friday, August 28, 1942. Beth's birthday, Jim's birthday two days before—passed unobserved. But Beth received cookies from Catholic nuns, a handkerchief from one child in camp, and one of five quintuplet dolls brought to camp by another child. Also a washcloth made from a piece of diaper cloth with BETH embroidered on it by donor. All makeshift and secondhand gifts but a big day for Beth.

Monday, August 31, 1942. Queen Wilhelmina's birthday, and her name was spelled out in orange and yellow leaves of croton plants pasted on a bed sheet attached to the wall above long cafeteria serving stand in the dining room. Five Dutch priests in camp were requested to sing the Dutch national anthem. With tears in their eyes they stood and sang in Dutch. Others in camp rose too, in deference, clapped and hurrahed at end of anthem. Orange marmalade spread on top of mashed carrots as a tribute to our Dutch internees. Large yellow

---

†Rafael Alunan, member of the Commonwealth government who served throughout the war in various posts in the puppet government.

trumpet-like blossoms of alemanda in clusters between huge pots from which food served as we pass in long line to sit in our low school desks to place food on back of another desk. This cramps our knees and makes dainty eating impossible.

A large group of new arrivals, twenty-two, came by boat today from Dumaguete, on the far side of Negros, normally an eight-hour drive from Bacolod by car. As the bridges between Dumaguete and Bacolod have been destroyed by Filipino guerrillas, the new internees had to be transferred by boat. They left Dumaguete on Saturday in an open boat—no covering from sun or rain. Went into foul smelling, stuffy holds when it rained, no toilet facilities, squatted with buttocks over edge of deck without modesty or privacy for necessary functions— very limited drinking water; no food provided by Japanese, previously cooked supplies brought by concentrainees—ten women and twelve men—two American couples, an aged American father with his half-Chinese son, fathers without wives and children, and wives without husbands, and, the most interesting, two American young missionary school teachers evacuated from Japan a few weeks before the out-break of war and who were trapped in Negros when the war started. They speak Japanese fluently, startled Col. Ohta on his last visit by addressing him in his native tongue. They say life has not been easy for them among their own nationality group since the outbreak of the war as they have been suspected and accused by Americans as being pro-Japanese, yet they received no benefits from the Japanese and lost all their money, clothing, and other personal belongings in Japan when forced to flee. In all, there were eight missionaries—teachers, preachers, and a nurse—in the last group to arrive in camp—these from Silliman University (supported by the American Presbyterian Church) at Dumaguete. The American president of the university and his family, however, fled to the hills before Japanese occupation of Negros and have not been caught by the Japanese. The story of Ameri-can missions in the Philippines is a strange one—great competition between Protestant groups in this Catholic stronghold, so not to be at cross-purposes with each other and to conserve funds and concen-trate efforts. Baptists agreed to try to Protestantize Panay (Iloilo, the capital) and Negros was left to Presbyterian efforts. There are a Baptist college mission and hospital in Iloilo and a Presbyterian college and mission hospital at Dumaguete. A voluminous and readable book could be written about Protestant efforts in the Philippine Islands— how in Iloilo three times a year a "canon missioner" came from the Episcopal Cathedral of Saint Mary and Saint John to conduct services in the stock exchange (the only auditorium in Iloilo except the theaters, and the theaters being owned and patronized by Filipinos who are almost solidly born into the Catholic fold)—the stock exchange being run by a Britisher still loyal to his home church. Prior to the visit of the American Protestant father, hasty preparations for services are made. Chapels for church services built and maintained by American missionaries in the provinces are generally crude structures in the midst of native sections, with rough wooden benches—the building inaccessible and uncomfortable to the white population—regular Sunday and weekly services conducted in native dialect, which few foreigners except missionaries ever attempt to learn. As most of the native population understand and speak a little English (from the public schools) or a little Spanish (there are almost no pure Spanish strains left, so great has been intermarriage between Spanish and Filipino). An American businessman who knows English and Spanish finds knowledge of native dialects unessential. I remember surprise at my casual remark that I should like to learn Chinese while I was visiting in China and the American friend whom I was visiting said, "No one here (in the foreign community of Shanghai) knows Chinese or we'd be ashamed to speak it if we did. One just doesn't use the natives' tongue. Our servants would lose respect for us if we addressed them in their own language." So only missionaries and priests speak Visäyan, Tagalog, the Moro dialects, or one of the hundreds of other dialects of the P. Islands. White Protestants do not attend the missionary churches, though foreign Catholics do go to mass in beautiful Catholic churches for mass in English or Spanish in churches often built during the Spanish regime, some of the most beautiful and lasting missions of Spanish architecture in the P. Islands. One of the missionaries from Japan said, "The Japanese government requires Protestant denominations to elect a Council, Council representatives to elect a Bishop to represent all denominations in conference with government officials. So Northern and Southern Baptists united, as did the Northern and Southern Presbyterians. These denominations then elected the Protestant Bishop." Imagine Baptists electing a Bishop! So Japan has brought about a union of different denominations when God has failed. Japan did, but God couldn't.

New arrivals in camp brought the following stories: Japanese went to Palimpenon and asked for U.S. soldiers and when people replied in negative began to machine-gun and bayonet. Killed six. One bullet went through right shoulder of girl five years old. Tied up three of the dead to posts as a warning. Bayoneted one man in town of Bakong because he did not know where USAF [soldiers] were.

Mr. Caballero, father of six children all under 10 years, cashier of Dumaguete Bank, evacuated to mountains. Japanese went to his home and broke up dishes. To protect his family, he surrendered. Refused to tell where cash of bank was hidden. Tied rope around chest and put end over acacia tree and beat him on chest with wood till blood ran from his mouth. Dropped forcibly to ground till confession made. He took Japs to hiding place of money, also rice. Found USAF uniform belonging to his brother. They then shot him in the back at the edge of a hole. As he fell in, they put a log on top of his still moving body and then dirt over that. Four women were shot for stealing rice.

Saturday, Sept. 5, 1942. Party for all children in camp between ages of one and twelve. Eighteen children attended. Pinned paper tail on donkey drawn on small portable blackboard, played Musical Chairs to accompaniment of camp piano (out of tune with sticking keys), drank pink juice (strawberry Jello), and carried home a package of candy and cookies. Sweets were provided as gifts by four or five adults in camp from their private stocks hoarded in their rooms. Also played games: Drop the Handkerchief, Grand Duke of York. I asked permission of the camp director, Mr. Pope, to have the party and was told that refreshments could not be supplied from commissary as there would be adults objecting to unnecessary use of food for children; there were women objecting to use of canned milk supply for children.

There are now five babies in camp under six months, two bottle-fed, three being nursed by their mothers. These babies and nursing mothers receive a generous milk allowance daily. Beth and Clay, as do all children to twelve, receive one glass diluted Carnation milk from camp daily. Their ages are 2 and 3 years. No milk is used in cooking, though four cases of evaporated milk are set aside for use in coffee and tea in the dining room. This is to be discontinued if voted on favorably by a majority of internees. There is much open antagonism to children in camp. This is shown by men and women both, some with older children not in camp, but mostly by those without children who sh-h-h small children when they are laughing happily on the long verandah which runs the full length of the two wings of our schoolhouse camp. Children and adults must travel back and forth on this verandah for the outdoor toilets, drinking water, shower baths, and to go in and out of room for outdoor play.

The children had a wonderful time at the party, almost laughing themselves sick at the antics of Mrs. Oss (mother of five-year-old daughter) who, blindfolded, took the donkey's tail from the blackboard, through door of children's playroom, out on porch, to pin the tail on one of the greatest sh-h-shers of children—a youngish English married man who has no children of his own and detests all children and is rude and cruel to them. Children appreciated the little joke. Children in camp are from varied homes. The three Teeheras and the five little Porters speak only Visäyan dialect, Helena Van Kaufman speaks Spanish, the other nine children are from English speaking homes. There are different cultural backgrounds, some children definitely "tough" in their free use of curse words and their abuse of younger children and younger children's property. Difficulties arise for the mothers.

Sept. 10, 1942. *Nippon Philippines*, a dateless magazine published in Tokyo in English, Tagalog, and Malay, was passed around the camp by Mori [Yasamori]. Profusely illustrated with photographs of plane production in Japan, capital ships of the Japanese navy, the surrender of Corregidor, booty captured at Shonanto (new name for Singapore) and at Hong Kong, and the following statistics to the credit of Japan:

War planes shot down & destroyed	3,910
Tanks	1,440
Artilleries, etc.	3,763
Machine guns	11,548
Rifles	216,714
Motor trucks	31,584
Railway cars	12,200
Shipping	
Seized	220,000 tons
Sunk or damaged	1,419,000 tons
Prisoners	342,000

A profusely illustrated article, "Long Live Nippon's‡ Silk," shows the kimono on a living Japanese model, smiling, "the most beautiful wearing apparel in the world—with undergarments especially gorgeous!" Sample patterns of kimono silk, a double page of Nipponese bathing beauties in beach costumes of silk, an article on the taki, or Nipponese sock or stocking, and on the zori, or Nipponese sandal. In the comic section is a full-page cartoon, "Sacked in Australia," showing MacArthur hiding in the sack of a huge kangaroo with his military arm sticking out and a lady's undergarment hanging beside his arm, his military boots and a lady's high-heeled slippers beside the kangaroo, MacArthur's hand sticking out to receive a sealed envelope from a U.S. soldier but his head and body still in hiding. The caption: "MacArthur, the newly appointed commander-in-chief of the kangaroo battalion, receiving orders from President Roosevelt."

Samples of jokes: four U.S. soldiers walking stealthily forward, each holding a cross in both hands in front of him, eyes fixed to the cross— "Onward Christian Soldiers." Below, the same four soldiers walking in the opposite direction, covered in bandages from head to foot with a cross on the bandages—"Backward Red Cross Soldiers."

An Eastern proverb says: "A child who lies grows up to be a thief." A new American proverb would be: "A child who lies grows up to be a Roosevelt."

A distracted queen, peering through a lorgnette held with one

‡Japanese name for Japan.

hand, holding tulips behind her back with the other hand, as she looks at globe on huge pedestal: "Queen Wilhelmina, we urgently need a new continent or islands, now that our East Indies have been lost."

Sept. 11, 1942. Four days of unremitting rain—camp grounds of 2 hectares (four acres?)* inches-deep in mud. We stand in puddles with umbrellas and raincoats (the few fortunates who have raincoats) for roll call twice daily. Unless there is an actual typhoon we are not permitted to have roll call on the verandah. Our guard seems to enjoy seeing us shiver in the rain, shifting from one wet foot to the other, as he stands under the shelter of media-aqua extending over steps of the verandah.

During rainy weather I made a mattress for Clay's bed as he has been sleeping on three pillows tacked together, making three big bumps. The pad for his bed was lost coming from the mountains to concentration camp. Also made a pillow cover for my pillow from two of Clay's old diapers as I have no other material. Need pillow slip as my last one is coming to pieces.

September 17, 1942. Shakeup in the kitchen, supervisor of the kitchen wasting food, serving too many canned goods, and throwing away native fruits and vegetables which she did not know how to use. Kitchen now in charge of a committee of men and women, food greatly curtailed with more native dishes and almost no cans opened. Committee includes a trained hospital dietitian, a supervisor of home economics teachers with the Bureau of Education on a visit from Manila and trapped on Negros, and a former hotel proprietor. Breakfast now daily one cup of weak coffee (native grown beans roasted here in camp) and a big spoon of rice (white polished rice and red unpolished rice interchangeably) with a bit of coconut honey (coconut juice squeezed from the coconut meat cooked with sugar till it forms a honey-like syrup). There is a large pitcher of hot water for those who feel like they must have a second cup. That is all for breakfast.

*Actually two hectares equals 4.942 acres.

Luncheon varies, but the main dish is always rice. At tea the first and main dish is rice and there is always a second helping for those who wish it. This is wonderful "chow" for Filipinos, but too starchy for foreigners, and efforts to counteract this one-sided diet are seen in endless walking around and around camp buildings in an effort to take exercise and endless drinking of hot water and coconut milk (when the latter is available). Also a great rush for spinach juice on days this is served. There are almost no laxatives in camp and people must use other measures for common stomach and intestinal ailments. Children are allowed one cup of carabao (water buffalo) milk per day and no more canned milk is to be used. Carabao milk is delivered to the camp hospital where it is boiled. The milk is white but thickish and contains a much greater proportion of fat than most cows' milk. It has a strong taste. Clay drank the milk without noticing difference from Carnation, which also has a strong taste. Beth wouldn't drink the new milk (perhaps she noticed my turned-up nose as I gave it to her!) so I put a spoonful of molded locally grown chocolate and a spoonful of sugar in it, then she drank her chocolate milk. When supplies are spoiling in the kitchen we can take them to our room—there was a large quantity of chocolate spoiling and sacks of sugar which were wet in the leaking bodega.

There has been a general tightening of camp rules. We must rise and bow deeply every time a Jap officer passes, no matter what we are doing, and officers pass unexpectedly and some days frequently. This is an old rule but some obstinate ones in camp always manage to be looking in the opposite direction when an officer comes. Then, too, the fact that the Japs seldom return the bow or even acknowledge it is irritating. We bow and smile and receive a cold stare in return, but there is the threat of severe punishment if we fail to bow. No more talking by husbands and wives on verandah after "lights out" at 9:00 P.M. as before. Almost no visitors allowed now. The food still comes in on trucks, the number and variety of livestock considerably increased. We have pigs of three sizes—between twenty and thirty pigs in all— sheep and goats and baby chicks all over the place. It's country life for the children with a one-room tenement existence also. Beth and Clay have at last learned that only one corner of our small room is our "home," as they call it, and that to get from our "house" to the door of the verandah they must pass the "houses" of three other families—though no line and no division for privacy mark the boundaries of each "house." Always open to view, the toys of children in two of these families whose "homes" are in the same room with us are not to be touched. This training has been my most difficult. Thora Ann Oss, blonde, Norwegian ancestored, who sleeps almost within touching distance of Beth and Clay if they hold out their hands from their beds, came to concentration camp later than we did and brought many pretty dolls, blocks, a tea set, and other things children love. Beth brought her "Eva," in a dilapidated state, and Clay only a small rubber piggie from his babyhood days. Those new toys which Thora Ann keeps on a small child's table beside her bed kept Beth and Clay in such an unhappy state of mind because they could not touch them. It required many spankings to teach them. How Beth has looked longingly at Thora Ann's doll carriage, but she has not been offered the "push" of it once these three months she has eyed it daily. And how she has softly cried, asking me if she might not sit in Thora Ann's child's rocking chair when Thora Ann is not using it—and how I have had to deny her and try to explain at the same time that her own little rocking chair and other furniture do not exist any more as they were lost (along with toys) in the Central fire. Now Beth and Clay have learned what is theirs and what is the property of others—training not necessary as long as we lived the isolated family life of Bacolod where the children seldom left our own garden and almost never saw other children.

When Beth and Clay pass Mrs. Canova's (lovely American school teacher married to naturalized American of Italian birth) section of the room where her cot looks temptingly like mine and they linger beside it, I call out frantically, "Don't you touch that bed. You can sit on my cot (it sags so badly the children cannot hurt it unless they cause it to collapse completely, in which case I simply prop it up again) but you must not touch anyone else's." The children, taking another step, pass under rows and rows of wet diapers on wires strung across the room and by the bed of Scott, a five-week-old Scotchman who with his mother occupies the space nearest the door. "Don't touch the baby," I

caution as they approach the door between our room and the verandah. On the verandah are chairs other people brought in and which
the owners forbid children to touch. "Don't touch. Don't touch." And
I guide the children down the long verandah to a school yard filled
with grass-cutting blades dropped here and there as the cutters tired,
and lawn mowers left here and there. There is an open fire burning all
day under caldrons of water heating for washing dishes and other
kitchen uses and one huge tank boiling for drinking water. There is no
fence around the fire and it is attended only when in need of fuel.
Children play so precariously close to this danger. Under the schoolhouse there are innumerable broken bottles, rusty tin cans, pieces of
wood with old nails protruding.

Now that we have less food I enjoy it more. A surplus nauseated
me—knowing that Jim might be starving in prison in Manila and
knowing that there are U.S. Army prisoners on this island who would
grab and consume the refuse we throw our pigs. Waste and extrava-
gance have always distressed me, now a waste of even a small amount
of food angers me. I want to go a little bit hungry if it means food for
someone who is hungrier than I. We have been too fortunate in our
food—since we are civilians the Japanese have made no effort to stop
food supplies from coming in as long as we ourselves have to pay for
it, cash or credit (all is on credit), but we all know this generous food
supply can't go on indefinitely. Especially has the use of canned foods
been inexcusable.

How faded we all look! Most of the women here have three or four
wash dresses which are worn in rotation, no dress being worn more
than one day without washing, due to the extreme heat and to perspiration. Strong, cheap soap—the only soap available after the start of
the war—and the blazing sun combine to destroy dye. And ceaseless
rubbing—as soap becomes more scarce we rub the more, depending
more on muscle than on a foreign cleansing agent—has removed not
only the color but the fabric as well. Patches sometimes, but not always, match the garment they adorn. When the Yanks do come to
liberate us we'll be a bedraggled sight to meet them. For shoes the
camp—men, women and children—have adopted bakyas, flat wood-

en shoes with one wide rubber strap (from old inner-tube) across the toes. These can be bought for $.30 from the men in camp. Beth and Clay go barefooted all the time now, as their last pairs of shoes have soles and tops separated and the leather on top is cracked open so toes stick out. Danger of cutting feet is great. (Clay was barefooted when a nail went through his foot.) Also children are sure to get worms from animal excreta everywhere on the grounds—dogs, sheep, pigs, goats, fowl, rabbits, and native cows, all of which develop intestinal worms in the tropics and have to be treated. Children need to wear shoes in a place with the filthy soil of our camp, but most children have to go barefooted. Though I can walk with comparative ease and speed in bakyas, neither Beth nor Clay can keep them on and Clay almost stumbled down the concrete verandah steps trying to wear his, so I have discarded theirs for the present.

Sept. 21, 1942. Yasamori's birthday—a chocolate cake from the kitchen, a "Thank you all" from him at morning roll call, a "Happy birthday to you, happy birthday to you, happy birthday Mr. Mori, happy birthday to you" and clapping by all of his prisoners. A funny situation. We pretend to love our head guard so much, and he us. It is to our advantage to be friends. He is afraid for his life after the war if he does not treat us kindly. It is an open secret that Bacolod Filipinos have sworn to take Mori's life as soon as the Japanese army no longer protects him. He must look to the foreign population for help and for work after the war. He is wise and we understand his attitude of curtness when Japanese are here and his laxity when they are away. He is married to a Filipino woman, considers the Philippines his home, not Japan.

Action, action all around us. Machine gun emplacements have been made at the corners of the concentration camp grounds—emplacements concealed and protected by sandbags, and sandbags disguised by grass soddings on top and sides. A big Jap boat at the pier. Hundreds of empty alcohol drums brought from the pier in a long line of trucks—most of trucks now semi-armored with iron plate over windshield except for small slit and iron shields on sides of truck cab—and the same trucks repassing camp later in the day moving more slowly with drums filled with alcohol from nearby sugar Central's alcohol distilleries.

A huge Standard Oil storage tank at the pier being taken to pieces bit by bit and loaded on boat, probably to go to Japan as scrap iron. The deliberateness of the Japanese as they go about war business is the most discouraging aspect of the war to us. There is no hurry. They seem so confident and so well organized in their occupation of the Philippines.

Truckloads and truckloads of soldiers coming fully equipped from pier and twenty truckloads of hand grenades and small bombs (they were unpacked in front of camp and most cases opened for inspection there) delivered to the houses of guards at our camp. A young American in prisoner overalls winked at those of us looking at activities outside the fence through the wire. This American was driving one of the large trucks and was never out of sight of three guards, who sat beside him on the seat of the truck. There have been many instances of American soldiers who have mechanical knowledge having been removed from prisons and assigned mechanical work, including truck driving and truck repair with the Japanese army.

More days of rain, and though Beth and Clay have running noses and coughs, the rain means good drinking water again. When the tank of rainwater is exhausted we find how unpleasant is boiled water through which smoke from a wood fire has blown. Oil drums in which drinking water is boiled are suspended on an iron rod over green wood flames. The smoke is terrific. Drums have no covers. The drinking water is full of small charred pieces of wood and has an unpalatable, smoky, dirty taste. Strange that we never have water with our meals and do not miss it now. At first I missed water and bread at meals and took a bottle of water and glass to meals. As more people came to camp water became more scarce, so that it is never served at meals and we drink what we have—quite often still warm from being boiled—slowly and deliberately that it might last the longer and be enjoyed as fully as an iced mint julep. And speaking of alcoholic drinks, since there is no alcohol except what some of men have been brewing on the sly from ginger root and camp molasses, there is a great demand for "dulce" or sweet desserts. Men and women who never craved candy before now request the dining room committee to make candy for general camp consumption. And at least once a week each person is given a small bag of sugar and water candy, sometimes flavored with coconut milk and sometimes with native chocolate. Not the creamy variety of candy we enjoy at home, but a great treat to us in camp. How excited grown men and women and children are over these sweets. Some of the men who drank regularly and sometimes heavily by States standards (for it is undoubtedly true there is more drinking in everyday life in the tropics—it fits in with the leisure of the tropics) now fill a coffee cup in the morning and a tea cup in the afternoon half full of sugar to satisfy the void left by lack of alcohol. The old adage here, that the way to break a drinker is to stuff him on sweets, is probably true.

Sept. 25 to October 2, 1942. Spent a week in the hospital with Beth and Clay both sick with high fever and colds. Continuous rain and high winds, typhoon weather, which made cure of sore throat, fever, and earache accompaniments of colds more difficult. While we were in the hospital Clay opened the refrigerator and ate a handful of sawdust packing in a box of eggs and cried all one night with stomach ache. No hot water bottle in hospital and no medicine for earache. Dr. Jara was called—gave three prescriptions (which is being done now, due to scarcity of medicine), first, second, and third choice. Shelves of drug stores are almost empty. Dr. Jara bought a secondhand bicycle for $125 cash (old currency) to use if his car is confiscated, as he expects. Tetanus serum has been stolen in large quantities by Japanese and an ampule for which I paid $3.00 in Bacolod now costs $25.00. Near Giahoulngan a child who lost his leg from bombing (leg held on by slender thread of skin when brought to hospital) later died from loss of blood and fright.

Washed the children's clothes standing in rain, caught cold and sinus headache. Returned to room to be received coldly by roommates, who had found the quiet while Beth and Clay were away very enjoyable, and who also had made use of room vacated by us. We had to take our own beds, mosquito nets, etc. to the hospital. Our "hospital" is an empty room to which patients take their own beds, thermometers, hot water bottles, bed clothes, toilet paper, soap, towels, as well as medicines.

The place left vacant in my room was so attractive that our return was not welcome. We returned at the time of day when we could find two men free from work or play (poker, bridge, checkers, and chess inside, and horseshoes, badminton, and baseball outside) to carry my cot and mattress and children's beds. Men here do not like to be called away from these pleasures to do little chores requested of them as favors. There are exceptions—notably among the Dumaguete group—but on the whole the attitude of men here seems to be "Why ask me to do this, why not ask somebody else?" which has the desired effect of minimizing favor requests.

Wed., Oct. 5, 1942. Death in camp. The Japanese are burying Mr. Bill Williams after all. When warned by Dr. Smith that Mr. Williams—who came to camp with one toe recently amputated, not healing at all, and with foot swollen to twice normal size—would die unless proper medicines were made available for treatment and further amputation of the foot, the Japanese had replied they were sorry not to allow the requested medicines to be transferred from the Fabrica Hospital. That hospital, prior to the war, was owned by Americans (now in camp) and Mr. Williams had been a patient there. The Japanese said that Mr. Williams and Dr. Smith need not worry for the Japanese would bury him in case of death. He is being buried today. Infection spread from his foot to his leg and the whole was amputated by Japanese doctors in Bacolod yesterday. Mr. Williams died this morning. Funeral services were held in camp this afternoon at 3:30 in children's playroom where body lay in inexpensive casket with a few wreaths of alamanda and hibiscus blossoms made here in camp from plants on grounds. Mr. Williams, a lovely character not unlike many other Americans found in the Philippines, came out 42 years ago and has not returned to the U.S. since. He was in his sixties at the time of death. Some of the people who have known him longest—and no one knew him well— say he has spoken of being married in the States before he came out, but whether his wife died or they separated is not known. He has always listed himself as "unmarried" and has but one close relative, a sister in the U.S. with whom he has not kept in touch. He was a brick-mason by trade, drew good pay during construction times, then went without work to extent of being a "bum" at times. So his life almost ceased 42 years ago when he severed all relations to come so far from his home. Probably he planned to return—to return rich in money and experience—but he's one of many Americans the tropics "got." He died alone, his fortune unaccumulated, his mind full of dreams and memories he alone knew and which died with him unfulfilled and unshared. His suitcase of personal belongings—a watch, a few coin charms, pipes, and small savings—are a problem to the manager of the Central where Mr. Williams had been employed for the past year. He has worked at many places for short periods of time, so there is no one organization which feels particularly concerned for him. Three school benches were put together, covered with a sheet and white lace bedspread, on which the coffin rested. Simple Protestant service which Baptist missionary read from an altar of a Catholic priest—three of which altars have been built individually by three dif-ferent priests. The body stank—gangrene had set in, in the unampu-tated hip, and was the cause of death. This putrid odor cannot be disguised. The lid of the coffin was left open for friends to see the face of the deceased, but had to be closed again quickly because of the stench. The body was carried away to be buried by the Japanese.

Hospital used by a Filipino woman who is paralyzed on one side. She and American mestizo husband in camp, but left three children with wife's mother. Wife in camp cannot wash own clothes due to paralyzed arm—husband does work for her—and together they go to toilet in hospital when she wishes to go, as he must unfasten clothes for her and place wife on toilet seat. Husband then remains outside door until wife calls him to come in again and help her from toilet seat. A most devoted couple—both always smiling—and she walks around camp grounds with him, limping and leaning heavily on him for support with her good arm, the limp one hanging loosely by her side.

How embarrassing to remove meat from one's teeth with an au-dience and to give one's scalp a good workout to prevent dandruff with three or four other women—even one's friends—watching. There is never a moment's privacy. We have learned to bathe together—sometimes three women under one shower at one time, as the water is flowing only a few hours a day in the shower due to low water pressure in camp. Toilets are only little open stalls without doors under a common roof—but it's brushing my teeth in public and cleaning them in any way before others which embarrasses me. Even ten minutes of privacy a day would be heaven.

Friday, October 16, 1942. Six aeroplanes circled camp today, landed at Bacolod airport. A few hours later a Japanese colonel, visiting Negros by air, was our guest. He came with a military escort of ten soldiers of varying rank. The colonel arrived about 10:00 A.M. Some men were gardening, some cutting grass, five men were amateurishly cutting up a pig just slaughtered, a small group was playing horseshoes, while women were mopping camp porches, washing clothes down at outdoor wooden washtubs beside the outdoor toilets, preparing vegetables for lunch, etc. Word spread that a colonel was arriving and not to forget to stop all work or play, rise and bow low. As the colonel approached, an empty verandah (half cleaned), an empty garden, a deserted butchery job, deserted horseshoe court, and unattended washtubs met his eyes. How people disappear when "inspectors" arrive! Where they go, how the ground swallows camp inmates up to keep from one low bow is amazing. There is a rush for toilets and showers, usually safe from visitors' eyes—but not always, as these have been visited also by Japanese military and civil authorities in camp. The colonel today was more friendly than some. He did acknowledge the bows to him with a short nod—too often our bows are demanded but ignored when given. To bow and smile and receive a frozen stare is like shaking a limp, clammy hand, responseless to feeling. Yet we were warned again, as we have been often before, that failure on our part to rise from our seats and bow everytime an officer or soldier, even a guard (this is a new regulation), passes, will cause the offender and the entire camp to be punished.

A cotton blossom in camp. Mrs. Davis, from Rome, Georgia, saw a stray cotton plant outside the eight-foot wire fence enclosing the camp grounds. A friendly looking guard stood outside the fence, leaning on his gun. Mrs. D., by sign language, asked him for the blossom. He seemed surprised but picked it for her and handed it through the fence. She kept it in a glass of water like a flower of rare and unusual beauty. The blossom is a white bud. I said that I thought cotton blossoms were pink, that I remembered acres and acres of pink blossoms in the Georgia summer sunlight. Mrs. Davis seemed surprised that I did not know cotton blossoms are white in the morning and pink in the afternoon. Two Georgians, we are from the heart of the "cotton country," uncertain about the color of a plant so common we have passed it for years without note or thought. I almost said, jokingly, "If you keep the blossom a few days you may have a boll of cotton," but we don't joke like that for fear of a head shaking and an aside, "Too bad, she's cracking up. Camp is too much for her."

Our one real mental case has been removed from the camp hospital to Bacolod Japanese hospital. He is a man of sixty who had epilepsy as a child but apparently recovered completely in young manhood. The excitement and uncertainty of war has brought about a complete physical and mental breakdown. The invalid showed only the faintest signs of motor ataxia when brought to camp and no mental symptoms, but he rapidly lost the use of both legs and arms and became incoherent in speech after three months of confinement here. His wife was also in camp and has been permitted to go to the Japanese hospital with him. The Japanese hold out no hope for his recovery, though according to latest reports he has learned to play Chinese checkers slowly and can take a few steps alone.

Georgia has pupped! Poldo came from the mountains yesterday and told me Georgia had two pups, Sejio is wanting money, and all goods stored half-way up to the mountains were gone. Included were two carved camphor wood chests containing clothes, shoes, linens (table and bed), Jim's dress suit (black trousers with white mess jacket and also short monkey jacket with vests to match), a coat Harvey (my brother) brought me from Scotland five years ago, which I still love and always receive complements on—real Scotch tweed cut on moderate princess lines with lovely and unusual button trim. I hate to lose these things. Also there was a box of dishes and glassware—water goblets, wine glasses and liqueur glasses to match. But somehow I don't mind the loss of dishes, as service for 18 with glasses for serving 24 seems incongruous without table or a single chair of household furniture. (Can picture myself in evening dress, sitting on floor, drinking a creme de menthe from crystal liqueur glass.) There was also a box of miscellaneous articles, including two bedroom lamps, but having no beds or dressing tables, the loss of lamps is not serious.

I would like to see Georgia's pups. Their father was evidently a "wonk" of the "Heinz 57" variety, but I was not permitted to talk long enough with Poldo to find out. Two Jap guards listened to the conversation and told me when to stop talking. I told Poldo to ask Miss Ganahan to pay Sejio half salary each month and of course he has use of garden we planted and is living in my house. Sejio will not come from mountains, I think, due to fear of becoming conscripted labor. Truckloads of Filipinos have been passing daily with armed Japanese guards standing over them. They are being carried to the rice fields to gather the ripened grain. About twenty sullen Filipino men and boys passed walking today to a rice field across the road from the camp. Five Japanese with guns pointing forward followed these Filipinos and leaned on guns on the edge of the field as Filipinos stooped to gather rice. Fifteen women and girls were brought from another direction with an armed escort. Shortly after beginning to harvest the rice a sudden and heavy downpour of rain broke from the sky. There was no shelter for workers. Guards ran to hedge of hibiscus for temporary shelter, but Filipinos were instructed to keep on working. They were drenched. Sun came out after half an hour and, with hair and clothes dripping, workers went on with back-breaking rice gathering by hand. Another downpour of rain, another respite by sunshine, and then at noon a heavily overcast sky indicated rain for the rest of the day. The sullen, unhappy, drenched, and already sneezing workers were not permitted to stop until three o'clock. The Japanese pick up any able-bodied man, woman, or child who might be used to harvest rice, repair roads, plant sugar cane, load lumber on trucks, or perform other miscellaneous jobs. For this reason Filipino traffic on the roads and streets is almost entirely limited to the old and decrepit. So I think Sejio will stay in the mountains with my few belongings there, though the prospect of paying him for a year to do nothing, when I have so little cash—Miss Ganahan has this—appalls me. I shall need badly what cash I have when we are released from camp.

Saturday, October 17, 1942. A Japanese holiday and flags flying, flowers on the caramotas bringing soldiers to the houses around camp. About fifty people in camp—over sixty years old, the sick, and Filipinos with American citizenship papers—were expecting to be released today but this did not happen. Yasamori had virtually promised them release—like gubernatorial clemency on Christmas when prison doors are often opened to a group of pardoned sinners—but release does not come to the encamped.

Time and usage have taken toll of the dishes and glassware in camp. Dishwashers are men—a Catholic priest, a Presbyterian missionary, a chief engineer of a sugar central, a chemist, a beachcomber, and a pensioned veteran of the Spanish-American War. Not any of these was an experienced kitchen worker. The present group rotates in service with other groups of similar varied composition. As a result there is seldom a day that more than one dish, glass, or cup does not crash to the concrete floor of the kitchen.

We now eat soup from coconut shells—the half without eyes, neatly cleaned within and filed without to remove roughness. About 150 of these smooth, rounded half-discs rest on nails on the dining room wall when not in use and the playful in camp draw faces in white chalk on the rounded surfaces, sometimes putting glasses and hats on these fantastic skulls. Some bowls tip a bit but drawings are on flat bottomed ones. For our breakfast coffee (it gets weaker and weaker and weaker and is the color of tea) and for tea we have tin cans with wire handles. The carpentry committee has for some time been saving all tins from kitchen. "Gold" or brass-colored, lined tins have been found to resist rust longer than the all-tin cans. Many fruits come in the lined tins as well as babies' and children's foods. Some milk tins rust too quickly to be used for drinking purposes, but condensed milk cans have been found to be hard, wide-mouthed and rust-resistant. The top of the can is completely removed and the open surface smoothed. A wire handle is attached through two tiny holes at the top of the can and attached also by a ring of wire which encircles the can near the bottom, a satisfactory handle arrangement. Most people now prefer cans for hot drinks because cans hold more than cups and no "seconds" are allowed at present.

Sunday, October 18, 1942. Why I and others from the H-P mountain camp were allowed, and in fact encouraged, to talk to Poldo has leaked out. The Japanese want to know from our questions to Poldo and from his answers how much foodstuffs and personal goods were left in the mountains and how much was stored in bodegas in the hills which have been looted—whether by Filipinos or Japanese, we do not know. I fell into a trap when I said Miss Ganahan had money of mine (a small amount only) and asked Poldo to ask her to try to locate two carved chests of clothes for me. If she locates these—only a Filipino could get them from another Filipino unless they were removed from the bodega by friends to protect the goods from Japanese or Filipino looting—there is the possibility the Japanese may take them from her. Admittedly I talked too much and I am sorry to have involved my friend, Miss Ganahan. Others from H-P, also under the thrill and charm of being permitted to talk freely to our one link with our mountain hideout, regret having given unnecessary information to Yasamori and guards taking in every word of conversations. The loss of material things doesn't affect me now. I have looked forward to putting on nice clothes again after the war—and I have dresses in the chests never worn—and to wearing stockings again (new nylon ones in the chests). Wear cotton socks in camp and as these wear out we wear wooden sandals on bare feet like natives. More than half the adults in camp, men and women, are shod in wooden sandals without hose. The single wide cross-strap on the block of wood usually rubs blisters on feet of foreigners wearing bakyas for the first time, but repeated use turns the blisters into calluses and the aching arches and ankles adjust themselves to the flat wood surface on which the foot rests. The bakya is held on by cupping the toes under and gripping the top of the bakya with them. This necessary use of toes to keep sandals from falling off when the foot is lifted in walking causes great pain in toe joints until the wearer becomes accustomed to bakyas. When I first came to the Philippines I was advised to buy a pair of them to

Between 1935 and 1937 Elizabeth Head served as a research assistant to Dr. Howard W. Odum at the University of North Carolina. Her training as a sociologist and her analytical skills would later make her a particularly astute observer of life in the Philippines. This photograph was taken in Chapel Hill in 1936. (By permission of the family.)

While traveling in the Philippines in 1937 Elizabeth Head met Jim Vaughan, a civil engineer from Mississippi working for the Pacific Commercial Company. They were married the following year. These portraits of Elizabeth and Jim were taken in Manila shortly after the couple became engaged. (By permission of the family.)

In August 1939 the Vaughans' first child, Beth, was born; a year later a son, Clay, joined the family. The Vaughans settled into a house in a residential section of Bacolod and the comfortable life of American colonials. This is Beth on the lawn of the Vaughan home in Bacolod, December 30, 1940. (By permission of the family.)

Like many other young men from the depression-ridden United States in the 1930s, Jim Vaughan chose to work in the Islands because salaries were higher and perquisites generous, which allowed his young family an opportunity to save for the future. This photograph of Jim and daughter Beth was taken in early 1941. (By permission of the family.)

Rumors of a Japanese invasion prompted some U.S. citizens to return to the States. Many others, including the Vaughans, not knowing when or where, or even if, such an invasion would occur, went on with their lives as usual. This photograph of Beth and Clay was taken not long before the Japanese attacked Pearl Harbor and the United States entered the war. (By permission of the family.)

The University of Santo Tomás, the Philippines' oldest educational institution, was used by the Japanese as an internment camp for Allied nationals. Elizabeth Vaughan and her children were held here from March 1943 until February 1945, when they were liberated by American troops. Three to four thousand Allied nationals were interned in this camp during the course of the war. (U.S. Army Military History Institute.)

The patio of the Santo Tomás Internment Camp as it appeared in February 1945 when American troops entered Manila. The Japanese had permitted internees to build "shanties" so families could eat in privacy and so extra food could be prepared by those with money to buy it and funds for a charcoal stove and fuel, but there was little food for anyone during the last months in the camp. (U.S. Army Signal Corps, SC200307-S.)

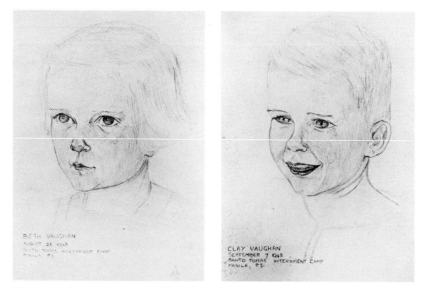

BETH VAUGHAN
AUGUST 28 1943
SANTO TOMAS INTERNMENT CAMP
MANILA, P.I.

CLAY VAUGHAN
SEPTEMBER 7 1943
SANTO TOMAS INTERNMENT CAMP
MANILA, P.I.

These sketches of Beth and Clay, dated August 28 and September 7, 1943, respectively, presumably were made by an unknown artist to commemorate their birthdays. On July 10 Elizabeth Vaughan received confirmation of her husband's death; her diary entries stop on that date and do not resume until October 29. (By permission of the family.)

Soon after she and the children returned to the States, Elizabeth Vaughan began to plan for the future and to take steps to rebuild the life so changed by the war. She reentered the University of North Carolina, where she wrote a dissertation based upon her experience as "a participant observer" in the internment camp and was soon granted a Ph.D. in sociology. This photograph of the family was taken several years after the war ended. (By permission of the family.)

wear when standing under the shower in hotels and other public bathing places, and to use on beaches when dressed for swimming as water in no way harms bakyas and if they are lost in water they float on top. By consistent practice I learned to carry the sandals with me when I took a step under the shower. (Athlete's foot is common here, as well as other foot diseases. Houseboys always walked barefooted when cleaning bathrooms, spreading any infections they might have, as well as carrying infection from previous guests.) Learning to wear the bakyas is like learning to use chopsticks. After the first try one wonders how it is possible for small children to show such dexterity in manipulation of fingers. But if small Chinese and Japanese children can pick up small grains of rice between two sticks held between fingers of one hand, surely an adult of a superior (?) race can learn the trick. So it is with the wearing of bakyas—even the smallest toddler among Filipinos toddles on them without danger of stepping right out of his shoes as foreigners do. Just as the art of using chopsticks—and the ability to think of something else while using them—comes suddenly to the hungry Occidental in parts of the Orient, so the ability to move along in bakyas—and to forget the feet—suddenly comes to the persistent foreigner in the Philippines. Beth learned to wear them more easily than I. She has a little pair painted bright red with yellow and white flowers painted on the flat surface covered by her foot. The single strap is a one-inch strip of black automobile innertube. Most bakyas are painted bright colors and decorated with painted flowers to attract buyers. They are usually tied together in pairs with a piece of string and hung on walls of market booths. It seems a shame that the art work on them is covered while the shoe is being worn, though colors are ornamental when shoes are beside the bed or standing in a conspicuous place in the bedroom. Clay likes to try to wear his little red bakyas—just like Beth's—but he has tripped several times and he came so near to falling down the steps of the verandah when his foot came from one that he is forbidden to wear his yet, except to practice in the camp bedroom. The noise they make is a terrific clatter, clatter, clatter, as the heels of shoes leave the feet and drop to floor if the wearer is a novice. But there is no more sound than if the shoes were of rubber with an experienced walker.

A quiet Sunday. Even the air is calm and still. While Catholics were at mass in the children's playroom which serves as church on Sunday, little Scott MacWilliams, now six months old, was being christened by a Presbyterian missionary in the adjoining room, the camp library. Only Scott's mother and father and the preacher were present. The christening bowl was a rose-colored soup bowl. There were no flowers, there were no godparents, no witnesses. Both godparents are in Scotland, not knowing for certain that they are godparents. Scott's father's brother and his mother's aunt had been asked by letter to be godparents in the event the child was a boy, before the baby's birth. Others had been asked in event the expected baby was a girl. Scott was born after invasion of the Japanese and after all communications with Europe and the U.S. were cut. Scott's parents wanted him christened and so he was, in the only absolutely private ceremony since we came into camp almost five months ago.

Spent Sunday morning sewing selvages of children's sheets together after having ripped them down middle lengthwise. During past week Clay has ripped two sheets badly in turning over in sleep—that is how thin sheets have become. To extend life in the center of the sheet where wear is heaviest, I have put two outer edges together in center seam. This bit of sewing done by hand with navy blue thread on white sheets, also outer edges whipped in navy thread. Towels are wearing out at ends. It is the thin, untufted, ornamental strip at each end of a bath towel which wears out first. As these ends are less absorbent than the center of the towel and serve little practical use, I cut off the ends of two formerly white bath towels—now a pinkish yellow from stains, poor soap, mineral water, and just poor washing on the part of the present washerwoman (myself)—and cut off lavender stripes on the ends of two other small bath towels of indeterminate color and age. These four towels—now all bob-tailed—are my complete chest of bath linens except for one badly stained, pinkish wash cloth and a square of diaper cloth to be used as bath cloth when the present one has gotten beyond use and repair.

Pork for dinner today—pig killed yesterday in camp—and soup with spinach, cauliflower, sugar peas, green beans, and asparagus in it, and sliced bananas with whipped cream. Elegance of soup and whipped cream explained as due to careful check of food committee on canned goods. Found cans of vegetables and of Nestle's cream were puffed at ends and badly rusted. Gave these cans to kitchen for immediate use if products in cans were not already spoiled. Cooks decided canned vegetables all right for eating but the quantities were too small for individual servings, so all were lumped together in soup. Four large cans of cream, mixed with egg whites, made one table-spoon serving for each person in camp.

Killing off livestock and poultry in camp, due to heavy toll by disease and death. Out of sixteen small pigs brought into camp a few weeks ago all have died except five. Other pigs, sheep, chickens and rabbits have died. The goats have almost ceased giving milk they are so thin, and Ferdinand the Bull is looking pale and wan. He will go to the butcher in a few days. Death of pigs has been due to improper food and to improper protection from weather. Pigs raised for foreign consumption are always kept off the ground in pens with wooden floors a foot or more above the earth or in larger pens with concrete floors. They are never in mud or wet by the rains. Such was background of pigs brought to camp. Here their shelter is a leaking roof, without sides or floor. The pigs trample around in rain in inches of mud. From a warm, cooked mash served twice daily their diet changed to rubbish—food refuse, coconut shells, and tin cans not good enough to be used as cups—thrown out in the mud for pigs to pick over. The change was too severe and too sudden. Also, it seems, the pigs here must be dewormed regularly and often, and facilities and medicines for this care are lacking in camp. Whether it is true that worms get to the heart of pigs and cause death, I do not know, but so 'tis said. The sheep are starving to death, having eaten all the hedges, flowers, and grass within their reach on camp grounds. Chickens have died of a sorehead epidemic among them and the rabbits died of neglect and starvation. So we'll have meat in camp now. It seems better to eat what we have than to take a chance on losing it by saving it for an uncertain future.

Tuesday, October 20, 1942. Last night I sat on the steps of the camp verandah and watched drinking orgy among Japanese soldiers directly across from camp. There are about twenty soldiers—our guards in different shifts—living within speaking distance of us and our Jap director. Whereas there were formerly one hundred soldiers barracked in the three houses adjoining camp—houses occupied by the North Bacolod Elementary School principal and teachers in pre-war times—two of the three houses by the school have been vacated recently and the troops transferred by boat to other places. Three Japanese transports arrived empty at the pier near camp yesterday and after unloading empty alcohol tanks re-loaded with full tanks from supply evidently brought to Bacolod from sugar mill distilleries and stored for shipping. We wonder if the drinking, singing, shouting, and drunken fighting among our Jap guards might not be in the nature of a "despida"† to themselves as they will likely leave Bacolod with the shipment of alcohol. When soldiers assigned to concentration camps have been re-assigned to the battlefronts there have been drunken farewell orgies before. As the commanding officer either stands silently by or participates in the riotous drinking these desperados undoubtedly have his sanction, possibly sponsored by those in still higher authority. There was loud singing of Japanese songs accompanied by hand-clapping and foot-stomping, then breaking of beer and saki bottles on tables, then tossing of empty bottles through window panes, then mock fencing with sticks of wood. As some punched too hard with the wood or were playfully tripped by opponents, a free-for-all fist fight ensued amid shouting and screaming. The soldiers' guns stood in corner during their "party," but we wondered if it might occur to them to pick up weapons and pop off a few of the "enemy" they were guarding. The guard on duty on the verandah at this time solemnly marched up and down with bayonet fixed on end of gun gleaming in bright moonlight and lights from room doors. We rose and bowed each time he passed, but when it became obvious that he was passing and re-passing the group of foreigners looking in on the actions inside the windows of the well-lighted house across the street, we took the hint and went into our own hot, stuffy rooms. As we are never permitted to close doors of our rooms, we know, as we have known all the time, we have no protection whatsoever if drunken soldiers cared to come into camp and molest us. Our unarmed Japanese director

†despedida [Spanish]—party given for people who are departing.

would be helpless before armed soldiers, as was demonstrated recently. Two guards came on duty after drinking heavily and spat in the face of a Scotch woman in camp and slapped Mrs. Oss heartily across the buttocks with an open hand as she passed by on the verandah. The same drunken guard followed me from the dark porch into a darkened room where the children were sleeping, but seemed flustered when I turned suddenly and put on the light. After pointing to the sleeping children and touching me on the shoulder he left the room, tottering. The smell of him as he touched me was nauseating—not the smell of beer, but the smell of a filthy body, accumulated perspiration, and body wastes.

I sat for a while on the verandah between the aged wife of a Baptist missionary and a young Presbyterian minister. Both seemed fascinated by the drunken revelry and said they had never seen anything like that before.

Thursday, October 22, 1942. Soldiers have gone and with them, it is rumored, American soldiers (23 officers) who were transferred to prison camp in Manila. Whether this report is true or false we cannot tell but it seems to be authentic, having been whispered by a Filipino friend of one of the inmates of camp who came in disguised as a deliverer of coconuts. People in camp began activity in packing one suitcase each to take with us to Manila. With others I hastily repacked the largest of my three handbags with one towel, a sheet each for myself and Beth and Clay, toilet soap, a bar of cheap, sticky homemade laundry soap, two cans of milk which I have been hiding out so carefully since they were saved from early allotment to children in camp, a change of clothes for myself and a half-dozen faded sunsuits each for children, mercurochrome, cotton, cod liver oil, calcium powder (a glass jar I have kept so closely for the time when the milk supply is completely cut off), scissors, a ball of string. No change of shoes for any of us. Comb, brush, and toothbrushes will go in handbag.

Scales which were in the schoolhouses when we entered have been returned by soldiers. Soldiers took the scales from school shortly after our arrival and moved them to a house across the street. Greatest loss in weight by Mr. Wiley, who lost 75 pounds. Mrs. Harbart, former manager of the kitchen, has lost 45 pounds since we came. My loss 8 lb. Beth and Clay have each gained only one pound since the outbreak of war a year ago, and with their increase in height they are both underweight, especially Beth who has not regained appetite lost when she was sick in the hospital with a cold and sore throat. The scales will probably remain in camp so we can check our slow deterioration.

With the return of the scales came a gift of a radio—of course stolen by the Japanese—to Yasamori. How anxious were the engineers in camp to help him install it! How eagerly they turned the dial to "test it," once installed! But Mori refused to let his benefactors tune in a station in English or other spoken language. Only musical programs could be listened to for the "testing." After the installation was complete Mori's assistants were asked to leave his room and with closed door he proceeded to hear what we so eagerly sought—"KGEI, San Francisco, the United States of America"—we heard faintly before being ordered away from the door by an angry guard. "Anyway it's still U.S.A. and not United States of Japan, as Japanese would have us think," one camp member remarked.

A paper bag of cookies—principally egg whites, sugar and crushed peanuts—and peanut brittle (homemade) from Mrs. Simke. An unexpected and delightful treat. Mrs. Harblentzel came to the camp gate with a pass from Japanese civilian headquarters at Mansion House in Bacolod, but was refused entrance to camp by Mori. Mrs. Harblentzel had small cakes and candies for a few women and brought a bag to me from Mrs. Simke. I was forbidden to thank Mrs. Harblentzel in person—the guard took the packages from Mrs. H. and delivered them to persons whose names were on them—but was permitted to write a short note of thanks to Mrs. Simke to be delivered by Mrs. H. Note was censored twice and then passed. I wonder about the Simkes, German Jews, who may or may not be suffering in Bacolod. His business—branch of a jewelry chain store throughout the Islands—cannot thrive in times like these if his store is permitted to be open at all. People do not buy watches and silverware during occupation and it has been the custom of soldiers to take what they wanted without paying. I wonder how people outside camp, like the Simkes, pay for their food. House rent is unknown now—owners of rented property are begging tenants to remain in houses to protect the property from sabotage by Japanese and Filipinos—but food is on a strictly cash basis.

Empty wooden boxes of various sizes and shapes were brought to guard houses around camp before the soldiers left. These boxes have been filled with silverware and the hand-hammered pure brassware so common in the Philippines. These items were loot collected from homes in or near Bacolod and probably are to be shipped to Japan to be melted down.

A real wave of excitement in camp among Fabrica Central group. These residents stood on the verandah "oh-ing" and "ah-ing" as truckloads of boxes and suitcases were unloaded by soldiers who had just arrived in other trucks to replace the group leaving Bacolod by boat. These new troops were transferred from Fabrica to be our camp guards. The people from Fabrica had had unpleasant experiences with the soldiers and their commanding officer, Captain Kakucha, and recognized the troops as they moved in across the street from us on the other side of our eight-foot wire fence with electric connections still in place should we venture too close to the fence. "That's mine," swiftly exclaimed Mr. Pope, our camp manager and former manager of Fabrica Central, as he saw a large, square wooden box with number 9 painted in red on all sides. A leather gladstone bag, also numbered and initialed in red, was Mr. Pope's personal property. Other boxes contained food and clothing packed by Fabrica people and left in their mountain camp for safekeeping when they were ordered to Bacolod with a half-hour's notice. The people were beaten and bruised when they failed to comply to the satisfaction of the Japanese—like Dr. Smith, who could hardly walk, who carried severe black bruises on his thighs when he arrived at Bacolod Camp. Two small end tables unloaded from a truck had held a lamp and ashtrays on the ends of a sofa in Mr. Dalba's Fabrica house. The captain himself arrived in the Studebaker car of the MacWilliams—formerly assistant manager of Fabrica. (His wife and son, my roommates.) Fenders of the MacWilliams' car were badly battered and it was distressing to the family to have this abuse of their property constantly before them, the captain and the car becoming established at one of camp's guard houses.

What a premium is placed on empty bottles. Even the "gold" lined tin cans used for drinking purposes are rusting due to difficulty of drying them immediately after every use and keeping them dry. So bottle tops are coming off and bottles converted into odd looking drinking utensils with wire handles. Clear bottles, brown bottles, green ones, round bottles, square bottles, eliptical ones, large or small, all have a use. Easiest method of removing top of bottle is Boy Scout way of tying a heavy string saturated in oil around bottle at place it is desired to cut it off. When string is lighted, bottle will break off at point of contact. Another simple method is the use of wire, bent to encircle the bottle to be cut. The wire is cut into two pieces, each piece with a wire handle and the two pieces hinged together. The connected (hinged) wires are heated in fire and then put around the bottle and held in place as bottle is dipped in water. Fortunately we were able to bring a roll of wire into camp, which has been most useful in stringing across rooms as support for mosquito nets, stringing from one wing of building to the other for laundry lines, and for cup handles. Another method to remove bottle top is to fill bottle with water to the point where it is to be cut off, pour oil on top of water and light oil. Several women in camp have used one or another of these methods for converting attractive bottles into vases or water containers for wicker flower baskets.

October 27, 1942. Dr. Jara brought into camp, to be charged to camp, a 25-gallon drum of cod liver oil priced at $180.00. The oil will be doled out in small quantities for emergencies only. Milk of magnesia is now $12.00 per medium sized household bottle and a roll of sterilized cotton formerly priced at 80¢ is now $5.00. Quaker oats, formerly 70¢ per box, are now $4.50. The camp bought some last week for the hospital. The children are eating cornmeal mush (corn grown and crudely crushed on Negros) or unpolished rice for breakfast.

The most interesting woman in camp is Bertha, 5 feet in height, a hundred pounds in weight, a super-charged dynamo from whom sparks fly when speaking or in action. As a child she was quiet, demure, self-conscious, diffident. At high school graduation in Texas, the vocal comment was, "She's so little, so quiet, so easy to educate." And she rebelled that night. At sixteen, with her high school diploma, Bertha set out to show the world that though she was little and quiet she just wasn't going to be passed by without notice and taken for granted. She applied for teaching position 5th and 6th grades. In personal interview with principal of school she gave her age as 35 and was employed. Next year, at seventeen, she became principal of a six-teacher school. Still little but no longer quiet, Bertha took matters into her own hands for many years. She returned to school and took a college degree, applied to the Bureau of Education in Washington, D.C., for an appointment to teach in the Philippines so she could see this part of the world without expense to herself. Bertha wanted to know the Philippines and she knew the way to learn the customs of the people was to live in the smaller isolated barrios. She taught Filipino children in the wilderness of Luzon, on Panay and on Negros. Often she was the only white woman within several days' travel. She loved it. Then she had her fill of native lore, native food, native religious and patriotic festivals at first hand, native domestic mores, even a study of native flora and of animal and bird habits. So Bertha came out of the wilderness and taught the children of the white and Spanish staff members of one of Negros' largest sugar centrals. She became engaged to the chief engineer of the Central, an American 15 years her senior. Bertha, still the individualist, did what many women in the P. Islands secretly wish to do and yet seldom do—saved money. She rode buses. (No white person ever does. They must ride in sleek, shiny cars behind a uniformed chauffeur.) She did the unheard of thing of passing by Chinese peddlers with their packs of embroidered linens and underthings, bronzes, carved chests, and other desirable but unnecessary objects. She didn't try to outshine other women on the Central with too-many-course dinners and saved her husband's $1,500–$2,000 monthly salary. With free house, lights, water and fuel provided by the Central, this saving was almost complete. While others are wailing and bemoaning hourly—at washtubs, at shower, at toilet, on verandah, in bedrooms, dining room and kitchen, Bertha smiles—her money and her husband's money is safe in U.S. banks. Everywhere one hears, "I lost forty-five pure Irish linen sheets, twenty-five untouched new bath towels, fifty luncheon sets, etc., etc." and then the next thing, "But I lost fifty sheets hand-hemstitched and monogrammed, ten beau–u–tiful Chinese rugs, four inlaid Chinese screens, etc., etc."—each person out-losing the other in losses. Many of these losers, with managers' salaries far in excess of her husband's generous one, don't have boat fare home after the war unless salaries are paid for the duration of the time we are in camp. No one's credit is acceptable at this time so there is no spending money "due you."

Bertha and her husband plan to retire to Colorado City or New Orleans when the war is over—picked these two cities from tour of all U.S. on last six months' "leave" in States, which they spent in car looking for likely place to spend remainder of life, any spot between Atlantic and Pacific, large town or city.

In camp Bertha is librarian the two hours each day the library is open and has made a special children's library of school texts and supplementary reading books found locked in a closet in the school building when we entered. In addition she spends three days a week over a small wood-burning stove roasting native coffee beans for camp use. She volunteered this service—it's a hot, slow process as roasting pans are small, oven space limited, repeated refueling of stove necessary—and no one else has come forward to relieve her. In addition she serves her time on kitchen duty preparing food, serving, drying dishes—and takes her turn at sanitation, keeping toilets and ladies' showers clean. She has organized a two-hour daily kindergarten and made by hand American-Spanish picture books for children.

Bertha's biggest handicap in childhood and adulthood has been her beauty. As a child she had long curls to the waist, big brown eyes, and lovely, noticeably straight white teeth. Beauty is a handicap to an ambitious girl. Other girls resent beauty. In my college experience there were two candidates for the presidency of the Literary Society in the girls' boarding school I attended. One was the campus brains and beauty, the other a homely, unattractive, rather unintelligent student. To me the former seemed so much better qualified, and I had my earliest lesson in petty politics when I was told by a wiser student than I that the beauty would be defeated by the other beauties and near-beauties in school who were jealous of her—that an unusually attractive girl was seldom liked "en masse" by other girls, that women can be cruel to other women more blessed by nature than they.

So Bertha developed a way of meeting the jealousy of others, and though she has true and loyal woman friends she is aware of the foibles of both men and women. She has "worldly wisdom" without cynicism.

Mrs. McMartin, of London, told me today that she has learned since coming to concentration camp that "Two in One" paste shoe polish is not polish for both black and brown shoes in one container as she had thought. She said she had always thought this was what the name implied and so brought only one can to camp for two colors of shoes. What different people have learned from war!

Friday, November 6, 1942. Five months in camp. Today Japanese guards cut up American flag in front of camp and tied pieces of starred or striped material to small wooden posts for staking off field for new recruits to practice war maneuvers. About thirty Negros Japanese youth—or of Japanese-Filipino blood—are being trained by our camp guards when off duty. The recruits, with aid of conscripted laborers picked up and stopped from their personal tasks as they passed on the highway, spent the morning filling sand bags (sugar sacks stolen from one of the centrals) from a nearby plowed field. These piled at the entrance to the camp, recruits then loudly sang Japanese war songs as they attacked an imaginary enemy in woods to the north of camp and in clear view of "campites"—our word for selves. The use of the American flag was to humiliate and annoy us and to give zest to the recruits' activity.

We are being tantalized in little ways now. Last night Yasamori let some of men in camp listen to his radio to a Berlin broadcast in which it was stated Britain is on the verge of collapse and the U.S. has decided to send no aid to the Far East. This broadcast had the desired effect on few listeners. One man said that the next time he tuned in KGEI, San Francisco's broadcasting station, he expected he would hear the announcer say "KGEI, San Francisco, the Voice of Tokyo speaking." The vast majority of people in camp refused to show annoyance or lowered spirits or morale. We don't expect to be out for Thanksgiving, or Christmas, but have almost unanimously agreed we should be freed by next June—one year after our imprisonment.

Our thoughts are constantly on release. But perhaps some of us are wise enough to know that aid of such proportions as to be decisive cannot be sent in a day. Yet time passes slowly. (Quote from *Mary Queen of Scotland and the Isles* by Stefan Zweig, Viking Press, N.Y. 1935, p. 285, 2nd para . . . "The prisoner, the solitary, thinking day and night of his own sad fate, is always inclined to believe that those who live in the free and active world must be thinking as much about him as he thinks about himself. Of course, it is not so.")

We sometimes joke about the possibility of being freed by a regiment of Chinese instead of the Yanks whose coming we await. Or the surprise we'd have if Dutchmen singing "Heil Wilhelmina" stormed our camp fence, or British troops, or American Negroes. We whisper to each other as we pass in the corridor, "The Yanks are coming!" as a sort of cheery password, and somehow we've come to expect Yanks literally. I think most Americans here had rather spend an extra month or two in prison and be ultimately freed by soldiers under the American flag than to be released earlier without our own soldiers to join in celebrations. Yes, the Yanks are coming.

To pass time pleasantly and as profitably as possible in camp two Spanish classes have been started by Spanish-speaking prisoners in camp: one class for beginners and a second for more advanced students. These classes meet in the evening between evening roll call and lights out. During the day beginners sit in all available corners of steps or on grass in shade of buildings (there is not one tree on camp grounds to protect from glare of sun) in effort to find quiet and near-privacy to memorize Spanish verbs or write assignments given by teachers. In the other (advanced) class groups gather for Spanish conversation. Probably our greatest physical inconvenience is due to lack of chairs in camp. For 140 people there are no more than 25 chairs, these privately owned and brought in for private use. Since school desks have been moved from bedrooms and verandahs to the dining room and surplus desks cut into firewood, sitting has become a major problem. In rooms we sit on beds, on the porch we sit on high railing or wooden boxes, or upturned waste baskets. Most people here are agreed that a comfortable chair is one of the greatest blessings of home. But lack of seating facilities doesn't deter us. We have learned to stand for hours, to relax leaning against a wall, and almost to sleep afoot. Pupils take their own seat, if any, to Spanish class. In an enthusiastic burst of pride in learning the language the daily menu appeared on the dining room bulletin board in Spanish words. As long line of hungry diners filed up to cafeteria-like counter to be served by group on kitchen duty for day, a grumble at having menu in anything except English arose. One man, American, stepped from the line, strode to the board, whipped out his handkerchief and erased every Spanish word, replacing it with its English equivalent. Applause went up from the line. "We are an American concentration camp. The Spanish residents of the Philippines have not been imprisoned, they are not allies nor sympathetic to our cause, we are proud of our language and do not need a foreign one for public bulletin board announcements," he said. Due to this outburst, doubtless only English will appear in future.

Saturday, November 7, 1942. One of the sudden windy days that makes little and grown boys run for their tailless Chinese box kites and makes women and girls stay indoors or tie scarves around their hair. (Filipino women never wear hats, but have triangular scarves which they wear around their waist or shoulders and put to their head to protect from sun, rain, or wind, and each has a black net veil for mass and other church affairs.)

At tea, wind blew soup from my spoon as I lifted it from the coconut shell to my mouth and spattered my dress and Clay's suit. Beth's dress whipped over her head as we left the dining hall and I held tightly to the children's hands so that they themselves not blow away. Back safely in room found towels blown from rack, bedspread whipped halfway off cot, waste basket (empty lard tin) blown from window with contents emptied on floor, two tin can drinking cups under bed. When windows closed, room became dark. Wind sounded like wintry blasts as it skirted corners of building. Two hours later stillness was death-like and all windows flying wide in effort to secure air. Such is the caprice of weather in P.I. During the night rose three times to close windows as mosquito nets on children's beds had blown loose from pads they were tucked under and there is danger if mosquitos get inside nets. When wind suddenly ceased in lulls between blasts, had to reopen windows.

November is probably the windiest month in P.I. It seems hardly possible that it was only twelve months ago that Jim and I stood in our garden watching a small group of Filipino boys and their fathers flying huge box kites like stars, like brilliantly colored flowers, like dragons, like birds in flight. And the thrill of watching smaller satellite kites ride up the string holding in check the huge spot of color in the sky and joining the parent kite, then by proper manipulation of the string the smaller kite crawling back down the string to earth again. Kite building and kite flying can well consume adult time and talent as well as that of youth.

As we watched kites in November a year ago Jim decided to utilize wind for toys Beth and Clay could enjoy. He spent afternoons and Sundays with bits of wood and tin and with small cans of paint—red, yellow, blue, the primary colors which small children love—constructing windmills for the children's chubby hands to hold in the breeze, and a larger windmill on a tall spiked pole to stick in the garden whenever the wind was blowing.

A few weeks later ordered lives turned into chaos, including the closing of my house and the frantic move to a sugar central to be with other white families in this crisis which had snatched my husband from me and left the children and me alone in a place classified by the army as "dangerous." How suddenly and how cruelly fate sometimes plays her hand.

November 8, 1942, Sunday. Discussing English language today with Scotchwoman in camp—she inadvertently said "tomāto" in conversation with fellow Scotchman in camp and was scolded for becoming too Americanized. (The Scotch say "tomăto." Also they say "prīvacy" instead of "prĭvacy.") From the differences of pronunciation we went into beauties of English. My Scotch friend thought correct use of "shall" and "will" and their corollaries "should" and "would"—these fine distinctions—make English more resonant than languages lacking such fine points of difference between persons in the same tense. And how English meanings change ("awful" no longer means "full of awe" but has taken on a common and vulgar interpretation; "unravel" means literally "not to ravel," yet the negative prefix before "ravel" does not negate its meaning).

While others are studying Spanish I am reading French. There are two books in French in the school library.

Monday, November 9, 1942. Swiss family from Bacolod brought in candy and bright pink flowers for couple from Insular Lumber Co. celebrating 35th wedding anniversary. Visitors not allowed to talk but excitedly pulling "thumbs up" sign. Managed to whisper as handed over gifts and purposely stumbled, to be caught by receiver, "Thumbs up, new battlefront in Italy."‡ Then rudely pushed away by guard who suspected mumbling and doubted necessity for stumble. News spread like fire in dry timber over camp.

Truckload of bicycles brought to guards' quarters across street, some bicycles with one wheel missing, some with handlebars twisted, but all apparently new and unused. Evidently a bicycle store or several such stores had been raided and bicycles brought here to be broken down to go to Japan for scrap iron.

New foods in dining room:

poto—rice flour cakes, small, puffy, snow white, gelatinous-like in texture.
tinola—fish head soup, fish eyes glaring from pot, one head with each
    serving, ghastly and nauseating to think of eating head and wide-open
    eyes, but favorite dish of Filipinos, often served in camp.
cincomas—tasteless, turnip-like white root, eaten boiled or sliced and
    fried and called in camp "Dutch fried potatoes."
patola—a stringy, okra-like vegetable sliced and boiled in coconut milk.
Coconut milk now used in tea and coffee, bowl of it on counter by drinks
    and those desiring it allowed one teaspoonful per cup of coffee or tea.
Carabao milk being saved for infants, children and invalids.

Friday, November 13, 1942. November 11th passed uneventfully, though we wondered if there was a big offensive somewhere. Death has laid hands on camp life again—murder of a father and four-year-old child, within earshot and view of camp, the wife and mother confined in camp.

Mrs. Amechagurra, twenty-six-year-old American mestizo (Ameri-

‡Since the earliest Allied effort in Italy did not occur until July 1943 when Sicily was invaded, this information was mistaken but is a good example of how readily (and understandably) the internees accepted hopeful news.

can father and Spanish-Filipino mother who later married Filipino stepfather), was brought into camp from her Bacolod home one block from camp site. Her Spanish husband and three young children were kept outside. Occasionally, but not often, the husband and children were given passes to visit in camp. The separation seemed so cruel and unnecessary. The sight of the mother embracing her children with tears in their eyes (two boys, Luis and Herman, aged 5 and 4, and Amaya, a curly haired girl of 3) brought tears to the eyes of adults in camp. Each afternon at 5:30, as regularly as the Jap bugles blew his fellow occupation-area soldiers to roll call, Mr. Amechagurra and the three little tots came out in the field separating their house from camp and stood silently looking at their mother through the camp fence. She stood on the camp steps so they could see her and she could see them. There was no waving, no sign of recognition which might be interpreted by the guards as signalling, but mother and children let the other know they were waiting, waiting. In the rain the little ones came out to look and return sadly to their empty house.

In October Mr. Amechagurra secured a pass to visit his wife and bring the children to see her. On this occasion he told her—in the presence of guards, of course—that he no longer felt safe in Bacolod and planned to go to Manila and take the children to live with his mother there. Mrs. A. wept at thought of dangers of trip on small boats available for passenger travel under Japanese pass now, and at distress of being unable to see children or even know if they arrived safely—there is no mail, of course, for civilians. In answer to Mrs. A.'s pleas her husband postponed his planned trip, though his life had been threatened in Bacolod. On Tuesday night, Nov. 10, he was murdered in his house and his four-year-old son, running to get in his arms as the assailant fired at close range, had his head blown off. Mr. A. was hit in the abdomen, the bullet passing completely through his body, while the other two children whom he was putting to bed stood looking on. There are no telephones permitted by Japanese in Bacolod, so Mr. A., mortally wounded, could not call aid. From information brought to camp, the servants in the house fled, leaving the boy of 5 and girl of 3 alone in the house all night with the bloody corpses of the father and brother. The bodies were buried privately by

Japanese army next day. Mrs. A. went to the hospital in camp on Monday with a sprained back and so was not at her usual look-out on the day preceding through the day following the tragedy. She knew nothing of the murders until yesterday when a Japanese civilian officer came to camp to inform her that her husband had been killed and buried and that the Japanese army was investigating the affair. Mrs. A. became hysterical. She felt her pleading with her husband not to go to Manila had led to his death. When she asked if the children might not come to her in camp, or if she might not be allowed out under guard to see them, she was told the children were with relatives of Mr. A. in Silay and that they would be brought by Japanese to see her in a few days. Today she was calm, awaiting the arrival of her three children, when the same Japanese officer returned to bring still further torture to her by telling her that one of the children had been buried with his father. He had thought it better not to tell her of two deaths at once but on different days. He still refuses to bring the other two children to her or to allow her to leave camp. "Once a person is placed in concentration camp confinement," he explained, "he cannot be permitted out again for any purposes." Mrs. A. is being given sedatives to calm her. She says she fears for her sanity, that she must see her remaining son and daughter.

Though there has been a shadow over camp, there is romance here also. Mr. White and his motherless son, Douglas, are about to be taken care of. Mr. White has been thin and sickly since the death of his wife in childbirth not long after the beginning of the war. The strain of being trapped among strangers with the responsibility of a motherless babe has been almost too much for him. The baby, Douglas, is hale and hearty under the care of a Catholic nun nurse in camp, but Mr. White has still had—until recently—a forlorn and distressed manner. Now romance has come into his life again—not by his own will, neither against his will. A six-foot bundle of determination and efficiency has chosen him for herself and everyone, including Mr. W., accepts the situation with satisfaction. When a woman decides a man shall be hers, the battle is half won, especially when the man is harassed with infant care and ill health. Mr. White is glad to share his responsibilities and worries. There has been no formal announcement of matrimonial intentions but the situation is obvious. There are Baptist, Presbyterian and Catholic ministers in camp, but as our lives are, by prison order, celibate, it is hardly likely that the Japanese would permit marriage sacrament in camp. This romance brings joy to all in camp who are watching the unembarrassed principals, who—of course—will have not one minute of privacy during their entire stay in camp. Privacy is impossible in a jail—privacy from other inmates or from jailers into whose care we have been placed.

A bit of scandal and a disgusting illicit affair are adding zest to camp tongues at the same time of the romance. A sugar central manager showers his attention and gifts on the wife of another camp inmate. She is a pure Filipino, he is an American whose own wife is in the U.S. A mestizo girl in camp is involved in the other affair. She was engaged to a boy in Persia at the outbreak of the war, more recently "officially" engaged (by "officially" I mean she made a public announcement and had a gift shower) to a U.S. Army officer fighting in Mindanao, and now she is engaged (?) to a young American in camp who is waiting for a girl from the States who is to come out to marry him. The mestizo girl has had no opportunity for telling the first two men who are waiting for the end of the war to marry her of her change of mind. To all appearances she's playing it safe so if one lover doesn't come back, there will always be another to fall back upon. Again privacy would be a boon, as the last two "affairs de couer" are as disgusting to unwilling onlookers as the Mr. White affair is quiet, unassuming, and pleasing.

Boxes containing typewriters and electric fans were placed on trucks in front of the camp to be sent to the pier. Bicycles have gone also. The typewriters and fans evidently were collected from homes and offices in Bacolod. Japanese desire for scrap iron must be great— unless fans and typewriters are to be used as such in other places.

November 14, 1942. The Amechagurra children came to camp today—Luis and Amaya. The children came in, cowed and afraid, accompanied by a dour looking Japanese officer whose pinched face was half hidden behind thick shell-rimmed glasses, wearing polished boots and a glistening sword sheath at his side. At seeing his mother crying, Luis said, "Aren't you glad to see us, Mother? You should smile if you are." So Mrs. A. smiled through the tears she had been shedding since she heard of the double murders in her family. She answered him, "I promise you I won't cry again, then you'll know how happy I am to have you two children with me again." This was the cure for her hysteria. Bertha, the indomitable, has offered to look after the children while the mother is still weak. She spent the afternoon with Amaya, who is shy, pulling empty spools on a cord and filling empty cans with sand. Luis went immediately with older boys in camp where they vied with each other in showing off before the "new boy."

Japanese "reveille" bugled at 4:30 this morning and packing of more trucks was noisily accomplished by camp guards. Everything taken from three houses across from camp—even to waste baskets and brooms. Corrugated roofs were removed from temporary guard stands erected to protect the gate guards from rain, wind, and sun. Roofs replaced with matting.

All trainees, who had only two weeks of army maneuvers around camp and who received uniforms two days ago, left with the last trucks. Men and trucks went to the pier. News came in today that Luzon had been bombed by U.S. flying fortresses.*

November 15, 1942. Commonwealth Day, the seventh anniversary of the Commonwealth of the Philippines, but a most unhappy one. Seven years ago today Manuel Quezon took office as the first President of the P.I., elected by the people for a term of six years and not subject to re-election. As the end of the first President's term of office drew near he desired to continue in office so the legislature changed the rule of non-reelection. This amendment, with others (increased pay for legislators, change from a unicameral to a bicameral Congress), was proposed with no choice of approving one and rejecting another. Party tickets must be approved or rejected as a whole, candidates on the party ticket all are elected or none, there is no choice between candidates as individuals, but between party tickets as a whole—a vicious system in P.I. since the party in control has complete control.

*Again, EHV's information is faulty. No bombing raids occurred in Luzon during this period. Flying fortresses (B-17s) were medium-sized bombers operational in the USAAF from 1937 to 1946, used most frequently in daylight bombing raids in Europe.

In reality there is only one party, the Nationalista. Mr. Quezon went into office for a second term and presidential terms were changed to four years as in the U.S. An unhappy day for Quezon and his Commonwealth today to sit in subjugation to the Japanese.

Clear evidence of Japanese occupation of the Islands. Long line of carabaos going to the fields to plow, all arriving at fields at the same time (with their drivers) and plowing from early to late (no time for siesta) on Sundays, too, and even today, which is a national holiday. Planting one crop, corn.

Clay has suddenly developed a somnambulistic trait, walking in his sleep at 5:00 A.M. in total darkness this morning. I heard his footsteps as they approached the door. Was frightened and will put his bed closely between mine and Beth's in future. Fear he may walk the length of verandah and fall down concrete steps or fall from window of room.

There is a certain anti-Filipino sentiment among some of camp inmates. Instability, lack of dependability, lack of appreciation—even honesty, courage and loyalty—have been subjects of conversation among "white" groups since these first came to the Islands. Certain small groups continue in this vein. The wise are realizing the danger in talk of this kind as lists of "enemies" are being made in camp by mestizos here and by Americans married to Filipinos. Tales go from conversations to Mori. There are some in camp who frankly prefer Japanese occupation to continuation of American administration of the Islands' affairs. There are currents, crosscurrents, and strong unseen undercurrents. We are all becoming wary and careful in most casual conversations.

Monday, November 16, 1942. Rainbows in the sky daily and for the past few weeks many times daily—in west in morning, in north at noon, in east toward sunset. The bow is brilliant, arch is complete. Yesterday there were two bows in sky at same time—a low one slightly above horizon curving gracefully and another arch in perfect symmetry curved above it—a beautiful and unusual sight. There are showers daily and seldom does a night pass without refreshing rain. Crops are beautifully green, corn luxuriant in growth, onions, lima beans, cowpeas, camotes, papaya trees which are bearing green fruit (planted from seed of fruit eaten in camp), cincomas, and a large Japanese bean (large as the end of a man's thumb) which is boiled, skinned, then opened in half and fried and which has a taste similar to chestnuts.

November 20, 1942. Up in total darkness at 6:00 A.M. (Electricity is off from 6 A.M. to 6 P.M. daily to conserve fuel for running the small electric plant of Bacolod.) Stumbled around room, as did other adults in their dressing, trying not to disturb the children, then down the dark verandah, trying not to collide with other gliding figures or bump into makeshift seats. Then down the concrete steps for which the camp's carpentry committee has this week secured secondhand lumber and nails (which they pulled from walls here and there) for badly needed banisters. Steps are dangerous at any time and treacherously slippery when wet. Then along walkway to toilet, walkway irregularly dotted with large and small puddles from which frogs hop with a splash as pedestrians approach, only to splash back in again when footsteps have passed. On to the wet, foul-smelling toilets, so continuously wet at this time of year that mushrooms six inches in height spring out from wooden partitions separating one narrow stall from another. Then in darkness an eerie sound from roof of toilets and, as heart stops, one wonders if it's a python (a few small snakes have been seen around toilets), a nest of scorpions, large cockroaches scurrying, or the lizards which abound in the Philippines—and a cock crows on the roof and you realize with relief that the sound came from this fowl changing position. A kerosene tin can is filled and poured in toilet for flushing. In the darkness the toilet seat cannot be seen and it is hardly possible to pour water in with force necessary for flushing without splashing water over sides of toilet and on walls and already wet floor.

Beth proud in new sunsuit today. The trunks, or legs, made of blue denim legs cut from a pair of man's overalls. (Overalls are cut off for shorts by men and women as shorts are easier to wash, also cooler.) Top of Beth's suit made of unbleached muslin or "coco crudo," the belt and pocket trim made of mattress ticking, buttons on the suit made in camp from coconut shell—small, dull buttons but when sewed on with red thread became attractive—to complete the outfit. Beth and Clay are outgrowing all their clothes, growing so rapidly now. We have been in camp five and a half months and in mountain hideout before that, so neither children nor I have had new clothes for almost a year, since shortly after the war started.

Thursday, November 26, 1942. Thanksgiving Day. Regardless of Rooseveltian decree changing Thanksgiving (which we heard was done in the U.S.), we observed it today.†

Swiss visitors during the morning were permitted passes to bring cakes and cookies to friends and relatives in camp, but no talking was allowed. Food was passed by Japanese guards from Swiss to friends.

Promised something "special" in dining room. Dinner consisted of native port, native sweet potatoes (camotes), a vegetable goulash and squash pie without crust. The "special" was an awesome "turkey" lying in state on a table in the center of dining room. A large pumpkin-type squash, shaped surprisingly like the torso of a fowl, had legs of long bananas fastened on with copper wire, which also formed the feet sticking high in the air. The turkey's wings were long, curved slices of camote, the neck was the stem of the pumpkin, painted darker than the rest of the body. The handsome fowl lay on its back on a large platter of red rice which looked, at first glance, like dressing.

For Thanksgiving tea there was chocolate coconut fudge for everybody, made by some of the women of camp on an open fire for several successive afternoons. Over one thousand pieces were cooked so each of the 146 persons in camp was allowed a few pieces to take to his room.

There were two birthdays in camp today—Mr. Pope's (our director) and an eight-year-old boy's [name blurred and unreadable]. After "Happy Birthday" we sang "God Bless America." There were tears in most people's eyes as they were thinking of Don Bell, Manila radio

†EHV refers here to Franklin Roosevelt's action in 1939 changing the traditional Thanksgiving holiday from the fourth Thursday in November to the third. His action was unpopular, and in 1941, by a joint resolution of Congress, the holiday celebration was returned to the fourth Thursday. Hence, the internees were correct in their choice of days.

newscaster who conducted campaign to keep the song out of dance halls and cabarets where it was being jazzed up for dancing, and who was ordered by Japanese to announce the fall of Manila. He refused to go to the microphone and say that the Filipinos and his fellow Americans had surrendered their capital city. He was shot in the back in the broadcast studio—one of the first and most popular martyrs to our cause in the P.I.

Friday, November 27, 1942. Col. Ohta came at 3:00 P.M. today and called us all together in the camp dining room. He called Miss Hereford, who was a missionary in Japan for many years, to be interpreter. Col. Ohta said, "I leave you now and go to another place. I hope you will remember my kindnesses and tell others about them. You have been well treated here, much better treated than Japanese civilians who were interned in this same place.‡ These Japanese were abused, their clothes half torn from them, their personal effects and money stolen, the camp windows were barred, the prisoners were allowed freedom of only part of the camp grounds, guards had holes in toilets, showers, and rooms, through which they spied on prisoners. You have suffered none of these abuses at our hands. However, I do not blame Americans and British for these unfortunate incidents. (The guards were Filipinos and the Filipino provincial government made regulations concerning war prisoners.) I hope this war will end soon and you can leave the concentration camp. After the war I hope also that I may meet some of you pleasantly in your homes in the U.S. and in England. Remember *Bushido* (the interpreter said Knights of the Round Table). Keep your spirits up, and courage and good-will high. Take good care of your health. My successor will be as nice as I have been. I have brought a remembrance with me (cigarettes) for you all and bid you all good-bye."

Mr. Pope responded that we had found the Colonel a true gentleman, regardless of nationality differences, that we truly were saddened by his departure and we would all give him a rising vote of

‡At the very beginning of World War II, before the Japanese invasion of the Philippines reached Negros, Japanese civilians were interned as a precaution. It is this experience that Colonel Ohta is referring to.

thanks. (There was much loud hand clapping, even joined in by the children, who knew nothing of all the verbal batting back and forth.)

As we filed from the dining room most people shook hands with Col. Ohta, who had an unceasing smile on his lips beneath his flaming mustache, but I slipped out unnoticed in the crowd.

Fires on the horizon every night and much smoke during the day. Whether houses are being burned and nearby fields are being cleared for replanting or new lands are being cleared for cultivation, we don't know. Every bit of land around camp is being plowed and ditched for drainage by Filipino labor under direction and supervision of Japanese soldiers—often soldiers ride around fields on horseback to see that no laborer is neglecting tasks assigned. Wages paid these conscripted laborers are not known, but rumor says $.40 per day, in Japanese currency, of course.

November 30, 1942. Mr. Pope was told today that there is only enough alcohol for alcohol stoves and wood for supplementary outdoor cooking for three weeks. (Rice for all three meals is now cooked to a smoky, sticky mess over open wood flame.) The alcohol and wood we have been buying with our own money to cook food bought by us is to be cut off, and the Japanese show no concern; and Col. Ohta wants us to tell others how kind the Japanese have been to us! They have done nothing at all for us, really and truly *nothing*. They have furnished no food and no aid to facilitate the preparation of the food we have furnished. Even the large cisterns for catching rain water were bought and delivered to camp by Swiss and Filipino friends outside who used our money. The camp kitchen was built by our men with their own tools, of materials bought with our own funds.

Had we not been able to afford transportation to bring in our mattresses and mosquito nets, we would be sleeping on the floor (unswept without our own brooms) or on haystacks for all the Japanese cared. And now our fuel is giving out and so is food and the Japanese only smile and say, "Look out for yourselves and tell others of our kindness."

For supper tonight we had soup, one small coconut shell bowl per person, and rice and watery tea—nothing else. For breakfast we had

rice with sugar (brown sugar now, as white sugar is all gone) and coconut milk on it.

December 2, 1942. Picked a boiled fly from Clay's soup tonight at
supper. Put fly on floor under the desk rather than walk with him
balanced on spoon the length of dining room to garbage can outside.
Also tired from day's activities and getting through cafeteria chow line
with bowls for children and myself.

Dr. Smith, camp doctor, called me aside a few days ago to ask
whether I had noticed puffiness around the eyes of Beth and Clay. Had
noticed how flesh under their eyes was swollen each morning. Dr.
Smith said he was going to ask the food committee to put them on the
"sick list" to get two spoonfuls of butter per day.

December 5, 1942. My birthday. One year ago today telegram at
breakfast table, "Happy Birthday. See you soon. All my love. Jim." And
then a telephone call from Manila when Jim said, "Have a nice birthday surprise for you." I asked if it were an Ormosolo painting. He
answered that it was not that, it was something that was less difficult to
carry than an oil painting but that I had wanted just as much. Am still
wondering what Jim had gotten in Manila.

Today rice with sugar for breakfast (rice slightly molded); dried
beans, native sweet potato roots, bananas for dinner; bean soup and
rice for supper. This all-starch diet is beginning to tell on everyone.

Water supply low, none for washing clothes and none in the showers today. So I soaped clothes and hung them out in rain for a rain
rinse. Got soaked to skin, but put on gown and to bed early to keep
from catching cold.

Since Clay has gotten out of bed the second time in his sleep, at
night, and headed for the door of the room I have been pushing our
three beds together, Clay's little bed between Beth's bed and my cot.

Have celebrated our wedding anniversary, Jim's birthday, Beth's and
Clay's birthdays and now mine, in camp.

Situation becoming more and more serious. Food difficult to receive, no visitors allowed in camp at present since burning of business
and residential houses in Bacolod and burning of Managua. Bacolod's

water plant was destroyed to inconvenience the Japanese, without realizing perhaps that we prisoners would likewise suffer by tightened regulations as a result.

Monday, Dec. 7, 1942. Today is the first anniversary of war in the States. Tomorrow will be the anniversary in the Far East. People in camp are jittery, fearing there may be a local uprising among Filipinos. No visitors allowed at camp. There are no cars on highways anymore as all private cars have been confiscated by Japs and permits for driving on Negros have been withdrawn. No buses running, mobility stopped for the present. Carabaos being driven to fields by laborers (walking) only sign of life.

At 7:30 P.M. came first sign of anniversary "celebration." A Japanese barrack beyond back fence of camp burst into flame. Flames were fanned high by the wind. Great fear in camp due to nearness of flames. But wind blew sparks toward the sea. Many people hastily threw what articles were not already packed into open suitcases preparatory to throwing them from windows. A terrific explosion at front of camp shook the building. Nothing was to be seen in the darkness but shapes of coconut trees and a few houses. Then a second, a third, and a fourth blast rent the air and shook camp.

Most people slept in their clothes, ready to go out into the windy night air if necessary. After the fire and the bombs, or dynamite, a car of Japanese civilian officers rushed out from Bacolod to have a conference with Mori. Real purpose of conference unknown but rumor has it that we are to be moved to another part of Negros.

Tuesday, December 8, 1942. Real anniversary of war. Air filled with smoke from the destroyed barracks and nipa houses. Whether Filipinos set fire to buildings so near us or whether Japanese wished to burn them is still a mystery. But each one can lay the blame on the other.

At 9:00 o'clock electricians (Filipinos accompanied by two armed Japanese guards) arrived at camp to connect large light outside our building. Tonight grounds around camp are aglow in the glare of the high-wattage bulbs. Many people say sleep will be difficult as rooms once dark after "lights out" are now bright enough for reading all night or until there is darkness for a brief period after 6 A.M. when the electric current goes off.

Food shortage becoming more serious. Pilfering and thievery from kitchen supplies common. A new dish in camp—soy bean fritters— made from soy beans that have been put through the meat chopper, mixed with rice flour and water and then fried. The soy taste is strong but fritters of any kind are such a novelty the "campites" are asking for more.

Many cases of illness in camp, some serious, due to diet deficiencies. Mr. Gibberson, age 65, was recently transferred from camp hospital to Japanese army hospital in Bacolod due to severity of illness. The first patient, Mr. Williams, moved from camp hospital to Bacolod under Japanese care, died. Second patient, Mr. Davis, in Japanese army care is slowly dying, having lost use of limbs as well as control of speech. Japanese admit his case is hopeless and they do not expect his recovery. There are chronic cases in camp with illnesses not traceable to confinement and prison fare—a severe asthmatic, an elderly man with an ulcerated leg which has been an open sore for years, a case of recurring fever accompanying passage of gall stones. When it was suggested to these sick that they go to the Japanese army hospital for treatment, all refused. Though facilities for treating severe illness here in camp are almost nil, and foods necessary for the sick cannot be secured in camp, these men prefer to face death among friends than with the better equipped medical staffs in the confiscated Philippine hospitals.

The kitchen has almost run out of sugar, the chief commodity of this island, with our camp in sight of one large sugar mill and within a few kilometers of another. But the Japanese have confiscated all sugar on the island and refuse to allow us any. They are evidently planning to ship the thousands and thousands of tons in the bodegas of Negros, which could not possibly have been looted by Filipinos or early arriving Japs. Notice was posted on the dining-room bulletin board that there will be only one spoon sugar (brown) per serving of coffee or tea. This limitation is hard on some—especially elderly men in camp—who are accustomed to putting three or four tablespoons of sugar into coffee or tea to kill the bitter taste of the poor quality of the beverage. Members of the camp food committee stand by the cracker tin from which sugar is served to see that not more than the allowance is taken.

Notice on the bulletin board also that no more extra table salt can be allowed—there had been a tin from which anyone desiring extra salt could serve self. And we live in sight of the sea! But we have no coconuts (such a useful fruit in cooking) and there is a large grove just outside the fence which separates the camp and the free (?) world outside.

December 12, 1942. Mrs. Simke came to see me today. She brought one can Carnation milk, small-sized can pineapple butter, cake of Lifebuoy soap, three eggs, six bananas, lollipops for children, and two one-meter lengths of cotton material for dresses for Beth. Seeing her brought tears, the first time I had seen her in almost a year. Life has not been easy for the Simkes in Bacolod. German Jews are not loved by the Japanese, yet they have not been sent to camp. Mrs. Simke said she dug the milk and butter from a small supply of canned goods she had buried (the cans are badly rusted) when she heard we were almost starving in camp; she wanted to make these donations to the children. It is almost impossible to get eggs in Bacolod at any price. Filipinos have eaten the chickens (all not previously eaten by Japanese in sukiyaki) and the Filipinos in the hills are not coming into Bacolod. Mrs. Simke brought with her in the caramota two live sheep which her husband had come across and had bought for the camp. These were a gift from the Simkes to all the camp—the first gift of food to the camp since we came in. All food sent us by Filipinos, Swiss, and especially by relatives of those in camp has been paid for in cash or charged to us on a pro-rata basis at exhorbitant prices. Everyone has tried to exploit our predicament, most especially the wealthy relatives of people confined here who have brought produce from their haciendas at two to six times its value. Such, unfortunately, is the spirit of this camp.

The selfishness of human nature shows itself in everyday affairs. The rain tanks (used to catch rain water for drinking purposes only) are raided at night by persons in camp who fill buckets or kerosene tins to use it for washing hair or clothes.

Bananas are counted out and put on the center table in the dining room for each person to take one, yet persons passing in line slip extras in their pockets so that the last twenty or thirty people have no fruit. One man slapped another because of short words over the selection.

Tempers are on edge and there are curt remarks of one woman to another as they wait for use of washtubs. Only four tubs for all the women in camp and some women wash slowly, deliberately dawdling, while others fidget to get washing done and on the line. There is pushing in the food line and persons in camp act more and more like savages as life becomes less comfortable and food less satisfying.

Sunday, December 13, 1942. To church tonight while Bertha kept the children. Mr. Wynn, Presbyterian missionary from Dumaguete, preached. He sat on the bench between a Baptist missionary who announced the songs and an elderly Scotch woman who sang a solo. The church altar was a Carnation milk case on top of a bridge table, the whole poorly disguised with a lace tablecloth, property of the minister's wife which she brought to camp in order to save. On the walls were three desk tops nailed about four feet above the floor, used by different Catholic priests for their altars; in the corner a large tin box—locked—contained the Catholic church paraphernalia.

The church audience of twenty sat on low benches with knees higher than hips and pressed against backs of desks in front. Two Catholic women (evidently not permitted to enter by their priest) stood in the doorway throughout the sermon, listening to every word. The noise of chattering and laughter on porches, Japanese guards talking under windows, interfered, but the service went on. Mr. Wynn gave a timely sermon, well delivered.

Mori was sick and away from camp for the past three days. That is why Mrs. Simke was allowed in, the substitute warden is more lenient than Mori. The new temporary warden also allowed talking with visitors while he left the room. When Mrs. Simke realized the opportunity she briefly summarized the news. (The Simkes have kept a radio concealed in their house, contrary to regulations, so her news is up to date. Still fighting in Libya, New Guinea taken by U.S. and Australian forces but re-attacked by Japanese, Russia advancing slowly but no decisive victory in Europe yet, Germany being bombed by R.A.F., troubles against Mussolini being squelched in Italy.) Seemingly nothing had happened which would affect us. The news when we came into camp six months ago and that of today are the same.

In answer to my question "Is Japan being bombed off the map and has the British army resting in England joined the U.S. forces in Ireland for invasion of the continent?" Mrs. Simke replied, "No, these things have not been mentioned on radio recently. But Roosevelt made a speech in which he said that 1943 will see things never before seen in the world's history."

Small consolation that, for if we starve in the concentration camp in 1943 that itself will fulfill Mr. Roosevelt's prophecy. If Mr. Roosevelt had been more concrete in his prognostication we might in turn be more optimistic. The outlook is anything but cheerful.

Mrs. Simke said the Bacolod post office has been reopened under the Japanese and is accepting mail for Manila. She will write her mother in Manila to find out if Jim is in army prison there. She said there is no Red Cross organization on Negros which might help. The Bacolod telegraph office has also reopened.

The warden who is taking Mori's place is not sure of the regulations and therefore unexpectedly lenient at times. Yesterday when one of the older boys playfully threw one of Beth's socks over the camp fence into a gully on the outside and I rushed over to prevent the other sock and shoes from going also (one of those rare occasions when I had put shoes and socks on Beth) the warden watched me admonish Beth for removing her socks and shoes and the boy for tossing the precious article away. Then the warden pointed to the gate and advised me in broken English and through signs to go outside the fence and recover the sock to use with the lone mate held in my hand. Outside the gate I blinked like a mole coming from darkness into the sun, and like the woodchuck, frightened by my own shadow in the free light, I almost ran back inside the heavy iron gates.

December 15, 1942. Radio in the warden's office playing loudly, strains of a waltz program. My mind carries me back to the Manila Hotel* where Jim and I have spent so many evenings dancing in the semi-darkness of shaded intra-mural† lights in the cool breezes of Manila Bay as these wafted between columns of the open dancing pavilion facing the bay. And the hundreds of colored balloons tied in a huge bouquet in the center of the ceiling to be released as the last waltz played. The billowing chiffon evening dresses blowing in the breeze, the trimness of men in black and white and glistening evening studs, the drinks while discussing life and love and watching the moon's reflection in the bay, the night I kissed Jim on the cheek on the dance floor among the hundreds of other couples—I loved him so, we both loved dancing so, the other couples ceased to exist.

Sunday tea dances in the air-conditioned Dao Room of the Manila Hotel—so named for the tree which provided beautiful timber for paneling of walls—on Sunday afternoons. Church upbringing at first rebelled at the thought of Sunday dances, but life is different in the Orient. Tiny cakes, wee sandwiches, ripe olives we nibbled with tea, a pleasant part of the afternoon.

There is not a dance floor small or large (and Manila's Santa Anna Club has the largest dance floor in the world) or a dance orchestra good or bad in Manila which we do not know. And after all clubs had closed for the night we went to Tom's Dixie Kitchen (run by an American Negro) for breakfast of black coffee, sausages, and waffles before going home.‡ How people in love can live without sleep! And the Sunday we left Manila at 7:00 A.M. straight from Tom's Dixie for Pagsanan Falls,* an all-day canoe (banca) trip up a lovely stream between coconut trees alive with monkeys, over rapids through which the Fil-

---

*Luxury hotel on Manila Bay, particularly popular during the U.S. colonial period; still in business today.
†Probably Intramuros—the walled old Spanish city of Manila bordering the bay.
‡Built in the second decade of American rule, this after-hours cafe became the best known restaurant in Manila by World War II.
*Falls at Pagsanjan, small town in Laguna Province of southern Luzon; popular tourist center, site of scenic rapids and waterfalls.

ipino boys paddling us had to get out and pull the boats through the shallow water. How we arrived, dripping and sunburned (in spite of the shadows cast over the water by heavy tropical foliage on both banks), at the base of the falls for a swim in the pool hollowed out of rocks by the force of falling water, for lunch on the rocks in mid-stream, and the most exciting riding of the rapids downstream. Or the Sunday after Saturday night revels at nightclubs we went to Malaban† to see the bats pour from caves in an unending stream, like heavy smoke. Such was Jim's and my life in Manila. Our excursions outside the city were limited to Sundays and holidays because of my classes during the week and his business.

How continual confinement makes a longing for the frivolous things of life—the insignificant things which become so significant in memory. To put on an evening dress again (and our wardrobes in the tropics contain a long dress for every short one, sometimes the after-daytime frocks excelling in number and variety the street costumes).

Our nerves are frazzled in the concentration camp because we find no release in the social life we are accustomed to. And a woman who feels herself poorly dressed and looking her worst is no pleasant companion. The same woman with a new coiffure, a bright nail polish, matched shoes, dress, bag, and hat is a different person. We are friendly not according to appearances of the other person but according to the way we feel ourselves seen by others. If a woman feels herself to be unattractive in the eyes of another woman she cannot help but act unattractively, though it would seem she might be the more gracious to balance her ungracious appearance. Women are not made so. We act as we think we look. And the concentration camp's formless, girdleless, colorless clothes, the long hours of being a washerwoman in a broiling sun which reddens and dries the complexion. (The oils and creams and lotions for soothing such skins simply cannot be bought if one had old currency for them.) Hair that has never been without a permanent wave now must blow—disheveled and straight in terrific and drying winds—as there is no recess from the winds, with dining room, toilets, shower, washtubs widely separated and far

†Town in Rizal Province of southern Luzon, just northwest of Manila.

removed across our unsheltered and unshaded concentration camp grounds. Fingernails are broken and shapeless, feet sore and calloused from bakyas, shoulders a little drooped from the endlessness of it all. Teeth taking on an ochreish tint—toothpaste $3.00 per medium-sized tube selling before the war for $.50 Our dispositions mirror our lack of self-appreciation.

Women in camp seem to show the effect of camp routine most about the neck. And a reddened, scaly neck, with a definite mark outlining the V of blouses worn with shorts (the almost universal camp uniform) will be most unsightly in evening attire. What luxury to wallow in a bath of cold cream, to feel softened and genteel again! And, oh! for a dash of perfume to sweeten the soul as well as the nostrils. As a roughneck feels himself to be, so does he act accordingly.

Among the losses I feel greatest were two newly-arrived from-the-States evening dresses I had never worn: one yards and yards and yards of turquoise chiffon which was Jim's favorite color because it made my eyes green, and a print with splotches of color so unexpected and so vivid the dress frightened me when first I unpacked it. It was to have brought oh's and ah's from envious friends at last year's New Year's Eve party—the biggest annual social event on Negros. Now some Filipino or Geisha girl has both dresses, with the rest of my worn and unworn wardrobe.

December 17, 1942. Our lives are a series of real and imagined crises. No lights tonight until after 8:30. From early sunset and nightfall at 7:00 P.M. we sat in huddles on the porch tormenting ourselves with plans of the nightly forced blackout which meant no reading, writing, sewing, bridge, or other pastimes and necessary work occupying evening hours before "lights out" call. From bedtime of the children at 7:30 till 9:30 is the most fruitful time of day for me—but fruitfulness would be stopped by darkness. There is not enough kerosene in camp for lamps and, of course, no more can be bought. Lights were off due only to necessary repairs to lines.

Speaking of fuel—families of Bacolod are cooking with coconut husks now.

Seen from window today: fifty Filipinos (men, women and children) hoeing at one time on one hectare of cultivated land. This hectare completed, they moved to another under the direction of an armed Japanese guard who sat in an automobile while the workers toiled. Those hoeing cotton recently planted at $.20 per day. Therefore whole families work together to make even sufficient cash for living expenses. Rumor has it that Filipinos come to cotton fields at night and pull off tops of cotton plants to insure no crop to Japanese. This is highly probable.

Filipino soldiers, prisoners of war, three open tightly packed truckloads of them, standing as closely as could, in ragged shirts and trousers (no uniforms, as these had been confiscated by Japanese) passed camp on way to Pulupandan‡ pier for loading on Japanese boat. Prisoners being moved from this island due to danger of release by Filipinos, who are definitely getting out of hand. Fires at night still lighten the night horizon. Last evening there was a glow on Panay—twenty miles away across water—as well as fires to the north toward Talisay* and Silay. Mr. Yangco's lovely home has been burned to the ground at Victorias Central. He was the second man in my life whose most impressive point was fingernails. The lacquer on his fascinated me and when he folded his lacquered hands on the smooth rotundity of his obese abdomen and half closed his eyes, as he pondered a bridge or poker play, he seemed more like a mystic of the Orient than any pure Chinese I have ever seen. Mr. Y. was a combination of three, possibly four, Oriental and European races.

The only other man whose hands dominated his personality was Forrester B. Washington, a Negro, president of the Atlanta School of Social Work in the upstairs offices and classrooms in Atlanta's Negro business section. Forrester B. Washington (don't know whether related to Booker T.) had carmine lacquered nails. Undoubtedly he was sincere in the work he was leading to ameliorate the suffering of his people, but whenever I heard him talk—and I did on several occasions—my eyes and mind could not rise above his brilliant fingertips. I remember nothing else about the character or personality of the

‡Town on western Negros Island, on Guimaras Strait, 14 miles southwest of Bacolod.
*Town on western Negros Island, on Guimaras Strait, 4 miles northeast of Bacolod.

man. So with Mr. Y. I can see only fat fingers with finely tapered gleaming ends, contentedly rising and falling with slow respiratory movements of his rounded abdomen.

December 18–23, 1942. Clay with a nightly temperature of 103 degrees with fever disappearing during the day. Torrential rains and cyclonic winds outside. Kept children in my corner of room with Clay in bed as much as possible. Room dark, no electric current during day. Sat on cot trying to amuse fretful children and do Christmas sewing at same time. Poor job of each in dreary dampness. My corner really "smelled" since it was toilet, dining room, kitchen (I brought meals from the dining room to the bedroom and washed dirty dishes in the room), wash room (damp clothes hanging just at head level), bathroom (children bathed in same small basin in which had to wash greasy dishes), and bedroom. The room reeked with human and food odors and the children, one or the other, cried almost incessantly to get out of this hole. Rain whipped about on the porch and I could not let the children near the door, which had to be kept open for ventilation. Did finish hand-sewed dress for Beth from two quilting squares given to me for that purpose by Mrs. Stevens, and a suit for Clay with blue trousers from an old dress of Beth's, now too small, with white blouse of a baby nightgown of Clay's. The children have become long and slim whereas they were short and chubby on arrival at the concentration camp six and one-half months ago. Children have been promised a party for Christmas by the missionaries in camp who will sponsor it, and new clothes are for the occasion.

December 24, 1942. Christmas plans suddenly disrupted by dismissal from camp of eight of our members. Four Philippine-born women of half or full Filipino blood were let out of camp with their four children. Three women, with the exception of Mrs. Amechagurra, young mestiza widow of Spanish-Philippine citizen, and her two children were also released. Two of the women did not want to go and leave their husbands here but were ordered out by ten o'clock on Christmas Day by the Japanese, a Japanese truck to call for their personal belongings. There are other Philippine-born women in camp to be released later. These people must sign a pledge to remain within the city of Bacolod, not to go beyond the airport on the south and the concrete bridge near camp on the north. No east and west boundaries necessary as Bacolod is bounded by the sea on these two sides and only the highway through the city proper goes north and south. Paroled camp prisoners cannot leave the city limits of Bacolod. Other women in camp are to be released when living arrangements can be made. Mrs. Fleischer, with a paralyzed arm and leg, was granted release but she asked to stay as she has nowhere to live in Bacolod and cannot look after herself alone. The Japanese said they had investigated and found Mrs. Fleischer was related to Mr. Weber, a German in Bacolod, and she could ask to live with him. Mrs. Fleischer explained that her brother married a sister-in-law of Mr. Weber but Mrs. Fleischer and Mr. Weber barely know each other and are not friendly and she hardly feels she can ask him to take her into his household as an uninvited guest, especially as Mrs. Fleischer's husband and Mr. Weber openly disliked each other prior to the war. Mrs. Fleischer's case is still before the Japanese. Camp personnel happy to see the number of prisoners reduced as there will be fewer to feed and the food shortage is becoming more acute daily, and also the camp's credit. We are still buying *all* of our own food.

December 25, 1942. Up in pitch darkness at 6:00 A.M. as Thora Ann Oss, oldest child in the room (6 years), climbed from her mosquito net amidst the squeaking of wires to which the net was fastened and the jolting of other nets in the room suspended from the same wires, and ran to her Santa-filled sock. The four children in the room— Thora Ann, Beth, Clay, and Scott (8 months old)—had put socks in a row on comb-and-brush shelf under small mirror for room. This sock hanging was made possible by gift of Japanese-made toys and candies to all children in camp from Mrs. Simke. Individual bags for Beth contained a celluloid three-inch doll, celluloid table and chair for doll, celluloid tub for doll, and candies of sugar, water, and artificial coloring. Clay's sock held a small balloon, which exposed the words "Made in Japan" in an oblique slant when inflated, and a celluloid horse, duck, and chicken, all with "Japan" (like Beth's) stamped prominently on each tag. Thora Ann's sock held articles similar to Beth's. Scott's Japanese-made rattle was as gaudily painted and as easily destructible as toys for the older children.

Beth was wakened by Thora Ann's shout, "Santa has been here!" And Beth in turn shook Clay from his deep slumber, sleep seeming more important to Clay than this unknown "Santa" the older children seem so excited about.

Then to the dining room where excited children crowded around the door waiting for it to open. Adults also out early for breakfast because a report had spread that the usual breakfast of rice and watery coffee was to be augmented by meat and by *real* coffee, perhaps two cups instead of the usual one cup per person. When heavy wooden doors of the former student manual training shop opened, "oh's" and "ah's" from children and adults alike. A Christmas tree glittered in the light of two kerosene lamps placed at the base of the tree. The tree (a large branch of the lime tree which grows just outside the camp grounds and which had been hanging over the camp fence and was "snitched" when guards were not looking) was decorated with stars cut from tin cans and polished till they shone and with chains of red, green, and brown paper—the paper found in book storeroom of school building and strips cut from sacks. A pitiful and a magnificent Christmas tree! Hanging from the center of the dining room wall above the long counter by which we file for our food was a huge star of green paper with the words "Merry Christmas" painted in gold lettering upon it. This was a gift from the Swiss living in Bacolod.

After breakfast of hamburgers, rice cakes, coconut syrup, and coffee—amid shrieks of the children—Santa himself entered the room. From the bag on his shoulder he produced gifts for every child in camp, crocheted balls made from wrapping string for boys, crocheted bags made from the same string for the girls of camp, and a little shiny cup with the child's name on it for each child in camp. These cups are the smallest sized condensed milk cans with handles and names soldered on—the names of shiny copper wire. Beth's and Clay's little cups have been put aside to be silvered or bronzed after the war as permanent mementos of camp. Clay's ball rolled in the mud while we were going from the dining room in the rain back to the bedroom and Beth's bag was "lifted" before the end of the day, but it was a wonderful Christmas morning. Their Japanese-made Christmas toys were all broken before bedtime.

Christmas afternoon the children gathered in the playroom to sing "Grand Old Duke of York," "Jack and Jill," "Hickory, Dickory Dock," and other nursery songs and to play games. Highlight of the afternoon was a marionette show with dolls made of handkerchiefs and suspended over the doorway by black thread as they danced and played on a platform in the doorway. A bag of candy and a bag of cookies was given each child at the party—these a gift from the Swiss of Bacolod. Though there were candies aplenty on Christmas Day, they were all the same in taste, though different in shape and color. This Christmas there was no butter, no milk, no eggs, no vanilla flavoring, no chocolate, no fruits, and no nuts (except peanuts and coconut) for candies. All were made from brown sugar and water colored with artificial dyes. Some pieces had peanuts or shredded coconut added but these candies all had the same brown sugar and water taste. The cookies also were of various shapes and sizes, but were uniform in content— rice flour, water, and sugar. This Christmas there were no raisins, no oranges, no apples, but it was a happy Christmas for children in camp. A Japanese guard stood looking in on our party but did not molest us. The Japanese are fond of children and did not interfere with Christmas plans in camp—in fact they were not consulted about the plans and followed their policy of "laissez-faire" as long as we pay for everything for ourselves.

Small gifts for some of the people in camp were delivered by guards during Christmas Day. The Yangcos sent to each of their women friends in camp a large brown paper sack decorated with a small bow of holly wreath paper (we wonder where they got Christmas wrapping paper) and containing three bars of toilet soap, toothpaste, a box of sanitary necessities, two small cans of natural milk, and a small tin of oatmeal. A strange, but wonderfully appreciated, war gift. These supplies came from pre-war stocks bought by the Yangcos and stored on haciendas all over the island. It is rumored they have twenty-thirty-forty thousand pesos of canned goods and medical supplies hidden away. How they were able to draw on these stocks for Christmas and send them through the Japanese to camp I do not know. The Yangcos have left the hospital in Bacolod and moved to a small house, believing in protection by the Japanese. The Japanese have taken the huge limousine of the Yangcos in which they rode behind a colorfully liveried chauffeur, and Mr. Yangco comes in a caramota, filling the little seat made for two and causing the tiny native horse to lower his head in an effort to haul the heavy load. Mr. Yangco's wife and adopted daughter come on bicycles on rare visits to camp. On Christmas Day Mr. Yangco came alone on an old open truck, sitting on a large overstuffed chair surrounded by paper bags on the floor of the truck. The truck was formerly used for hauling wood, but took on an air of distinction by the immobile, aloof manner of the sole occupant, except for the Filipino driver sitting in rags on the driver's seat.

I also received a card containing matched rouge and tiny lipstick from Mrs. Simke, a shoulder cape for combing hair from the Schulmanns, also refugee German gems and candy from Miss Toluba, a Filipino nurse formerly in camp in our room as nurse for Douglas White.

December 30, 1942. Rizal Day—the equivalent of Washington's Birthday in the States for Rizal was "Father of His Country" in P.I.† Rizal is a man and a myth—the man and the myth being inseparable. That he was both a Catholic and a Mason during his turbulent lifetime, that he was publicly executed by the Spaniards because of his belief in the sovereign and human rights of Filipinos makes him a satisfactory hero for Filipinos of all creeds. Beyond his few published writings and the facts of his death, little is known of the man himself and many stories of the "cherry tree" variety have grown up around him. Rizal is the hero of every school child in P.I. and the creation of Rizal Day and selection of a particular character for a national hero has done much to develop patriotism and solidarity in the Islands.

December 31, 1942. The end of a horrible year. Spent day reminiscing about my life back in Georgia in peacetime days. Mr. Thompson, a

---

†José Rizal (1861–1896), a national hero of the Philippines, executed by Spanish for revolutionary activities.

Scotsman, sitting on the verandah outside my door, directed my train of thought by his question, "Is sugar cane ripe in Georgia at Christmas time?" To my negative reply he said he was reading *Up from Slavery* by Booker T. Washington and the author mentioned going into poor Negro homes in mid-winter and finding people eating only sugar cane. To the best of my knowledge sugar cane ripens in the summer months in Georgia. Then to a discussion of Hampden and Tuskegee Institutes. Told him of a visit to Dorothy Hall at the latter school for commencement exercises—of courtesies of home economics students who prepared and served meals to guests, of fresh flowers and fruit and ice water kept constantly in room, of graciousness and gentility of President Morton and his wife, both Negroes, and the talent of their daughter who was home from studying piano in a New England university.

Then to a discussion of Warm Springs, Georgia, a place which is known by more out-of-state people than by Georgians—Roosevelt's "other White House." Here Franklin Delano Roosevelt goes for a part of each year for therapeutic treatment and hot water baths for his paralytic limbs. Here the President has his "other home," a neat white cottage with small pillars supporting high verandah roof which is approached by a wooden runway, not steps, as most of occupants of Warm Springs are in wheelchairs or on crutches.

Roosevelt's trim cottage in its quiet green forest setting has been the meeting place of groups from which momentous political decisions have come. Here Cabinet members who are also personal friends of the President are invited for intimacies and confidences not permitted in the busy life of Washington. To have an audience in the White House is something almost any interested and persistent person can secure—but to have an audience in the President's private retreat in the pine woods of Georgia—that is a token of real affection and personal esteem, an honor coveted by politicians and social climbers alike and awarded to few.

January 1, 1943. And so to wind up the year with reminiscences older than the year itself. For my New Year's wish I should like Gordon Smith's triumvirate to rule my life—beauty, laughter, love. There was so little of these fundamental virtues during 1942 and life without beauty, life without laughter, and life without love is a void, a vacuum, a cruel passing of time. The aesthetic, the emotional (other than hate)—may these find their place in my life and the lives of my children and of my dearly beloved husband if he is alive, during 1943. These virtues which war crowded out of life in 1942.

The New Year has brought no change and little hope for early release to us. I can hear Roosevelt's New Year fireside chat‡ (and in the U.S. people are literally at firesides while we go about in cotton short-sleeved frocks as during all months of the year). "My friends . . . have patience . . . the democratic way of life will prevail." Not words, Mr. Roosevelt. Action, please.

Camp life has become organized on a longtime basis. School classes have been opened by volunteer teachers and piano lessons cut short by war have been resumed by a piano teacher who finds herself a prisoner here with four little girls anxious to learn piano forte technique. Beth is learning to read entire sentences. (She does not know the alphabet and cannot write.) She learned in a preschool class organized by Bertha (B. Hill she likes to call herself). B. Hill, a modern teacher in every sense of the word, tells me learning the alphabet is out-of-date just as beginning piano lessons with scales, as I did, is now passé. Music pupils in camp begin with "Comin' Round the Mountain," "Song of the Volga Boatman" and "Home on the Range" with one finger. After beginner can pick out single notes of melody teacher plays bass for accompaniment—to banish lonesomeness of practicing and playing alone—and child feels himself a musician from the beginning.

January 5, 1943. Nineteen more people released from camp today: Mrs. Porter and five children, Mrs. Teehera and three children, Mrs. Fleischer, Mrs. Land, Mrs. Gurrisharri and baby, Mrs. Mercado and baby, Mrs. Toboyan, Mrs. Romero, Mrs. Jardelega. Most of the women are married to Filipinos, pure or half-caste. The husbands of some are

‡Throughout his administrations, Franklin Roosevelt frequently addressed his constituents via casual radio talks which became known as "fireside chats."

still in camp because they have British or American citizenship—the Filipino husbands of American women in camp who kept Filipino citizenship are outside to welcome their wives and families again. Mrs. Teehera, a Filipino married to an Italian who once served in U.S. Navy, is considered American by Japanese. Teehera, a bum, was glad to bring himself and native family in for three meals a day. Camp was glad to see Mrs. Teehera and children leave as many petty thefts traced to them. In fact, luggage of all outgoing campites was searched by Mori, at the request of Mr. Pope, to see if silver stolen from dining room was in Teehera luggage. This searching of luggage for items stolen from camp offended departing campites, but was carried out nevertheless.

Mrs. Land had peculiar status—wife of a Swiss and mother of a grown son and daughter who now reside in Bacolod. She was sent to camp because she "might" be British as she had lived in Hong Kong, had used a British passport and seemed of indeterminate blood and nationality. After her confinement in camp she claimed to be Portuguese, from Macao, the Portuguese island out from Hong Kong to which British and Chinese go for gambling. Her son made a recent trip to Manila on a Japanese boat to try to prove her Portuguese nationality and was evidently successful. The family have Japanese leanings and most people were happy to see her go from camp.

Action around camp: Galvanized iron roof being removed from shell of home begun before the war and standing incomplete near camp. The Japanese are not missing a piece of scrap iron on Negros. On the other side of camp twenty white-suited Japanese arrived in chauffeured cars to inspect cotton crop which is being sprayed with hand sprays by Filipino boys and men. Japanese cars all bore lettered flags on radiator caps, probably "Official Cotton Inspection Committee of Imperial Japanese Army."

And most important event of a full day—a boat at the pier with smoking funnel and masts in clear view has become cynosure of all eyes. It is rumored, with foundation, that we shall be herded in the hold of this boat at 6:00 P.M. tomorrow and carried to Manila. Such packing! Such anticipated terror!

All emergency money was taken from people leaving camp today.

We shall probably be searched also and have what little money we have left taken from us. I have $10.00 emergency funds in $2.00 bills and $2.00 in Japanese funds, the latter payment for a tube of toothpaste which I sold to Mrs. Doule. A medium-sized tube of toothpaste sells for ₱3.00 to ₱4.00 per tube in Bacolod now, Japanese or old currency, of course. The Japanese are making a desperate effort to destroy all emergency currency so people compelled to use pre-war money or Japanese currency, which everyone feels will be worthless at end of war.

Latest chatter about trip to Manila—in recent radio speech Roosevelt said he would bomb Manila. Is this why we are being taken there?

January 7, 1943. Everyone packed ready for trip to Manila. Two large boats at Bacolod pier, from which Japanese soldiers and horses were unloaded and to which truckloads of scrap iron from Negros were carried, as well as more drums of alcohol of the few remaining on the island. A few Swiss came to gate with fresh vegetables and fruit yesterday but were not permitted in. These carried such sentiments as "Good-bye. God bless you." "All our love. May God be with you." These messages passed censor. It is obvious the outside community expects us to be removed from Bacolod. Ten pairs of shoes sent out of camp two days ago were returned today unrepaired—with no explanation.

Friday, January 8, 1943. Breakfast: Oxford sausages, hamburgers, hot rice cakes with coconut syrup, Hills Brothers coffee (two cups per person).

Lunch: Spam—sliced and fried
           Candied sweet potatoes
           Sugar peas and carrots (canned)
           Rice
           Heinz mince meat pudding

Tea: Campbell's soups—assorted
           Corned beef hash with vegetables
           Lipton's tea—unlimited supply, thermos bottle filled on request

Priests received a coveted bottle of Worcestershire sauce for Christmas from the Bishop and passed this to all sitting near in dining room, thinking this might be the last meal in camp.

Were ever such meals served in concentration camp after seven months of imprisonment?

So sure is Mr. Pope that we are going to Manila and so slight the possibility of the Japanese letting us take our canned foodstuff that we are eating American canned goods rather than turn them over to the Japanese. Also, in the rush of packing, inmates on kitchen duty today had no time to prepare vegetables from our garden or slaughter sheep from our livestock. No fresh food supplies have come in from the Swiss for several days—they buy fruit, vegetables, and meat for camp from our funds in local Bacolod market and bring to camp on hand pushcarts. There are two large boats at the pier and the Swiss in Bacolod as well as Americans, British, and Dutch in camp are sure we are going on one of these. Of course one cannot pack intelligently not knowing what baggage will be allowed, but there is always the handbag with canned milk, soap, and change of clothes for children and No. 1 suitcase with more food, soap and clothes, No. 2 with bed linen, etc. No. 3 with towels, laundry soap, dishes, change of shoes, medicines, which might have to be left behind. There are few "non-essentials" in camp to be packed separately except linens and silver brought in by some of the women from other centrals and which were not heeded by the Japanese as we entered camp.

January 10, 1943. Both boats have sailed and we are still here, though belief we are to be transferred persists. Elsa Huni came to bring a bag of cookies for Beth and Clay and to say good-bye. Offered me a flannel nightgown for trip and also money from her purse, both of which offers were refused. Elsa says there is nothing for a young girl to do in Bacolod. Japanese soldiers on streets make it unpleasant for a girl to be out at all and dangerous for girls to be out alone.

Hard-boiled eggs sent to all Fabrica people by Swiss family in Bacolod connected with Central. These eggs for the trip.

January 11–12, 1943. Mr. Pope spoke to camp in dining room before lunch. Said strong likelihood of our being removed on few hours' notice and bodega of canned goods being padlocked by Japanese who came to tell us of our departure. To prevent confiscation of all canned goods and to assure persons in camp of food on boat trip (slow boats require now from three to five days for trip) emergency rations to be issued to each person in camp. These emergency canned goods are to be packed in suitcases or knapsacks of individuals and so could be taken out, whereas case lots of goods might not be allowed on ship. Emergency rations for each adult: 2 cans soup, 2 cans fruit juice (water supply on boats doubtful), 2 cans pork and beans, 2 cans dried beef, 1 small can (¼ lb.) butter. Later these rations increased by following for adults, 1 lb. Klim;* for children and babies, 1 tin cocoa, 1 Ovaltine, 1 peanut butter, 1 box crackers, 1 dried fruit, 1 jar honey or syrup.

Children also received one case evaporated milk each which is to be marked "Baby Vaughan" in my case for both Beth and Clay as goods marked for a baby or child are more likely to receive consideration of Japanese than baggage for adults. If possible, cases of milk to be opened and distributed through baggage of parents, at least enough for few days on boat.

After eight months the Japanese have made first reply to Mr. Pope's request that they assist in feeding us. Camp owes ₱12,000.00 for food bought by Swiss and others outside for camp, in addition to a thousand pesos cash paid by persons in camp to camp funds. Mr. Pope has received check for ₱1,500.00 from Japanese which was for month of December—an allowance of ₱.50 per person per day. (First six months—June to December—never to be paid by Japanese.) From December allowance were deducted electric light bills and water bills for camp for the entire period we have been in camp—bills charged to us by Japanese amount to about ₱500.00. We wonder if Japanese won't deduct rent for our camp from next payment. Mr. Pope said since it took seven months to get first payment he is not too optimistic about checks coming regularly from Japanese for purchase of our nec-

*Brand name for canned powdered milk.

essary foodstuffs. The fact that we prisoners should be forced to pay Japanese who control public utility plants for our own lights and water is appalling to everyone here. Also the fact that we must pay cash for all fuel for cooking.

January [?], 1943. As part of preparation to leave camp we decided to kill and eat Ferdinand, the internment camp Carabao bull. Men of camp made bamboo clubs and chased the animal for half an hour before getting him on his front knees in position to hit death blow over head. Slaughtering, skinning, butchering of animal carried out entirely by amateurs in camp with only ordinary kitchen cutlery. Women of camp pitched in and helped prepare the meat for cooking. Due to inadequate refrigeration to keep the meat, the day's menu was as follows:

Breakfast: Ferdinanders (hamburgers)
Lunch: Ferdinand steaks (choice of heart, tongue, liver, kidneys de
           Ferdinand)
Tea: Ferdinand soup

Brains de Ferdinand (for children and sick in camp) as Ferdinand was a young carabao and had led an easy life he was more tender than the work animals we had been eating. Carabao at its best, however, is a stringy, tasteless, dark meat difficult to chew and digest.

The men of the camp fought for the skin of Ferdinand to patch worn-out shoes. Ferdinand's bones were hand cut into buttons for shirts, trousers, dresses. His head was tossed over the fence to grinning, gesticulating Filipino women who had watched the slaughter through the barbed wire. Doubtless this went into soup also.

Camp livestock now fourteen sheep and ten lambs, the last born lambs being twins. The sheep that do not have lambs already are expecting so that we are not enjoying mutton at present. All of the pigs died from exposure to rain, and rabbits, ducks, and chickens have long since been eaten. The milk goats were the private property of Mrs. Guesachan (?) and were taken by her from the camp when she was released by Japanese, she being married to a Filipino.

Ancient, traditional laundry methods of the American Indians have been put into practice by the women of camp at the instigation of Mrs. Ramona Samilpa, our American Indian internee. The Indians believe that moonlight is better for bleaching than the sun, the bleaching effects of which every Filipino knows. Nature will assist in removal of spots and stains and give a new whiteness to garments left overnight in the full moon and the fall of the dew, Ramona declares. The camp grounds are now dotted with garments, soaped and wet, which are stretched out on the grass at dusk and there are those that say the combination of moonlight, soap, and dew does act as a bleaching agent. A brilliant tropical moon is now at its zenith and our always heavy dew was never more intense. Ramona has also taught the women of camp practical and useful hand arts. She has shown them the cuff of a worn-out sock makes a good sewing thread—that the cuff ravels easily and can be carried around in the sewing basket to be unstrung as needed. Ramona suggests drawstrings for the children's panties instead of elastic. A drawstring has proved more satisfactory than the elastic of Beth's pants which is fast losing its elasticity both from age and laundering. New elastic can be secured neither by purchase nor barter.

My last maternity smock worn while awaiting Clay has been converted into a badly needed dress. The smock was cut off at the waistline and drawn in to a snug fit; twelve inches of unbleached muslin, bartered in exchange for two of Clay's outgrown sunsuits, was added to remainder of smock for full, gathered skirt so I could take it for camp wear. Thora Ann Oss has a new dress from a bright blue bedspread. A tablecloth frock got admiring glances for its wearer today. The top of the dress was white damask, the skirt a green and white checked breakfast cloth. Extra sheets have been cut up for both men's and women's underwear. Scarlett O'Hara was not the only war-harassed self-stylist who saw wearing possibilities in window draperies. Bedroom marquisette has gone into ladies air-conditioned undies in camp and heavier curtains and odd pieces of draperies have appeared as original concentration camp dresses.

Hope this noon's cloudiness means an early "spring offensive"— we're getting a bit impatient. We waited for a "spring offensive" from February thru July of 1942 and never really gave up hope until the rigors of winter had fallen upon both Europe and the U.S. Now hope arises again with the approach of spring in the northern hemisphere. The seasoned prognostications of the groundhog have been known to be false—untrue—but school children in the U.S. probably still look to him, as I did as a child, to predict whether winter woolens and long drawers and stockings will be packed away early or late. However, in 1943 the groundhog's predictions involve more fundamental issues than season changes of clothing.

February 2, 1943. Groundhog Day. Cloudy at noon today, so the hog was not frightened by his shadow when he peeped from his hole in the ground at the stroke of twelve. He will stay out and that'll be an early spring. (Strange is the groundhog's comprehension of the international date line and time zone differences.) He's as busy today as Santa Claus on his day out.

Attractive red-roofed bungalow near camp with flowing bougainvillea climbing over trellises to shade the windows has disappeared as if by waving of magician's wand. Where neat little white house stood a few days ago there is barren space now. The house was carried away piece by piece by the Japs. Probably not even a nail remains on the ground, for eyes of corps of Filipinos who razed houses under Jap supervision seemed to watch for these precious bits of metal, and hands went to pockets as nails were discovered lying about.

Galvanized iron of roof was taken off first, gutter next, and loaded on boat waiting at pier. Beams, walls, window frames, doors were removed one at a time and loaded on trucks for Bacolod. Flooring damaged in removal went to incinerator in clear view of camp across cotton fields (cotton now thinned and about eight to ten inches high) where preparation is under way for cremation of one or more Jap soldiers. A hearse, a Jap military escort, and a group of civilians stood by while wood fire was lighted and box was moved from hearse to improvised funeral pyre (formerly used to dispose of Bacolod garbage). Flames roared for hours from the wood fire and when we opened camp windows at night (closed during afternoon because of a gale from the north) the stench of burning flesh was so strong, so nauseating, that we found sleep impossible. We do not know why the

Japs burn their dead so near us with facilities inadequate for quick and inoffensive cremation.

Labels appearing in camp:

Coca-Cola—Emergency labels put on by bottling plants in Cuba when syrup remained but no more standard Coca-Cola bottles.

Cigaret packages
    Kamel—same animal as on Camel
    Cesterfeld—Chesterfield design
    Pidemon—Piedmont style
    Lucky Stroke—tense of name changed only

"Lifeboat" soap in black letters on strangely familiar orange colored box, the soap an orange color also.

Japanese putting out cigarettes in Manila factories must have had fun deciding upon name and design for packages. Didn't know before the Japs had a sense of humor. The tobacco in all packages is identical, the packages themselves being made from old Philippine Island government forms and mimeographed public school record blanks. There is a shortage of paper in the Islands, a shortage which will become acute as time goes on.

We are beginning to feel shortages here. I wonder if I can find enough paper and other materials to go ahead with my diary. I'm now writing with a stub of pencil less than two inches long. When a gift of food is received in camp there is usually a cry, "Can anyone give me a small piece of paper for a note of thanks?" and the request goes from room to room until a scrap of lined or unlined, used or unused, paper is found.

February 8, 1943. Today Philippines to celebrate day of independence by Japanese.

Beth repeats almost daily, "Mommee, when is my daddy coming back? Maybe he isn't coming back at all." Whenever she begins the second sentence I always drown her out. I can hardly bear to see this doubt creeping into a little mind clearly perplexed by responsibilities that have been forced upon her.

February 14, 1943, Sunday. St. Valentine's Day. Wonderful alliterative beauty of the English language—from mendicity to mendacity.† While thoughts were on such a lofty terminological plane, I heard a strange gulp from Beth's bed where she lay quietly for a mid-day siesta. Scattered around her in bed were many paper valentines, an exchange of which had taken place between children this morning. Beth has a way of keeping new acquisitions at her side until something still newer crowds out older playthings for lack of space. She simply wallowed in volutions made from old Christmas cards and bits of colored paper and ribbons hoarded squirrel-like by foresighted parents. Yellow, green, and brown wrapping paper had also been transformed into heart-like symbols of the day. Beth's and Clay's more prized "valentines," however, were pasteboard with a shiny old-currency ten-centavo piece pasted in the center.

I feared, when I heard gurgles and gulps from Beth's bed, that it might be this coin passing down her throat. It was. Childlike, she had given the new toy the test of taste as well as of touch. For an awful moment Beth gasped as the coin hesitated in its downward course, then a smile broke on her face as she gave one final swallow and the coin passed safely to depths below. A glass of water, hastily handed her, helped lubricate the pathway of this indigestible item.

The four adults in our room—Bertha, Liddy, Jean, and I—sipped forbidden coffee in our room as our celebration of St. Valentine's. We have discovered that coffee can be made most palatable (or has our taste become desensitized or debased?) by adding coffee to a thermos of hot water and letting the mixture stand for an hour or two. This coffee, when passed through strainers, so far surpasses camp stuff that we brew the drink in our room whenever one or another of us is fortunate enough to secure coffee grounds. Jean was the recent recipient of a one-pound tin of U.S. coffee from friends in Bacolod—so our feast today. The boiling water was secured for Scott's bath—hot water is doled out, as this is itself precious due to lack of fuel for heating— and thus the baby splashed in a cold tub to make coffee possible.

---

†Mendicity: the practice of begging; mendacity: the quality of being untruthful. EHV may have meant this as a commentary on conditions in camp.

Beth's silver valentine coin is rare now—Japanese money is of course paper, even one-centavo papers are now in circulation. Needless to say I salvaged Beth's precious coin and put it in safety in her piggy-bank.

February 17, 1943. Spent the morning with a volunteer group hunting small game in rice. There are ten sacks of rice remaining in camp and these are so old, moldy, and bug-eaten. Under ordinary circumstances the stuff would be left to the worms and bugs which infest it. It could justifiably be labeled "unfit for human consumption." But now nothing is thrown away and when the starving, sickly pup which crawled into camp recently searching for food is becoming discouraged at the scantiness of kitchen scraps, we are very saving.

Volunteers each morning pick long worms, smaller white worms more easily detectable, weevils, and ubiquitous ants from rice allotment for the day. The worms remain in coconut shells into which they are tossed and from which they are later emptied into flames of fire, but the weevils have to be "popped" between fingernails to prevent their crawling back into the rice supply.

Saturday, February 20, 1943. Dr. Jardelega in camp today with pass to talk to Mrs. Gibbs and bring candies to Beth and Clay and Thora Ann. While Mori was called to the telephone Dr. Jardelega told Mrs. Gibbs that the U.S.A.F.F.E. had occupied our mountain camp—the Filipino soldiers living in our house there. This means the end of any foodstuffs we might have left there—those who refused to bring goods to camp for camp use have now lost these goods they refused to bring in because they did not wish to share them with others in camp, but for me and for others there are losses far greater than food—personal papers and photos. Whether the Filipinos who have taken over the mountain hideout will be orderly, disciplined, and show regard for property which is not theirs remains to be seen.

Mr. Pope says that his last resort for help to meet our food crisis will be an appeal to the International Red Cross in Manila if, of course, the Japanese will permit his communication. Without funds or credit for food the camp is divided into two thoroughly antagonistic groups concerned with the solution of our problem. One group, headed by Mr. Pope, feels that we should cut the daily food served in camp to a bare subsistence minimum until we have assurance that the Japanese will pay what they have promised us or that money is forthcoming from some other source—internees' pockets. The opposed group feels that we should try to serve at least one well-balanced meal a day until every can of canned goods in the camp bodega has been consumed and every leaf in the garden cut. Then, this group thinks, when the Japanese see that we are really starving they will come to our relief. After much discussion the meeting was adjourned till the following week.

Tuesday, February 23, 1943. At the urgent request of Mr. Pope— through Mori—the Commandant came to camp today to discuss our food situation with Mr. Pope. The new officer made a quick trip through the camp, looking sullenly into every room as he passed down the long verandahs. It was siesta time when the Colonel made his visit and most of the internees were in their rooms undressed in the mid-day heat. Many internees were asleep. Mr. Pope sent around a hasty message that everyone dress and be ready to rise and bow as the Colonel passed the door. To assist the solution of our food problem by making a good impression upon the big Japanese official, most internees carried out Mr. Pope's suggestion. A few lay-in-beds feigned sleep.

After a cursory inspection of the camp the Colonel called Mr. Pope into Mori's office for a conference at which the Colonel, through an interpreter, told Mr. Pope the following relevant and irrelevant facts: (1) Bacolod Camp has a good reputation for behaving, there having been no serious trouble here. (2) Should trouble of any kind arise, Mr. Pope will be held personally responsible. (3) The food shortage of which we spoke and the request for funds in support of camp will be considered. (4) A look at our worm-infested rice supply which we say is beyond salvage shows that this rice is no worse than that eaten by the Japanese soldiers.

This Colonel's attitude was entirely unsympathetic. There seems to be no getting around the belief of the Japanese that we are wealthy prisoners who can continue to feed ourselves while paying the Japanese for food, lights, and water. The Japanese seem unconcerned that there are people in our camp who go to their beds at night too hungry to sleep.

In recent weeks sundries of fruit, rice cookies, and of candies have been permitted at the camp gate. Those with cash have bought them and also papayas, eggs and other things at ridiculously high prices. This has fortified the belief of the Japanese that there is still much money in camp. We are not completely communal, however, and Mr. Pope cannot compel the internees making individual purchases at the gate to turn their money into the camp fund. Herein lies the basic cause of the discontent and discord in camp. Those with money might continue to buy privately what they desire for themselves without regard to the needs of those unfortunates in camp who for one reason or another are unable to secure funds. Those who cannot supplement the dining hall didn't say that their hunger would be less cruel if they weren't compelled to sit quietly by in a crowded room and watch a few gorge themselves on privately bought foodstuffs while they hug their empty stomachs, stomachs painfully distended by gas as a result of a diet almost wholly rice. In recent weeks baked whole chickens have been for sale at the camp gate and some internees have been buying three or four of these deliciously browned fowl a week for their private consumption. In reality there can be no privacy in a place like this and so these savory, tempting dishes must be consumed before envious and often acutely hungry eyes. The atmosphere in camp has become strained and tense. Friends of years' standing have ceased to be friends because of the food situation. There is hardly a conversation in which the words "selfishness" and "unfairness" are not repeated. There are many in camp who think that individual purchases should be stopped or reduced to a minimum and that all personal funds should be held in readiness for the camp in case no money is forthcoming from the Japanese. But this is, after all, a matter which must be left to the discretion of those with the cash in hand. Everyone admits that. Human nature being what it is, it is not strange. Russia's Five Year Plan ran into seemingly insurmountable difficulties of execution. And little wonder that we hate the communal system of living worse than we hate the Devil.

February 28, 1943. About 10:30 A.M. Mr. Pope was summoned to Mori's office for a conference with an officer who had come there. A few minutes later Mr. Pope came out wreathed in smiles and at a signal from him the Filipino driver of a car opened the car doors and baskets of foodstuffs were poured on the camp grounds. There were hundreds of lechs (onions) and small tomatoes, two sacks of camotes, two hundred and fifty Bantam eggs, and two sacks of dried fish.

Consternation was on the faces of the internees who were peering from behind the front verandah and out of doorways. Some people had prayed for manna from heaven, but they did not expect it to be delivered by the Japanese. Here was the first food that the Japanese had sent to our internment camp since we were confined here by them almost nine months ago.

Mr. Pope told us later what had happened. The Japanese officer said that he had come to camp to bring the allowance for the month of December—today the last day of February—of ₱.50 per person per day promised us by the Japanese. The foodstuffs sent us had been deducted from the cash allotment, as had been the light and water bills for January and February. (June, July, August, September, October, November, and December light and water bills had been deducted from the first and only allowance previously made to the camp.)

Our pleasure in the food brought by the Japanese was somewhat dampened when a check-up revealed that: the Japanese had charged ₱5.00 per sack when the identical sack can be bought in Bacolod by the camp for ₱2.75. Tomatoes were deducted from the allowance at ₱.08 each. The current price in Bacolod is ₱.05. We were charged ₱.02 more for eggs than the camp pays the Swiss who have been furnishing them.

At 2:30 many internees get up hurriedly from siesta to watch four unaccompanied bombers flying low over our camp toward a nearby mountain range. The planes circled the mountain range, picking their objective carefully before loosing their bombs. There was no reply from the hillsides where, in all likelihood, the Japanese had discovered a guerrilla hideout. Having completed this mission the planes returned toward Panay Island from which they had come.

March 1, 1943. Second funeral in camp. A bright, cool morning—one of the rare perfect days in the P.I. which follow months of rain and precede months of almost unbearable drought and heat. Mr. John Davis died in the Japanese army hospital in Bacolod yesterday at 1:50. At 2:10 Dr. Jara drove up at camp gate to inform Mr. Pope.

Mr. Davis, English by birth, had been an employee of the Insular Lumber Co. for over twenty years. When Mr. Davis came to the concentration camp he had a slight difficulty in walking. His legs became more unsteady as the months went by. After one or two severe falls on the camp grounds, Mr. Davis was assigned to the camp hospital, later to be removed and sent to the army hospital. It was announced by the Japanese that Mr. Davis's body would be brought back to concentration camp. Burial was at 10:00 today.

ABOARD THE NAGA
1943

2:30 P.M., March 2, 1943, Tuesday. Like lightning from a dark cloud came the order to leave for Manila in one hour. "The boat is waiting at the pier and trucks on which you will load what belongings you can pack in the time allowed are at the camp gate." There was pandemonium in camp. The order to break camp was not entirely unexpected, but the short time for preparation left us breathless.

Fifteen Philippine Constabulary‡ came to camp at 2:30 with Japanese officers and eight empty trucks. Constabulary went into rooms saying casually that they had come to supervise packing and loading of trucks.

What rushing about pulling down mosquito nets, folding cots, throwing clothes and foodstuffs into knapsacks. Packing washcloths, tin cups, foodstuffs, and change of clothing in bag to carry in hand. Boxes nailed tightly were ripped open crudely before being loaded on trucks and all boxes containing canned goods—especially milk— were set aside and "forgotten" to be loaded when the trucks pulled out.

Rode to the pier standing and bundled together tightly. Truck drivers seemed concerned only with getting driving done in shortest possible time. At the pier soap, rice, and odd pieces of clothing lay scat-

‡Indigenous police force established in the early U.S. colonial period.

tered about. The clothing had been spilled from boxes opened by the Japanese for inspection and incompletely and insecurely repacked before being put aboard ship. When the last truckload of internees arrived at the littered pier, it was dusk. We were told to form two columns for a final Bacolod roll call before we departed. A drizzling rain had set in and mothers did their best to keep babies and children covered as we carried out the contradictory orders of the Japanese— first to arrange ourselves by nationality groups, then by sixes [sexes?], then to segregate those with children from those without children— in whatever manner the Japanese demanded, for they seemed of different opinions themselves as to how they wished us to be counted and recounted. Before roll call was completed darkness had set in and we had to tread the steep and slippery gangplank by the light of a kerosene lantern which showed us nothing of the black interior of the boat on which we were to travel.

We soon found to our distress that the slipperiness of the gangplank was due not entirely to the rain, as we had thought, but that the boat was covered with the greasy, dirty overflow from a cargo of crude oil, loaded in leaking barrels on the boat shortly before us and which was to accompany us to Manila. From our unsteady and treacherous walking of the gangplank into the boat until our exit in Manila, crude oil and passengers mixed freely. The hand rail of the deck which we clutched to steady us as we climbed aboard left our hands gummy and slimy. As we felt our way along oily hand rails leading to second deck which was to house us, Japanese soldiers, barefooted and clad only in a G-string, watched us by a lamp which had been lighted as we filed past the deck space where they were sleeping. The soldiers were to sleep on one half of the deck, the women and children on the other. The men of our group were to sleep on the hatches on the main deck.

We filed aboard—three American Indians, one Negro, two nuns in their most inappropriate flowing robes, and the Dutch, British, and American priests who had long before abandoned ecclesiastical attire, and the run-of-the-mill internees.

"What do we sleep on?" asked someone. "On the bare floor," we were told. "But it's filthy with oil tracked by everyone walking over it," we protested. We got no response and began to take mental measurement of individuals and space to see if everyone could stretch out on the floor. We found, when this was tried, that we would have to try to relax on the hard floor in relays, half of the women to stretch out the first half of the night and the remaining women to have the use of the floor space the last half of the night. The children were to be allowed to lie down all night, though none of them slept well the first night due to the hardness of the floor, the crowded condition, and the excitement caused by moving and being aboard ship.

The men sat on top of the miscellaneous surplus baggage which cluttered the lower deck after the hatch assigned to our use had been filled. Men, like the women, found sitting more comfortable than lying on the unaccustomed hardness of the floor, which seemed to rub the very flesh from thigh joints when one stayed in a single prone position for more than a few minutes. The natural fleshiness of the hips made a sitting position more tolerable.

Wednesday, March 3, 1943. At dawn we pulled our stiff bodies from the filthy floor to stand on cramped legs while we planned breakfast for the children, crying and irritable from lack of sleep.

One of our women ventured out and squatted precariously over one of the holes on the rear of the deck. One of the Japanese soldiers quietly took the same position over the hole next to her. She left in haste and confusion. A council of women aboard was held. We decided to use the children's potties brought aboard ship, though there is no spot of privacy for the users. A bucket tied to the end of a rope thrown over the side of the ship for water will be used for cleaning the potties.

Our disappointments were two: we were still tied up at the Bacolod pier and were told we should probably be here for several days, and the Japanese had made no plans for feeding us—we were to provide and cook our own food. Someone opened a can of coffee and with hot water obtained from the Filipino cook for the Japanese aboard ship made a weak hot drink for each adult person. In the middle of the morning, when the Japanese had finished their own breakfast and the kitchen was empty, three mothers slipped into the dirty hole which served as the kitchen to prepare oatmeal for children who were by now crying with hunger.

Since the unexplained and unexpected delay in sailing would cause a drain on our personal food supplies, Mr. Pope ordered an immediate check-up on food brought aboard. Each person was supposed to have brought aboard his "emergency rations" given out some months before when the first rumor concerning our transfer to Manila caused a flurry in Bacolod for these "emergency rations." A food inventory of canned goods brought aboard ship by internees revealed the following: Many internees failed to bring "emergency rations" aboard with them in the rush of packing; other internees had already consumed a large part of rations during the night; many cases of canned goods from the Bacolod Camp bodega had been opened and looted by our own men during the night. Seeing cases pilfered by our own men, the Japanese pulled cans also from cases ripped on the sides sufficient for a hand to enter to draw out a can. One Japanese soldier showed other soldier large size tin of Crisco which was his loot. Later, Japanese soldier ate this happily with a spoon from the tin.

Daylight offered us our first real glimpse of the ship to transport us to Manila—the Naga, the name printed in dull letters on the grey side of the ship. The Japanese had not removed nor changed the name of the boat, a small inter-island lumber ship of 372,000 tons net built in Hong Kong in 1929 for the Manila Railroad Co. (for inter-island use in the P.I.). The Naga has fifteen tiny staterooms on the lower deck and ten on the upper, in addition to captain's quarters on the bridge. She carries a crew of twenty-three Filipinos. There are no toilet facilities nor provisions for bathing. No one understood the first night but now many of us plan to arrive in Manila in the clothes, already ruined by oil, in which we boarded the Naga. Most of us have too few clothes to ruin more than one outfit on this dirty boat.

A look around disclosed a small open platform built off the stern, extending out over the rudders. In the floor of the platform were three round holes. These were toilets for men, women, and children. (Due to size of holes and danger of children falling through, no mother would let her child venture out.)

Thursday, March 4, 1943. Still at the pier! First birthday of Douglas White, whose mother died a year ago today when he was born.

Friday, March 5, 1943. Permitted to walk on pier today and stretch our legs. We discovered joyfully that oil drums on the pier had collected an inch of rain water on tops. I took out a washcloth and laundry soap, disrobed filthy Beth and Clay for the first bath since coming aboard Naga. I scraped off much oil with my fingernails to the discomfort of the children, for soap and water alone failed to remove the heavy grease. Put their same clothes back on, stiff with dirt and oil, for these must last the trip, after which they will be burned in Manila.

The Japanese are openly perplexed at the sudden boldness of American women prisoners. We are no longer the humble internees of yore. Prisoners and soldiers are constantly bumping into each other due to conditions. No prisoner says, "Excuse me," but looks straight ahead into the slant eyes before him with an air which has in some instances brought an apology (in Japanese) from an astounded soldier.

As we have become more dirty, men have become more brazen. We are already so uncomfortable we have little to lose on the filthy, stifling boat. Our cockiness conceals a fear for the uncertainties as we wait at the pier for we know not what nor for how long.

A dark, narrow, slimy passageway leads to the kitchen. We stand in this to eat, after which we hold our plate for a minute under cold, soapless water which hardens grease rather than removes it. We wipe our plates and spoons with odd pieces of paper and scraps of cloth which we toss overboard and which float on the water around us.

Sunday, March 7, 1943. Today we left the pier, to which we madly rushed on Tuesday. A sigh of relief broke from every lip as we left the stinking, steaming pier. Our delay, we learned, was due to failure of our escort to arrive to accompany us to Manila. Two lightly armed motor launches had come to our side during the night. The snow-white flags on which the Nippon sun rose, above the masts of launches, was the first clean sight before our eyes in many days. On the Naga there flies a smoke-blackened insignia of the Japanese empire and also the black and white lightning flash of the Japanese army—a zig-zag perpendicular from corner to corner of a white square. This military flag adorned our "escorts" also.

Additional soldiers came aboard the Naga before we sailed. They were assigned to the captain's bridge, from which they urinated and defecated over the side of the ship, to the disgust of us below, as wind blew the matter on crowded prisoners who could not withdraw far from railing for lack of space.

We discovered that in addition to soldiers, taken on at last minute, we had also added a cargo of six large, lusty, live pigs, domiciled in a pen constructed under the steps from our deck to a lower one. In an undrained small enclosure the pigs wallowed in their own filth as well as the soured remnants of food waste tossed to them. We passed up and down these steps for our food. Having worn our own clothes for five days and nights without bathing or without a change we didn't want to protest too much about the pigs.

Pillow cases, grass bags of all sizes and shapes, overflowed with dirty towels, overripe fruit and a change of clothes to have handy in Manila. Baby diapers, freshly washed in the clear, pure water of the open sea, flutter from ropes strung across the deck at head level. Diapers washed in salt water without soap have given no baby a rash.

The sea wind is a wondrous relief for the days at the pier when we sat drenched in our own perspiration, limp and listless. Our sailing today at dawn eased tension of nerves, and the spirits of all were raised.

Monday, March 8, 1943. Stayed up late last night sitting on steps listening to discussion by two of our group as to whether parallel lines meet at infinity. Took off shoes and stepped over sleeping forms in darkness—we have been in blackout since we left Bacolod—to find room to lie down. I lay on my side, knees under my chin, and slept.

Tuesday, March 9, 1943. The Japanese soldiers aboard are putting their personal belongings in boxes in preparation for going ashore.

At 5:30 P.M. we sighted Corregidor. We were looking for this fortress by the sea. At the sight of Corregidor we saw our first real evidence of the struggle for the capital of the Philippines. From the sea protruded the funnels and masts of sunken craft—sharp and gaunt like the arms of stiffened dead protruding from a watery grave. On Corregidor beach lay the dry and bleached remains of barges and boats, large and small. Great holes gaped on the slopes of Corregidor (the Captain) where explosives had blasted the earth.* The sight was both awesome and depressing.

*With the development of air warfare, Corregidor's former impregnability no longer held and it remains now, as when viewed by EHV, barren and bombed, as a monument to the destruction of World War II.

MANILA
1943-1945

Wednesday, March 10, 1943. Pulled into the pier of "longest pier in the world"—Manila—at 10:00 A.M. Warehouse windows were shattered, glass gone, iron frames warped, but all rubbish removed. The hull of Casiana, Pres. Quezon's luxury yacht, being raised from watery grave near Pier 5 for scrap iron.

Roll call on pier, then walked in double file with bundles of food and clothing in hands for ½ kilometer to wait for transportation to new camp. American soldiers reassembling broken trucks and working on automobile parts waved at us through a wire fence guarding them.

Manila Hotel lawns and flower gardens are beautifully kept. The only cars on the streets are ones carrying Japanese army and naval officers. No civilian cars seen in use and no white face except American soldiers.

Monday, April 19, 1943.† First six weeks in "Stic" (Santo Tomás Internment Camp) with 3,500 internees of mixed races, colors, and creeds. Sitting under the acacia trees which are in pinkish splendor of

---

†Note the gap of nearly six weeks in EHV's account, probably due to the necessity of settling into a new environment. During this time the Allied effort in the Pacific remained limited, secondary to the war in Europe, and moving only slowly toward the Philippines.

full bloom on the front campus of the University of Manila. The children, tired of the kindergarten equipment at the Main Building, have wandered up to the front campus to play hide-and-seek in the well-trimmed hedges which border the spacious lawns. Fourteen or fifteen middle-aged men, without regard to previous wealth or position, and all stripped to the waist, sweep leaves, tend flower beds, or carry out other assignments of the Santo Tomás Concentration Camp.

On the baseball field the camp's ace pitcher is practicing with a few members of his team for the British-American series. An outdoor basketball court has teams of high school boys having a workout with their dark-skinned coach. The men's handball court is always busy and now two teams of fifteen men each constantly bat the ball over the net and back—over the net and back—it's good to keep the spirits up and the body agile, they say. The hockey field is deserted, so is the four-hole practice golf course.

It seems a fitting place for Americans to be "sheltered" and "protected" from the war that ravages the world about us, the reason given by the Japanese for our internment. But there is tragedy in every group, a tightness about the mouth of a seemingly carefree ball player, furrowed brows, quick and cautious whispers after a furtive look around to see that no one is in earshot.

Six weeks in Santo Tomás—a campus familiar to me because of pre-war and pre-marital frequent trips to the Dean's office to arrange for a transfer of post-graduate credits from American universities that I might be granted a Ph.D. from this oldest university under the American flag.‡ How much fun, I thought, to return to the U.S. with a doctorate from Harvard's predecessor! A change in graduation requirements postponed my enrollment for a few courses necessary for qualification for degree—all candidates for degrees from Santo Tomás must take an oath of allegiance to the Catholic Church! Indeed a thought-provoking request to a dyed-in-the-wool Southern Protestant. Marriage, the birth of Beth and Clay, and our life in the provinces

‡Santo Tomás, founded in Manila in 1611 (twenty-five years earlier than the founding of Harvard) by the Dominican Fathers, was of course "under the American flag" for only a brief period in its long history—approximately forty-one years.

away from Manila temporarily diverted my Santo Tomás ambitions. Now I am at Santo Tomás, not a student but a prisoner.

The history of Santo Tomás is as follows: "Founded in 1611 by legacy of Archbishop Miguel de Benavides. Authorized to confer degrees in 1624. Granted university privileges in 1645 by Innocent X upon Philip IV's request. Made a royal university in 1785 by Charles III and a Pontifical university in 1902 by Leo XII. Oldest university under the American flag. This building designed and constructed under the supervision of Rev. Rogue Rarama, O.P., was solemnly inaugurated on July 2, 1927."

"This building" is the Main Building of internment camp. The original buildings of Santo Tomás still stand in crowded Walled City in the heart of Manila. The new buildings are far out in a residential area.

The Main Building of the university, which formerly housed the administration offices and classrooms on the ground floor and dormitory space on second and third floors, is a large, square, three-story grey concrete structure built around a small open court. Iron bars in full-length windows on first floor and grill bars on doors opening into large lobby give the impression of either a large banking institution or of a Sing Sing. Bars were a part of the original plan of the building and have nothing to do with our tenure here. Each of the many houses in which my husband and I have lived in life in the Philippines has had barred windows—in fact, in looking for a residence window bars were a requisite for renting. There are too many persons on the Islands who do not have the American concept of the property rights of others. Stealing is so much less effort in a tropical climate—and only once in a thousand cases does one go to jail for stealing. The sympathy of police is toward the culprit, and the police attitude toward the victim may be summed up with the statement with which I was admonished after reporting a theft in my home, "If you didn't put your things behind a lock and key, what did you expect? Be more careful in the future."

The Main Building is approached by two tree-lined cement driveways from two gateways in the solid walls enclosing it. These driveways converge at the entrance to the building to form a wide open concrete plaza in front of the building. Here people unfold their chairs in the cool of the evening to listen to masses given on radio broadcasts.

The records of between three and four thousand internees (the exact number varies weekly as sick internees are permitted out for treatment and others to visit relatives and hundreds out in Manila on passes are temporarily or permanently recalled for one reason or another) are kept in some cabinets in the same room formerly designated for student charts. The camp library is also on the first floor. A magnificently wide concrete stairway leads from the center of the lobby to the mezzanine floor, housing a camp school library. There are valuable oil paintings, representing gifts of royalty of Spain and of the Papacy, all relating to the Holy Virgin, our Blessed Lord, or an interesting moment in the life of a reverenced saint. In other buildings on campus are other similar paintings—all original oils, beautifully framed—all devoutly Catholic.

The gymnasium, far off to the left, has been converted into a men's dormitory. Balcony seats have been removed and cots put on the balcony floors. Every inch of basketball court has been converted into sleeping quarters for men.

To the right of the Main Building is the Education Building, a new three-story structure, oblong and flat. Completed just before the outbreak of war, it was to have been a women students' dormitory. It now houses almost a thousand interned men.

Sandwiched between the Main Building and the Education Building is a little one-story structure formerly a cafeteria run for students. This is now the Commandant's office (Japanese Commandant) and is seldom approached due to inhospitable sign over door, "Do not enter."

At rear of the Main Building is the Annex for mothers of children under four years. A long, low building of sixteen classrooms has been converted into a home for infants and small children (lights out and in their beds at 7:00 P.M.), also children's dining room, a clinic and a dispensary, and a children's hospital for the more serious disturbances. A well-equipped playground is between the Annex and the Dormitory—the Dormitory is also a small, low building for children four to eight years and their mothers. Occupants of this building eat in the Annex: three hundred fifty children, one hundred fifty mothers, all told (Is this all children under 12 with parents?)

Lights out in the Dormitory at 8:30 P.M. Children over twelve years old live in the Main Building with mothers or in the Education Building with fathers. "Adult" buildings keeping lights on until 10:30 in rooms and 11:00 in halls.

These are the camp quarters, except for Shantytown, the hundreds of internee-owned private nipa-grass huts which dot the back campus and are the most unusual, most interesting, and most embarrassing phase of camp life.* The Seminary Building, housing the priests who normally administer Santo Tomás University and which also houses the beautiful University Chapel, confessional stalls, private library of the priests, etc., has not been taken over by the Japanese for camp. This three-story concrete rectangle has been set off by a barbed wire fence beyond which internees may not enter. The priests have the freedom of the grounds and also may leave camp if they wish, but rather prefer to remain secluded in their semi-privacy here, to be on hand to take over their property the minute relinquished by Japanese to prevent looting and vandalism during that interim of chaos in between evacuation by Japanese and the restoration of order in the P.I.

Shantytown—"Meet me at my shanty at ten this morning for a cup of coffee." "How about a game of bingo at the shanty this afternoon?"

There are nine mothers in my room in the Annex (whose twelve children bring total of small room to twenty-one) and seven of these mothers own shanties. These shanties cost from ₱50 to build at beginning of camp (most of the internees here are from Manila and came to Santo Tomás in January 1942). The shanties would cost ₱350 to build now, such has been increase in price of building materials. Most shanties are about 20 feet square, with wooden floor, nipa sides, front open but protected by overhanging roof, sloping roof of nipa also.

*EHV is probably referring to the fact that although internees were allowed to build individual "shanties" for family use during daylight hours, activities within them were strictly supervised by the Japanese, their construction had to allow for easy visibility, and no fraternization between family members was allowed after lights-out. These regulations were unpopular, sometimes disobeyed, and toward the end of the internment disregarded.

Section of a side wall opening on hinges and propped open all day serves as window. Since the "big scandal" all shanties must be kept open on one side at all times and must be vacated by occupant at 6:30 P.M.

Japanese granted permission to internees to build shanties so families could eat in privacy and so extra food could be prepared by those with money to buy it and funds for a charcoal stove and fuel. Smoke rising from Shantytown in mid-morning and smell of frying chicken or of steaks, the aroma of coffee, the sound of an ice cream freezer turning, are indications of food preparation in Shantytown, though for internees the camp budget allows ₽.50 per person per day. The amazing thing to us from Bacolod when we arrived at Santo Tomás was that so many internees seemed to have monetary resources as yet untapped. This outward appearance of prosperity and the almost flagrant expenditures of money by some of the internees simply bewilders the Japanese. It also bewilders other internees, some of whom must make every effort to keep alive.

Shantytown is not only for those affluent at present, for there are a few who built shanties for cooking but, finding funds depleted, prepare little or no food, taking camp meals to shanty to eat in privacy. This camp menu consists of cornmeal mush and coffee for breakfast, beans for lunch, meat and vegetable stew and weak tea, unsweetened, for supper. Children get special food in the Annex, including milk, eggs, and fish—foods never tasted by adults except at our own expense.

Supper parties and late coffee were frequently served in shanties. The scandal put the curfew padlock on Shantytown. In the eight o'clock (8 P.M.) daily broadcast of camp announcements, the names of five pregnant women were read one evening. Four fathers were married (women had husbands in camp). The husbands each pleaded guilty. The fifth was a girl of fourteen who herself gave the name of the father of her expected child—a married man whose wife and family are in U.S.A. The women were sent from camp to have their babies and the offending men were put in prison. The Japanese have always demanded segregation of the sexes, though husbands and wives—

and girls and their boyfriends—may stroll together and sit together at mealtimes and during daylight hours.

It was two days ago, Saturday, April 17, that Beth and Clay left "Stic" on a children-posted Japanese pass which, translated into English, gave the children permission to go to the home of Mrs. Ipekdjian by car for two weeks while I recovered from influenza in Santa Catalina Hospital, run by the camp and located just outside the camp walls. In the hospital all thirty-five beds in the women's ward were full, some patients on cots, others on old fashioned beds (brass and iron bed-steads). The men's ward and isolation ward were similarly equipped with miscellaneous beds. Ribbons tied to foot of each bed caught my eye. All the nurses were former U.S. Army nurses, caught on leave here at the time of surrender and interned. Seeing a nurse replace purple badge of last patient with a pink bow, "Your chow card," she explained, "and you'd better be glad your bed marker isn't yellow." As the woman in the bed next to mine was on a "yellow" diet I found how true the nurse's warning. A pink ribbon called for a liquid diet (tea, calamanci juice,† carabao milk); purple ribbon, soft diet (poached duck, eggs, mashed squash, brown sugar pudding); white ribbon, full diet of fried fish, eggplant, spinach. The despised yellow diet is for dysentery patients ("I'm in for loose living," one such pa-tient told me) and is a diet of rice, rice, and rice. Dysentery, amoebic or bacillary, is the most common illness in camp. More than half of patients in women's ward were dysentery cases at the time I entered.

"All patients who can walk must vacate hospital beds for incoming dysentery patients" was the edict before I began fever, chills, and a contagious cold that forced me to leave my children (we had been sleeping together in one bed since arrival in Manila) for their health's sake.

The arrival of the ward doctor for routine check-up and the ap-proach of the daily visiting hours, 3:30–4:30, resulted in a flurry of hand mirrors and powder puffs. Femininity in action, prison and hos-pital status notwithstanding. My yellow patient tucked a few blossoms

---

†kalamansí [Tagalog]—small, lime-like citrus fruit, native to the islands.

in her hair and adjusted her pillow so she would be more erect in bed, as much as to say to the world and to the Japanese, "I can take it."

There is a shadow hanging over camp caused by the murder by Japanese of three internees who, half in fun, climbed over "Stic" walls one night. The jest of the young men ended in tragedy. Caught by the Japanese soon after their more or less open escape, the internees were beaten into almost insensibility till their cries for mercy rent the air. Then, that the lesson might be more impressed, the battered, broken forms of the internees were tied up, propped up and shot. The lesson has had the desired effect. No one speaks of escape from "Stic." We do not forget that we *are* prisoners and that there is a war of which we are a part. The tragedy of the three young, gay internees has been told me, with slightly differing gruesome details, on at least half a dozen different occasions. The Japanese permitted a special memorial service in the Santo Tomás Seminary Chapel which was attended by about everyone.

Shortly after arrival in camp a mestiza woman married to an American soldier from Negros told me, excitedly and furtively, that her husband in the military, a prisoner at Cabanatuan‡ prison, one hundred twenty kilometers from Manila, had sent her a letter—via dangerous undercover route—in which he said my husband was in Cabanatuan prison also. What news! The first intimation that my husband was still alive, the first word concerning him since December 1941. I immediately made plans to send a note to Jim by the same long, dangerous, and circuitous route through which the message concerning him came. I hope someday for assurance that he is not suffering from dysentery, beriberi, or malaria which cause such steady depletion of American military prisoner ranks. To date there has been no other word concerning my husband. Caution is essential.

These war months have been months of endless packing, moving from our Bacolod home to the sugar Central, from the Hawaiian-Philippine Central to a mountain hideout, back to Bacolod for intern-

‡Small town in central Luzon, 60 miles north of Manila; site of the major prisoner-of-war camp for Philamerican troops captured on Bataan.

ment, then from Bacolod Camp to Santo Tomás. During this time there was an overhanging shadow caused by the inability to secure word of my husband as well as the drain of assuming all big family responsibilities as well as my own.

Fever, chills, and sheer exhaustion forced me to hospital bed, and since there was no one to care for them in camp, the children were sent, with the approval of the Japanese, to the home of the Ipekdjians. I could find happiness today in wallowing in a cool and salty sea of tears and self-pity. But such lachrymose joys are reserved for the emotionally unattached.

Wednesday, April 21, 1943. Message from Beth and Clay today, after they have been gone one week. Mrs. S. L. Jones, mother of Mrs. Ipekdjian, who lives in Manila, visited in camp. On first night out, Clay sobbing in his bed, found no comfort in caresses of household or the staff. Beth got out of her bed and went over to him. She put her arms around her little brother and said, "Clay, you might just as well stop crying, you'll have to spend the night in this house anyway." At Beth's practical suggestion, he went to sleep. On May 1 Beth and Clay will come to Santo Tomás to spend the day with me.

Saturday, April 24, 1943. Ciné tonight by permission of Commandant. No cinés for many months, entire camp being punished for pregnancies of women in Shantytown scandal. Four-reel Japanese propaganda film, "What do you think?" showing Japanese rehabilitation and re-orientation—Filipino children learning to sing Japanese song, to speak Jap language in American-built schools. With commentary in English there were flashed on the screen varied scenes from present-day Manila life: nightclub dancing, prize fighting, road construction, military drills in goose step, gardening, smiling passengers unloading from a transportation barge. One will notice a change in the passenger personnel—there's not an American face among those alighting! We were instructed before beginning of ciné that there was to be "no applause during nor at the end of the film" and that we were to report immediately to our rooms.

Sunday, April 25, 1943. Easter Sunday. The clear, clean sky of spring in the wake of a sunrise so dazzling that I wished to shout, "Arise, friends, the world is beginning." The spiritual and the material—peace and war—no one thought can completely master the mind, even on Easter.

There were eggs, colored with crayons, for the children and pineapple pudding for adults, in celebration of the day.

And vespers at sunset out of doors again. "Peace be with you." So Easter Sunday in Santo Tomás Internment Camp draws to a close, this world going to rest as "naturally and as quietly as a leaf dropping from a tree." The day has had its moments of poetry, there has been the "jingling of unexpected coins in the shabby pocket of life."

Monday, April 26, 1943. Class Day exercises of twenty-one high school seniors from the Santo Tomás Internment Camp High School. As all teachers and pupils alike were thrown into concentration upon the fall of Manila, teachers generously offered their services free to the camp. Classes were opened with unmatched and insufficient textbooks, almost no chalk for blackboard work, and stubs for pencils. Pupils from Manila's expensive and racially exclusive private school, the American School, entered classes for first time with students of Manila public schools. Many of these latter students are part Filipino, part Chinese, part East Indian, part Spanish, and pure or part American Negro. Some are a mixture of many races. There are about a dozen Negro men in Santo Tomás—men who came out as cooks on boats and came ashore to stay, or former soldiers with the U.S. Army. There are two pure black Negro women in concentration with large families of children, though most of Negro men have married Filipinos.

The pride of the senior class is the boy who had nearly completed high school in his native Scotland and was caught by the war while visiting in the Philippines. His Scotch accent has not suffered from the experience—in fact, under the admiration and envy of classmates his voice has become increasingly Scotch until now his fellow countrymen here have difficulty understanding him. Nationalities in the high school represent most of the allied nations. In addition to Americans there are English, Dutch, Scotch, and French students. Manila's large Spanish and Swiss communities have been unmolested according to their right as neutrals.

In the past month there have been three occasions for closing all offices in Manila, for parades, the display in all public places of the Japanese flag, speeches, and bands: (1) anniversary of the death of the first Emperor of Japan, (2) fall of Bataan, (3) Tento Setu, the birthday of the present Emperor. There are other events such as the occupation by the Japanese of each separate island. The Japanese have been quick to utilize pageantry as a means to an end.

Catholic holidays have not been deleted from the official calendar. Japanese pride themselves on being broad-minded regarding the religion of the Filipinos. This tolerance is expressed in such public press statements as, "The Japanese understand the religious fervor of the Filipinos." The Japanese know that it will require time before the Divine significance of His Imperial Majesty can be grasped by the Filipino. The Catholic Church is silent, except for the observance of masses and hearing of confessions, for its doors can be closed any moment it offends local Japanese officials who represent His Imperial Majesty. The Japanese would like to get their hands on church property in the Philippine Islands (and no one knows this better than the priests). The Japanese, however, have not yet won their East Asia War and desire and need assistance of the Filipinos in the final struggle. For this reason alone Catholic teachings are still tolerated and Christianity is seemingly condoned by Japanese passivity and by silence concerning its affairs, which nevertheless are watched with a slanted eagle eye.

Distress and fear in Australia prefacing more urgent calls to U.S. for immediate aid. The public execution in Japan of American aviators forced down in unrepeated raids there a year ago,* the scattering of American prisoners grouped at Cabanatuan to smaller and ever more miserable quarters, some sent as cargo to Japan, others to Formosa, still others left in P.I. in unknown and secluded hell holes so there can at no time be a wholesale liberation of prisoners and so that no one,

*See above note, p. 49.

not even immediate families of unfortunate prisoners, now knows whereabouts of loved ones.

Roosevelt's recent chat, "My friends, the war will be over in 1943," does not reassure us. In the evacuation of Cabanatuan I have again lost all trace of my husband.

Thursday, April 29, 1943. Tento Setu, forty-second birthday of the Emperor of Japan. Big Holiday in P.I. More planes than usual in the sky. Distant booming of guns indicated salute and bowing of populace to Imperial Palace in Tokyo. Parade in Manila—Filipinos love parades.

When I began teaching in the University of Philippines before marriage I was given a printed class calendar prepared for freshmen English students. The calendar ran like this: Monday, grammar; Tuesday, composition; Wednesday, holiday; Thursday, rhetoric; Friday, holiday. These holidays were largely Catholic events, saints days which called for special observance. Not only every Catholic member has his individual saint's day, every town, every tiny house has its patron saint whose "day" must be observed by cessation of all work on that day. All call for holidays and parades. There is Occupation Day, August 13 (the day Americans arrived in the Philippines); Commonwealth Day, Nov. 15; All Heroes Day, Nov. 30 (so no one will feel neglected). In addition, there are all U.S. holidays, the historical significance of day being unknown to most of the celebrants: Independence Day, celebrated with as much enthusiasm here as if the P.I. had a part in the occasion, George Washington's Birthday, Memorial Day, Thanksgiving Day—all call for closing of offices and classes, and a trip to the public plaza for the inevitable parades and speeches.

American holidays will not be observed in P.I. this year, but the Japanese are adding as many as they can.

Saturday, May 1, 1943. "In which queue shall I find you this morning?" asks an English friend. For Santo Tomás internees, when not on camp work assignments, spend the remainder of the morning in queues to buy ice (five pounds to a customer), Manila-made soap (one small cake to each person), vegetables and fruits ("Sorry, lady, can't let you have but ten limes"), rice flour bread called puto, and the endless "package" line. In the package line stand those who think they might have donations of food from friends outside camp. Food donations, cooked and uncooked, are received at camp gate between 9:00 and 11:00 A.M. Food containers vary from rusted tin cans and buckets to the most attractive porcelain and metal containers, sometimes brought to the gate with a sprig of flowers on top. Recipients of food are not permitted to talk with those who bring gifts. All packages are left outside gate at censor's office. Each food container is examined rigidly. Few people would dare risk sending a message this way, the examination of contents is so thorough and a violation of regulation would mean cessation of this important privilege, as well as severe punishment to offenders.

The daily package line moves like the body of a huge writhing serpent as men, women, and children, who compose the line, shift and fidget from both impatience and the discomfort of the glare of the sun on the driveway from the Main Building to the gate. When packages have been approved and arranged alphabetically the line files by and each standee is handed his gift through a square hole in the wall. Uncalled for gifts become property of the examiner.

Mrs. Aucoin from Bacolod has few friends in Manila and does not expect a gift of food. She heard that there was a package for her at the gate. She asked for it. She was handed the tag which was attached to the container: "Cookies for Mrs. Aucoin and children from P. Rosaria." "Where are the cookies?" Mrs. Aucoin asked. "Rats ate them. However, you didn't call for them on time. We can't keep food." "Two-legged rats ate them, I suppose," Mrs. Aucoin muttered, thinking how her three small children would have enjoyed cookies again. "What did you say?" demanded the guard angrily. "Only 'Good day,'" replied Mrs. Aucoin as she walked away.

The longest and most popular line of all is the chow line. An hour before the serving of food from improvised cafeteria begins, internees with tin plates, tin cups, spoons and forks in hand form a line. This queue grows at mealtime until it sometimes encircles the Main Building. This line is a cross section of internees. Here one can pick out bearded men of camp—most of them are men who have no razors or blades. The safety razor blade is a memory to most of the masculine population, the old fashioned "strop" razor having come back into its own. (The Japanese had to be convinced this type of razor was brought into camp for toilette uses only and not as a deadly weapon.) The razorless, bearded population of Santo Tomás vie with each other in length and care of beards. Some young men have nurtured beards, in the three and a half years of concentration,† which now reach from chin to chest. One young bearded internee told me that he thought his flowing beard such a beauty that it had become his greatest vanity and he dreaded the end of the war and the foolish resumption of the daily shave. There is a barber shop for those with money—an ex-barber in Manila even managed to put a barber chair into camp. The removal of hair from the head has become a camp problem—not individual. Free haircuts are offered those who cannot pay for this tonsorial service. The free barbers stand by their camp-made wooden stools and clip hair under the shade of a tree. Clay had his first camp haircut under the trees. As the barber stool was too low for comfortable cutting of child's hair, I held Clay. "Face the wind, please," said one barber. "Outdoor haircutting is so much easier," the volunteer barber explained, "if the hair blows away from the face." The wind changed before the haircut was completed and I turned with the breeze.

In the breakfast chow line this morning behind two patriarchal looking internees stood a man in black evening trousers, the shiny silk braid on the dusty trouser legs slightly out of place at this hour of the morning. Above the black trousers he wore a faded and patched blue denim shirt. The evening trousers were probably salvaged from his own belongings or were a gift from someone who felt he, himself, would have little need for such attire in the near future.

The most popular men's clothing in "Stic" is khaki or dark blue or brown shorts. As a top to these are worn undershirts, short sleeved top shirts, polo shirts, or no shirts at all. The only necktie I have seen in camp was one worn by the preacher on Easter. There were not

†Clearly EHV is mistaken here, since concentration in Manila and elsewhere in the Philippines began no earlier than January 1942.

enough white coats or ties in camp for the high school seniors so they were graduated in informal everyday camp clothes.

The women in camp are not so free in the choice of their dress as are the men. Women are forbidden by the Commandant to wear shorts. This rule of Santo Tomás concerning dress was a blow to women from Bacolod, many with wardrobes consisting primarily of shorts and skirtless playsuits. Unfortunately, many of the playsuits in camp have no third piece (wrap-around skirt) and so have had to go into seclusion for the present. Slacks may be worn but, as they are hotter than dresses and more difficult to launder, dresses are preferred by most of the women. There are a few culottes in women's wardrobes, and a few slacks cut off below the knee—for the knees must be covered. There must be pockets on everything, big pockets and deep pockets to hold a meal ticket (which must be punched in each chow line and for purchases of such special commodities as soap, lard, sugar), to carry a fork and spoon, a toothbrush, a notebook and pencil, a comb, a pair of dark glasses, and a vanity case (if one is foresighted enough to save one from bombings). Women without a vanity case may use empty space for a handkerchief, if they have a handkerchief. I must not forget to tell Beth what she will need for the next war. And as soon as she is old enough to remember she must know of Grandmother McMahan's recipe for war hunger, learned from Civil War days—to stay in bed all day and lie perfectly still. One does not get nearly so hungry lying down if there is nothing to eat as one does moving around. Surely Grandmother's own experience and mine should be of some value to my daughter, even if she is not yet four. Beth must be told about string, although it is possible that by the next war something new for women's war needs will have been discovered.

Beth and Clay came to Santo Tomás at 10:30 this morning to spend the day with me. At 9:30 I was as near the gate as the camp rules permit. It seemed the children would never come. At last the big gate opened and nine little children came rushing in, the short legs of Marie, Spanish governess accompanying the children, hardly able to keep pace. Beth and Clay were holding hands. They stopped short when they saw me. There was a moment's awful hesitation when I thought they might have forgotten their mother in the two weeks they had been away. With simultaneous shouts of "Mom-mee!" they were both in my arms, and I carried them, both at one time to the petate mat‡ I had put on the grass in the shade of a tree. There on the grass mat lay Jo-Jo, Beth's clown doll given her by a friend in camp to replace Eva, who fell overboard on the trip to Manila. Jo-Jo had on a new clown suit I had made. Clay's tin truck made in Santo Tomás, and his favorite toy at the moment, lay beside Jo-Jo.

Seated on the mat, toys in their arms, the children told me of their stay at Mrs. Ipekdjian's. "Mommee, we had an Easter party. I found an egg. It was yellow." Clay, it seems, had been naughty and had been put in a closet as punishment. "Mommee, we eat off a table with a cloth on," Beth went on, and I realized that the child could probably never remember having seen a covered table before. The crude life in our hideout, the school benches which served us as chairs and tables in Bacolod Camp, and the rough wooden slabs from which we eat in Santo Tomás must be quite different from a real table "with a cloth on."

At night Beth puts her hand under Clay's cheek, she told me, and he reaches his hand across to her little bed next to his and puts his hand under her cheek. And so they go to sleep. "Does anyone kiss you good-night?" I asked. "Kiss us?" "No," Beth said. I hugged them with tears in my eyes. I want them back but the doctor says for my own health and for the sake of the children as well, they must go back for a month or two longer.

Clay wept when Maria gathered up the children at 4:30 to take them out again. As the heavy gate closed and they passed out of sight Beth had one arm around Clay's shoulders, consoling him as usual. She is, at the age of three and three-fourths, in some ways sharing a mother's responsibilities.

Thursday, May 6, 1943. The Japanese have gone the U.S. one better in regard to holidays. It has been officially proclaimed that May 6 and

‡Mat or matting made of dried palm leaves or grass.

May 7 shall be Thanksgiving in the P.I. Not one day of Thanksgiving, but two. These days of Thanksgiving commemorate the fall of Corregidor, and coincide this year with the visit of Premier Tozyo of Japan.* Free rides on Manila's streetcars are offered to encourage a large attendance at the Premier's Thanksgiving address at Manila's Luneta Park. We shall hear more later of Tozyo's visit, I feel sure.

Friday, May 7, 1943. Turn quickly the spigot of my mind. Cut off this debilitating flow of war fears which leaves my life a dry and devitalized thing!

The agent who promised to deliver a note to my husband in Cabanatuan Military Prison brought harrowing and chilling news today. The "agent" is an American newspaper correspondent, wife, and their two and one-half-year-old daughter. The baby had infantile paralysis before coming into camp and is permitted to be taken outside once each week for therapeutic massage in a private hospital in Manila. One week the father takes the baby, the next week the mother. On one of these trips to Manila, this father took out with him a note I had written to my husband. He in turn gave the note to a Filipino friend of his who was to deliver a consignment of medicinal supplies to the Cabanatuan Hospital. The letter began "Dear Jim" and was signed "Libby." My husband's full name and army rank were written on a separate piece of paper. There were no names on the communication itself.

Ordinarily medicines are permitted into the prison hospital after only a cursory examination at the prison gate. But five prisoners had escaped from Cabanatuan the day the medical supplies arrived and cartons of pills were emptied and vials of serum, worth thousands of pesos and badly needed by sick and dying internees, were broken open in the search for messages which might give a clue to the escape. No less than eight or ten notes to prisoners were discovered in the destroyed medicines. The fate of those who could be identified from the messages is not known. It is known, however, that three of the escaped prisoners were recaptured near Cabanatuan, and shot, and

*Hideki Tojo (1884–1948), premier of Japan from late 1941 until mid-1944.

that the remaining five prisoners who made up the work-group of ten who were together at the time of the escape were shot also.

Diverting this stream of war thoughts I shall begin a dressing gown for Jo-Jo, Beth's doll, from a dress of mine which is beyond repair. The making of doll clothes is to me the most quieting and comforting of activities. In every crisis during this war I have gone to the sewing basket for scraps for doll clothes. When a momentous decision has had to be made, or a decision just made has left me exhausted with its labor pains, or a piece of news has momentarily stopped my heart, the sewing basket has carried me through the crisis. The last few hours in our mountain hideout before we began the long walk into the unknown concentration camp in Bacolod were spent in putting the final stitches on a new wardrobe for the smallest one of us to make the trip—Beth's doll, Eva, which came to an unhappy and watery ending on the S.S. Naga on the way from Bacolod to Manila.

A few statistics issued by Executive Committee as of May 1, 1943:

3,626	regular internees in Santo Tomás
11	special staff
129	internees at Holy Ghost Convent (orthodox Catholic children in convent school)
292	internees in hospital
4,028	total internees

From Mr. Earl Carroll, director of Santo Tomás internees:

5,890	American and British war prisoners at Cabanatuan (2,000 of these in the hospital)
18,000	Americans interned originally at Cabanatuan. Of these 6,000 have died, 6,000 have been moved to Japan or Formosa, and 5,890 remain (half of them are sick). Appalling figures!

One out of three American war prisoners has died and one of the two remaining has been sent away from the Philippines. In which group my husband is included, I seem unable to find out. It has been confirmed, Mr. Carroll said, that Cabanatuan will be evacuated completely by July 1. My chances of hearing from my husband after July 1 are even less than now. Is he sick, is he well, if he's still at Cabanatuan can I send the few aspirin tablets that I have, a cake of soap, and a little cash for cigarettes? Was he one of the five shot last week whose sole offense was that they were on a work assignment with other prisoners who escaped? Is Jim dead or alive? That is the real question. I avoid asking myself. Even those who have heard recently from their husbands find uncertain comfort in the news. For that was last week! What about this week, and next, and the next, before war prisoners will be released?

I moved today from the Annex with its child and baby population to the Main Building in a room totally adult. My new home is a strip of floor space seven feet long (six feet taken up by my springless bed) and 26 inches wide, the exact width of the bed. The extra foot at the end of my bed is for my clothes, shoes, tin plate, and cup. All other personal belongings are considered "non-essential" and had to be boxed and stored in the camp bodega.

Approximately two thousand persons sleep in the Main Building, and toilet and bath facilities are most inadequate. And in the tropics, during the hot, humid months of April and May, when the slightest exertion causes a deluge of perspiration, two or three showers a day are a necessity. There were ten persons in line ahead of me when I first went to the toilet this morning.

Saturday, May 8, 1943. Premier General Hideki Tozyo is of average height of a Filipino—about 5 ft. 6 inches—is well built, healthy and strong (in spite of his 59 years and heavy responsibilities) with a neatly trimmed mustache, a gait and bearing that reminds one of military school, a wide smile that wins people, and a Japanese military haircut, part of which is baldness.

General Tozyo came to the Philippines laden with gifts. He gave ₱100,000 to the fund for the relief of the poor people through Chairman Jorge B. Vargas,† chairman of the Philippine Executive Commission. Also he gave one ton of quinine as his gift to those suffering from

---

†Longtime Philippine politician and close ally of Manuel Quezon. Served as chairman of a puppet cabinet called the Philippine Executive Commission established by the Japanese in January 1942.

malaria. He and Chairman Vargas exchanged gifts and then the Premier said: "Having personally inspected existing conditions in the Philippines, Manchoukuo‡ and Asia, I am feeling convinced that the construction of Greater East Asia is making satisfactory progress and its future is very bright. The entire Filipino people under the leadership of Jorge B. Vargas and other leaders are positively cooperating with the Japanese military administration, understanding fully the true intentions of Japan.

"The United States policy toward the Philippines has always been to place America's interests first, completely hoodwinking the Filipino people by the glamour of American material civilization and deliberately denying the Filipinos their economic power and progressive spirit which are essential factors for the establishment of an independent nation.

"The United States maintained a policy solely designed to make the Philippines a permanent colony of the United States. In this manner the Filipino people were unwittingly paralyzed by the American poison, but with the progress of the War of Greater East Asia, they have now awakened to their true mission.

"If the Filipino people continue in their present effort, the formation of a new Philippine state will not be far distant."

So spoke Tozyo in Manila. After another scattering of gifts the General exchanged farewells with the Commander-in-Chief of the Imperial Japanese Army, the Commander of the Imperial Japanese Fleet in Philippine waters, Highest Advisor Syozo Murata of the Japanese Military Administration, the staff officers of the Headquarters of the Army and the Fleet, the Director General of the Japanese Military Administration, Chairman Jorge B. Vargas, and members of the Philippine Executive Commission and others. General Tozyo left Higasi airfield on May 7 at 10:00 A.M. enroute to Japan.

Of more importance to us in Santo Tomás was a small-type story inside the same Japanese edited newspaper which described Tozyo's visit to Manila. This story was headed "Enemy Planes Downed in Af-

‡Manchukuo—name given to Manchuria, a section of northeast China, by the Japanese after their occupation beginning in 1932.

rica." After lauding the German forces in the Mediterranean area the story closed with this sententious paragraph: "A German news agency this afternoon published without comment an unconfirmed Reuter dispatch saying that anti-Axis forces occupied Tunis and Bizerte."* This exciting news means, we hope, that major fighting on the North African front ended.

Sunday Afternoon, May 9, 1943. R-r-r-ing went the bell connected to the outdoor loudspeakers on the front and back campuses of Santo Tomás. "Attention, please. Everyone stand by for an important announcement," came the voice over the air. "This afternoon the Commandant issued the following announcement to the Santo Tomás Internment Camp Executive Committee. 'I am authorized by the Director General of the Japanese Military Administration in the Philippines to make a statement regarding the change of location of enemy civilians' internment camp to a more spacious place where more permanent accommodations can be provided so that you will continue to live there until the time when you will repatriate to your respective countries or peace will be restored. The new site is in Los Banos,† an ideal health resort noted for its hot springs, where new buildings will be erected for your housing and where you will enjoy fresh air and find an easy access to fresh meat and vegetables, part of which you may be able to cultivate yourselves.

" 'In carrying out the above plan, the first group of about 800 men to be selected from the present internees, which will constitute the core for the new camp, will be dispatched to Los Banos by trains on the 14th of this month. It is to be emphasized that this change of location is entirely based upon the humanitarian consideration of your own welfare. In this connection *you are warned not to make any careless utterance* which will distort the true intention of the Military Administration regarding the present plan, as they are sure that the new camp will promise a better and healthier life to all the enemy civilians in this country.

---

*Cities in northeast Tunisia.
†Small town on Laguna de Bay, south of Manila.

" 'The Commandant of the new camp will be Lt. Col. Narusawa of the Religious Section of the Japanese Military Administration who will have as his assistant Mr. G. Hayasaki.' "

We are to be moved again and there is no pleasure in the anticipation.

Tuesday, May 11, 1943. Everyone in Santo Tomás is indignant at the proposed change of campsite. For seventeen months the internees have devoted their time to making the surroundings here livable. When the first internees arrived at Santo Tomás the buildings were dirty and alive with lice, bed bugs, roaches and rats. The buildings—floors, walls and ceilings—have been scrubbed and kept clean and the insect and rodent pests have been put under control if not completely exterminated. Kitchen equipment has been made and installed. Dining sheds have been erected. Laundry tubs and extended water taps to all parts of the camp have been the work, not of the Japanese but of the internees themselves. Extra showers have been constructed from odd bits of tin and electric lights installed. Into Santo Tomás bodegas has gone thousands of pesos of internees' own money. These improvements, we have been told, are to be left undisturbed when we depart.

Ask anyone in Santo Tomás why the change is being made and the answer will be as follows:

(1) Japanese want this improved Santo Tomás for a Japanese military barracks or for a hospital for wounded Japanese soldiers as the fighting front moves nearer Manila.

(2) Filipinos in Manila are too friendly with internees. The requests of Filipinos for passes to visit in Santo Tomás shows an interest in alien internees which the Japanese wish to stifle. The failure of the Filipinos to forget the Anglo-Saxons, so recently and so closely associated with them, is retarding the complete submission of the Filipino people to the Japanese will. Los Banos is an out-of-way, sparsely settled spot. The Japanese will test the adage "Out of sight, out of mind" in an effort to hasten the complete control of the Philippines.

(3) Underground communications between Santo Tomás and Manila have become so perfected and well established that the Japanese

cannot discover the endless secret tunnels through which forbidden messages pass. The Japanese know that Santo Tomás is informed of all that happens in Manila and that Manilians seem acquainted with all that transpires behind the solid walls of the alien civilian internment camp.

There is not an important shortwave broadcast from the U.S.A. or England that is not picked up on concealed receiving sets in Manila and the news passed on to Santo Tomás. This flow of news, which the Japanese know about but don't seem to be able to stop, has led them to decide to move the camp away from Manila.

Messages come into Santo Tomás in cigarettes, from which the tobacco has been removed, the message inserted and the tobacco repacked at the end. Cigarettes are delivered in camp in fifties, tied together with a piece of string. The cigarette nearest the knot in the string has the message. Labels on a milk can are steamed off in Manila by friends of internees, news typed on the back of the paper and the re-labeled tin sent into Santo Tomás. The old method of inserting notes wrapped in waxed paper in the batter of a loaf of bread is still used. The want ads and the personal columns of the Manila newspaper carry select messages to watchful internees. Yesterday I saw a Manila mestizo, called to the Santo Tomás Commandant's office for a conference concerning his pass, drop a piece of crushed paper in a garbage can at the Commandant's door as he entered the office. This "rubbish," later salvaged by the boy's English father interned in Santo Tomás, carried an uncensored message and a roll of money.

In an effort to sever this and other established communication systems, the Japanese will move internees out of the reach of Manila friends and co-conspirators. There will be no package line at Los Banos and no camp visitors. We shall pay dearly for the privileges abused (or shall we say "fully used") at Santo Tomás.

It is likely that a combination of the three internee interpretations of our camp move have led to the decision for our transfer. It is true that the Japanese are not satisfied with their progress of Nipponizing the Filipinos. The Japanese are anxious to give the Filipinos their independence, but the Japanese feel that the Filipinos are not ready for it. This readiness means that the Filipino people must give the following pledge to Japan: (1) to declare war on the U.S., (2) to place one million Filipino men on the battlefront against the anti-Axis forces, (3) to guarantee the cessation of guerrilla warfare in the P.I.

The Filipinos are not yet in a state of mind to accept "independence" from the Japanese at such a price and Japan is becoming impatient.

The report of a small committee of internees who went to Los Banos on Monday accompanied by the new Commandant more than confirmed our doubt of the Japanese and rather terrified us at the prospect of the move.

The report of the committee of three internees who inspected the new site for our internment contained the following salient points and concluded with a protest to the Japanese against the transfer:

(1) The grounds of the new site cover approximately twenty-five acres, compared with the fifty-two acres of the Santo Tomás Camp. As it is planned to confine seven thousand persons on the new area instead of the thirty-five hundred now interned in Manila (two thousand now out on passes to be re-interned, and approximately fifteen hundred other internees from Baguio, Iloilo, and Mindanao civilian camps to be transferred to Los Banos), the overcrowding will work great hardship and discomfort on internees.

(2) The water supply at Los Banos is both inadequate and polluted, a condition which will endanger the health and the lives of the internees.

The protests of the inspection committee fell upon the ears of determined and somewhat angered Japanese. Plans for the camp transfer will go ahead as originally planned. The 800 men will go first. Other internees will be moved as accommodations on the new site permit.

The barracks in which we are to be housed are in the process of construction under a Japanese contractor. The contract, we were told, calls for seventy one-story barracks, each to house one hundred internees. The 800 men who are to form the first group to be transferred will assist the laborers building their barracks and will live in a few unused buildings of the Philippine Agricultural College in Los Banos.

Saturday night, May 15, 1943. Santo Tomás Internment Camp KGST broadcasting!

Tonight a radio program broadcast from our theater under the stars will feature the Karigzards (Annex Four mothers) against Fax, Inc. (Annex Four fathers). The mothers' team is composed of Mesdames Heine, Plowman, Vaughan, Watson. The fathers' team of Messrs Lewis, Crabb, Everett, and Solomon. Here is the first question: "Mrs. Heine, over what place besides the White House does the U.S. flag fly continuously?" Mrs. Heine puckered her brows in thought as the large clock on the stage ticked off fifteen of the twenty seconds allowed for an answer. "Pass," said Mrs. Heine into the loudspeaker placed before her on the brightly lighted stage in our camp's outdoor theater before an audience of 3,000 internees who sat in the darkness on the plaza before the Main Building.

"Mr. Crabb," called the master of ceremonies, and the microphone was placed before Mr. Crabb. Mr. Crabb hesitated for ten seconds before he answered, "The tomb of the unknown soldier." "Incorrect" came the decision from the questioner. Score two points for the mothers. The only place besides the White House over which the American flag flies continuously is over the grave of Francis Scott Key in Arlington Cemetery in deference to the words of the national anthem, "Gave proof through the night that our flag was still there." And so the battle of the wits was on. As an incorrect answer scored for the opposing side, guesses were minimized.

"Mrs. Plowman, who composed the opera Bohemian Girl?" "Balfe." "Correct, score one point for the mothers," and the score went up in big figures on a board behind the seated contestants. "Mr. Everett, what sculptor fell in love with the statue he had sculptured?" "Mrs. Vaughan, what was the loudest noise ever recorded?" "Mr. Lewis, the blood of the human body composes what percentage of the total weight of the body?" "Mrs. Watson, what is the Decalogue?"

Questions from mythology, music, history and science composed the oral test, as the men and women on the stage strove to outscore each other not only for the honor of victory but for the prizes stacked on the desk of the questioner: four cans of milk, four tins of coconut oil margarine, bags of salt, and of cornmeal, locally made tomato ketchup, and cigarettes, for each member of the winning team. The "jackpot" question, answered in writing by each contestant, carried a special award of Bataan cancelled stamps and souvenir Japanese-P.I.

stamp issues which would delight the philatelist. Also free shampoo and finger wave for the mothers, if they win.

Sunday, May 16, 1943. The first of eight hundred men to go to Los Banos were selected from the Santo Tomás able-bodied. They were men between the ages of 18 and 55 who were single. There were not eight hundred of these, and the names of married men without children were drawn to complete the roster. Two internee doctors and a half dozen internee nurses accompanied the men selected.

The baggage of these men went to Los Banos on Thursday. The men left Santo Tomás on Friday morning at 7:00 A.M. in Japanese (formerly American) army trucks which were to take them to the railroad station where a train awaited them. They rode to Los Banos, an hour and a half ride, in boxcars.

Saturday, May 22, 1943. Beth and Clay returned from Mrs. Ipekdjian's today, by order of the Japanese who are re-interning in Santo Tomás all children as well as the sick, aged, the special nationality groups, and others out in Manila on passes. Beth and Clay had each put on two pounds in weight and look better than at any time since the start of the war and our constant moves, each of which necessitated difficult physical and mental readjustments for the children. (Mrs. Ipekdjian lost her baby in November before the war and took children in memory of her own child. She is expecting another baby now, so loss of Santo Tomás children will not be so depressing to her.)

Current prices in Camp Bazaar (in U.S. currency):

Klim	$10.00 per lb.
Scott tissue	2.50 per roll
Lifebuoy, Camay, Ivory	1.50 per cake
Carnation milk	1.20 per tall can
Carnation milk	.70 per small can
Dutch Cleanser	1.40 per can
Dime store quality playing cards	3.00 per deck
White cotton thread	1.25 per spool
Bananas	.01 each
Coconut	.02 each

Tuesday, May 25, 1943. It was one week ago today that the word that Jim had died at Cabanatuan Military Prison reached me. Shortly after our arrival at Manila from Bacolod I wrote a Swiss friend of Jim's living in Manila, Walter Roeder, to ask him to try to find out any information he could concerning my husband. Last Tuesday he sent me word, by a Dutch family being re-interned in Santo Tomás after having been out on passes, that an examination of the records of Cabanatuan disclosed that Jim died of dysentery on July 8 of last year.‡

For days and nights I was frantic. Frantic from absolute frustration in any effort to prove or disprove the message of Mr. Roeder. I tried the Santo Tomás Executive Committee. "We shall try to find out something about Mr. Vaughan, but the Japanese are busy with plans for Los Banos and the internment of Manilians in Santo Tomás at the present time. We shall take up the request for information concerning your husband at the propitious period, if we expect any consideration from the Japanese. It is possible, though not probable, that they will tell you whether he is dead or alive. Come back to the office in a few weeks."

Weeks! When every day is interminable. So I began again a series of underground messages to friends in Manila, and friends in Santo Tomás made contacts with others on the outside to try to locate Jim. But I was warned by each one—do not expect an immediate reply, these things take time and require great caution. So on I go though the earth has given way under me and I feel I am pulling sagging feet through a muck of quicksand in which I half expect and half hope to submerge myself and forget once and for all time the tortuous uncertainties of this war.

The arrival of Beth and Clay from Mrs. Ipekdjian's helped to stabilize my life again, though it seems uncanny that Beth should have asked within half an hour after her arrival in Santo Tomás, "Where is my daddy, Mommee?" While I hestitated to reply, Clay answered for me, "Your daddy is riding in an airplane, Beth. When that airplane comes down my daddy will come out. There are many airplanes to

‡After EHV learned of her husband's death, her diary entries became more sporadic. Between July 10, 1943, when the death was confirmed, and October 29, 1943, no entries at all survive. From other accounts, it can be surmised that life in Santo Tomás continued as before.

come down and many daddies will come out. Yes sir!" This seemed to satisfy her for the present, but her question will be asked again and again, I fear, before she can grasp the real significance of this separation of our family group. The absence of her daddy to her means that she must sit and watch sorrowfully while the daddies of other children in camp romp about with small sons and daughters astride their backs "piggy" fashion, and while daddies toss their little ones into the air and catch them, screeching with joy as they descend ball-like into their parents' waiting arms. These things I cannot do, nor can I say to Beth as she hears other mommies in our crowded quarters tell their daughters, "Be a nice girl so I can let your daddy know how proud I am of you." There is no one to share my interest and personal pride in my children's accomplishments, and the children sense this loss as much as I. Home, within prison walls or out, falls short in its primary function when the parental duet becomes a solo and the family melody disproportionate and incomplete.

Even the air seems dense and heavy and uncertain. Occasionally the summer lightning cleanses the atmosphere like a swift and sharp knife penetrating soft butter, leaving no trace of its stroke immediately after its disappearance, and the air becomes the same solid mass as before.

Mrs. Morrison—cerebral hemorrhage on May 19th. Margaret Russ—missing on May 23.

June 7, 1943. Rain in Santo Tomás on the first anniversary of my internment under the Japanese. And the wet weather has brought out a Robinson Crusoe assortment of rain attire to replace rubber goods ordinarily worn during this season. Long fibre grass rain capes of fingertip length share popularity with grass hats whose waterproof brims protrude over the shoulders—the immense but lightweight native hats worn by the Filipinos for protection from sun and rain alike. The brims of these odd looking headgear have been widened to cover the broader shoulders of the Occidental, and a few internees have added a coat of bright paint to give the hats a gaudiness as well as an extra waterproof quality. The Japanese oiled paper, bamboo-ribbed umbrella is not so popular in internment camp as rain hats and rain capes, as the latter permit the use of both hands and the hands are usually filled as one goes about in the rain from canteen line to package line, to chow line, from the building where one sleeps to the place where one eats, to a shanty, or to the dining sheds.

Rubber goods are a thing of the past. Not even a child's balloon can be found in Manila, though children's knee-length rubber boots (of pre-war vintage) which normally sold for $1.50 per pair and are so useful during the rainy season have suddenly made their appearance from hidden stocks at $10 and $15 per pair. Knee-length boots or wooden bakyas, on bare feet, are the only sensible rainy season foot attire, and the standard at Santo Tomás.

Within the past few weeks about 250 cablegrams have come to internees at "Stic" through the Japanese censor's office from relatives and friends in the U.S.A. and Europe. Twelve letters were delivered to a dozen happy internees though the route by which these came remains a mystery. Cables may be sent from Santo Tomás through the censor's office to the U.S.A. at $.80 per word, including address. There is no assurance that cables will be delivered, the Japanese making no guarantees. Many internees, however, have sent messages at their own risks.

Last week ₱50,000 was received by the Executive Committee of Santo Tomás, through the Tokyo Swiss representative of the International Red Cross who had in turn received the money from headquarters in Switzerland, for aid to civilian alien internees in the P.I. By vote of the Executive Committee this money will go for medical supplies for Santo Tomás and for clothing supplies for the indigent of camp, as well as for aid to the non-internable families of internees who are in need of help. The Executive Committee bemoans the fact, however, that many of the medical supplies (especially quinine and narcotics of various kinds) are forbidden them by the Japanese, as these supplies have been withdrawn from the market and are reserved for the Japanese army and the Filipinos being courted by the Japanese.

A communication from the Japanese Military High Command in Manila stated that the request of Santo Tomás to the International Red Cross for specific and badly needed medical aids which cannot be secured in the P.I. at the present time had been delivered to the Red Cross Headquarters in Switzerland. The Japanese High Command stated that the Red Cross advised Japan that the medical supplies would be available for shipment on the first boat on which space was provided for this purpose. The Japanese High Command wished to inform Santo Tomás, however, that due to shipping difficulties and uncertainties at the present time there is little likelihood that the supplies can be expected anytime soon.

Internees are still talking about the two "comfort kits" each received on different occasions prior to the arrival of the Bacolod group in camp. These kits (small pasteboard boxes) contained a tin of powdered milk, canned meat, butter, raisins, jelly, pork and beans, and crackers. One kit was from the Canadian Red Cross, the other from someone unknown. Doubtless these came to the P.I. via Switzerland also, though the route was not disclosed by the Japanese.

We wonder if the American Red Cross has sent packages to us, and if so, where these are, what they contain, and what disposition the Japanese have made of them. And since twelve letters passed the censor's office, must there not have been thousands of others? It is not reasonable to think that only a dozen persons in the U.S. sent a special bundle of mail through the Red Cross to civilian internees in the P.I.

June 14, 1943. Clothes rationing system has been put into effect for internees—same system as for outside inhabitants of P.I. Eighty points allowed each person for year from May 20, 1943 to May 20, 1944. This rationing system allows a woman one dress, a pair of panties and a handkerchief (bath towel) for one year (no bed clothes—if she needs a sheet more than a dress she may take a choice, but not have both in a twelve months' period). A man may get one suit of clothes and a handkerchief a year.

Internees were asked to turn in cards to S.T.I.C. Clothing Committee, in order that this committee could buy cotton materials now available in Manila, but which will not be on the market for long, and these materials will be stocked in camp and drawn upon by each internee up to his 80 points. The chief disadvantage of this system of camp purchases is that materials will be bought by the bolt and only a few "practical" patterns selected. Therefore, persons securing cloth through the camp will choose pattern #1, #2, #6, etc. and there will be more or less of a camp uniform for these using their ration points.

On the other hand, if cards are not turned in to S.T.I.C. Clothing Committee the internee may have difficulty, and practical impossibility, of buying materials or ready-made clothes in Manila as ration tickets are non-transferable and the Japanese will not permit internees outside for shopping.

There are internees with sufficient clothes to carry them for several years and these persons have been asked to allow the camp to buy materials on their tickets to be given by the camp to indigent internees requiring more than their own 80 points. Shoes do not come under the rationing system.

Due to cost of coffee (locally grown), tea has been served for breakfast at Tuesday and Friday breakfasts. So many complaints of headaches due to absence of coffee, and requests for aspirin (also a local production), the Food Committee reversed its action reducing the coffee allowance to the kitchen and returned to a seven-day allowance.

Wednesday, June 23, 1943. Iloilo people arrived—96 of them, glad to be in Manila where the responsibility for feeding is up to the Japanese. They were promised repeatedly by the Japanese that money for food would be forthcoming, but the first payment was made only shortly before leaving Iloilo, after thirteen months of desperation due to the uncertainty of even a living standard. Children in Iloilo had no milk for a year. When payment was made by the Japanese for three of thirteen months just before departure of Iloilo internees for Manila, the camp received ₱600 instead of the ₱6,000 expected. (₱.70 per day for 100 persons = ₱2,100 per month. Three months = ₱6,000.) As in our camp, deductions were made for as many expenses as possible, the greatest being a ₱3.00 per day deduction for all internees who were in the St. Paul's Hospital in Iloilo, to which all sick internees were sent upon recommendation of the Japanese. The ₱.70 per day camp allowance for the sick internees was also stopped while the person was outside, so the daily cost for hospitalized internees was ₱3.70 to the camp. Wonder if Japanese internees in the U.S. are being charged, out of a bare subsistence allowance (which is not paid) for their own medical treatment? In Iloilo also, a few sacks of rice and beans that the Japanese gave to the camp with the understanding that these were a "gift" above and separate from the cash allowance for food were deducted from the allowance when it was finally paid.

Dateless cables typed on plain slips of paper were delivered today to about fifty internees. These were from U.S. and were almost uniformly the same—such general statements as "All well, thinking of you. Signed Mother" or "Family well, write to us." A woman in my room received one which said: "Writing to you often, please reply. Mother." She has of course received no letters from her mother since the outbreak of the war.

Friday, June 25, 1943. Per day food allowance raised from ₱.70 per day to ₱.80 by the Japanese. S.T.I.C. Executive Committee had asked for raise to ₱1.00 per person per day due to steadily increasing prices for food. Increase to ₱.80 only was disappointment to the committee.

Saturday, June 26, 1943. Shorts, not more than four inches above the knees, may be worn by women internees, it was announced today. The clothes rationing system permits so little to be bought that the Executive Committee asked that shorts be permitted on the lady internees. The Japanese, who seem to be in an agreeable mood at the moment, agreed. But woe to any woman who wears her shorts five inches instead of four inches, as prescribed by law.

Sunday, June 27, 1943. Father Kelly, Irish, who says mass in Santo Tomás on Sundays and Cabanatuan on weekdays, because of his neutral standing, told me today after 7:30 mass that Jim is not at Cabanatuan. He asked on his last trip out. Whether Jim has been transferred or is dead, Father Kelly does not know. This will require more time, but he will endeavor to locate Jim.

Tragedies in camp:

Mrs. Senick—husband killed in Corregidor. She, tubercular with only one lung, taking care of year-old baby in Santo Tomás. Baby died of pneumonia. Mrs. Senick has no one left who is close to her, and her own health becomes more uncertain daily. The torture the war has brought this woman is indescribable.

Mrs. X. Shortly after internment in Santo Tomás with her husband, she was sent out for a major abdominal operation—cancer. Six months later she was sent out again to have both breasts removed because of cancer there. The doctors tell her she is full of cancer, incurably so. The severe financial losses suffered by the war, the mental and physical strain of going through the bombing of Manila and the internment after the fall of the city, plus his wife's severe illness, caused a complete mental collapse of the husband. While his wife was recovering from her last operation the husband was transferred from Santo Tomás to a hospital for the insane. He, with two other Americans and two Filipinos, attempted escape from this institution. The other four were shot when recaptured. He was returned to the prison. Two days later he hanged himself. His wife ordered cremation of the body. She and fifteen of her friends were given passes two days ago to attend burial services, when ashes were placed in vault in a Manila church.

Mrs. Lippie, with whom I sit at long tables under trees where we now eat on clear days. Boys eight and four years, and baby girl 18 months. Her husband killed in Cavite bombings. She goes ahead gaily and happily saying she thinks of today, never of yesterday and seldom of tomorrow. "That's the only way to keep going," she says.

July 10, 1943. Was mopping floor of room, my chore this week (each of eight mothers in room is responsible for sweeping and mopping entire floor each day in turn), when Millie Booth called me to door. "Let me talk to you," she said. "Wait until I wash the mop at the faucet and fill the bucket with water and hang it on the fire prevention hook," I replied, "then we can talk while I polish Beth's shoes for Janice's birthday party this morning." The expression on Millie's face caused me to stop my chatter about the morning activities. "Is it bad news about Jim?" I demanded hastily and frightenedly. "It is," she said as she handed me a little square of notebook paper, a full sheet folded and refolded till it was no larger than a two-inch square, sealed together with narrow strips of adhesive tape. My name was written on the outside of this packet. In my haste in ripping off the tape I tore the outer paper. A penciled note from Mr. Booth was still legible. The typed note wrapped tightly, almost wadded, inside Mr. Booth's note gave me the definite and heartbreaking news.

"Don't let Beth and Clay know," I asked Millie, whose own note from her husband, which came via the same underground route as mine, had told her the news. "They are going to a birthday party this morning and they have been looking forward to eating the ice cream which Janice's mother has prepared."

In a way the truth is better than the suspense of these past few months since fears that Jim had died first entered my mind. After a squeeze of the hand Millie was gone. A mother bumped into me with a baby tub of warm water as she passed down the corridor, always crowded with children and mothers. Instead of apologizing she swore at me for standing so stupidly in the middle of the corridor.

Beth and Clay appeared from nowhere to tug at my skirt and to ask had I forgotten to dress them for the party. I suddenly remembered that I had an overdue library book which must be returned to the library before it closed, which meant go to the Main Building before taking the children to the shanty where the party was to take place. Also the alum crystals which I had asked the personal shopping service of the camp canteen to buy for me (interned women have discovered that alum crystals in water make a very sharp and effective underarm deodorant), and for which I had paid ₱.50 in advance, would not be held beyond today, Saturday.

I shook the children loose, told them to stay indoors—a drizzling rain made the bleak day more dreary—and set out, my mind calling, "Oh, Jim, Jim, why did this have to happen? You to die alone and suffering two days before our fourth wedding anniversary. Why couldn't I have come to you, to give you medicine, to answer your feverish calls for water?"

"Please take your place in line to return a library book. You cannot crowd to the desk ahead of others who have been waiting," I was admonished as I absentmindedly placed my book on the library "return" counter.

Library record clear and alum crystals in my hand, I returned to a cry. Beth had slipped and bitten her tongue and Clay joined her tears at the sight of blood coming from her mouth. A hasty trip to the children's dispensary for the nurse to put antiseptic on the punctured tongue.

"No one knows, no one cares." I realized the awful loneliness as I went from duty to duty, like the other people, always in motion, around me.

Back in my room with a partially consoled Beth and Clay. I reached up on the high shelf for a bottle of ink to fill a fountain pen for a birthday note to Janice to go inside the little bamboo basket with a close fitting top which was to be Beth's and Clay's birthday gift to Janice. The ink fell from my hand and hit on my head. The cork came out, ink spattered my bed clothes, my dress, my shoes, and the children. For the first time this morning I thought I was going to give up, lie on the bed and cry it out. Now the bed was too inky to be used until it was washed and had dried—there were four other disinterested mothers and six other variously occupied but all noisily engaged children in the room—and a quick, almost unconscious glance at the clock told me there was only a half hour to get two children of my own bathed, dressed and escorted to the party to which they were looking forward. Unshed tears stung my eyes. I was to help entertain the guests at Janice's party. I must hurry, hurry.

So the day passed—from party to lunch chow line, to be served after forty minutes of standing—faces and hands washed, dishes washed, then siesta, from which I jumped from bed just at relaxation point when I remembered ink-stained sheets and clothes should be put in water to soak.

I could turn to God for solace, but God seems uncertain and remote as infinity in mathematics. I agree with God on many matters—as honesty, integrity, love, because the dividends these yield make them worthwhile, whereas their opponents bring nothing but distress. But, still, I have never gotten to know God well enough to discuss the real values of life with Him, and it's not fair to place the burden of one's personal troubles on the shoulders of a casual acquaintance whom one has only admired and respected from a distance. Jim knew God better than I, and I loved Jim the more for it. Perhaps a kind and all-observing God made Jim's agony less in the awful days before his lonely death.

Friday, October 29, 1943. Outside the sawali* walls of Santo Tomás I stood in the scorching two o'clock late October sun, beside a Japanese guard as caramota driver after driver ignored my hail to stop, or waved me away as I approached his empty vehicle. The sun and the humiliation of being rejected as a passenger left my face as red as the scarlet arm band above my elbow which announced to all Manila that I was an "enemy alien," and to many, an untouchable.

Along Espana Avenue on which Santo Tomás faces, bicycle rickshas, an innovation brought to the Philippines by the Japanese, pedaled by their Filipino coolies and the horse-powered caramota appeared slow-moving indeed when Japanese army motor trucks thundered by. For only the Imperial Japanese Army and the Philippine puppet government were permitted the use of fuel for motor driven transportation!

After three quarters of an hour a bony, aged, and sick horse drew up to the curb and I gratefully and longingly looked at the narrow board which served for a seat. I picked up one end of my bedroll, which was beside me in the sun on the pavement, and the caramota driver, grunting and appearing displeased that I could not put the roll in his caramota without aid, reluctantly raised the other end to dump my clean mattress in the dust and beatle nut juice on the caramota floor. A well-filled suitcase and a native bayon† I laboriously pulled in with me and I climbed the high step into the rickety vehicle. The Japanese guard who stood immobile beside me smiled at my distress.

"To Remedios Hospital," I directed the Filipino driver, hoping he understood English. A grunt of assent, a touch of the whip to the horse's thin frame, and we jogged away from Santo Tomás. I didn't look back at the walls which had confined me till continued ill health resulted in my transfer from the Santa Catalina Hospital within the Santo Tomás boundaries to the convalescent Remedios Hospital in the

*Interwoven splits of bamboo for walling.
†bayong—large bag.

Ermita district of Manila. I had been weeks in bed, yet this was the mode of hospital transfer approved by the Japanese, a public vehicle secured and paid for by the internee.

From a high bridge over the Pasig River I looked down upon the slow motion of the stream, its filth concealed by the lavender water hyacinth coverlet which it carried into the sea. Filipino boatmen struggle to keep their streams as free as possible of this enemy of nature. Pushing their way through the hyacinths were clumsy barges propelled by poles, so shallow is the Pasig now. House barges afloat or tied along the muddy banks might have been Nipponese as well as Philippine.

From loudspeakers over the doorways of Filipino tiendas‡ Japanese music blared unceasingly, its high-pitched sounds piercing the ears from both sides of the roadway, competing merchants hoping to draw more attention to themselves by the greater strength of their receiving sets.

We passed Manila's beautiful jai alai palace, great neon-lighted Japanese characters over its chromium and silver entrance. This is the playhouse of Japanese high officials, we are told.

Remedios—room with five single beds, four occupied when I entered. Room larger than one in Santo Tomás in which I lived with nineteen other persons. Spaciousness of quarters frightened me. Three of the other occupants all over sixty—and I found out all definitely "queer." In fact I began to think I had been assigned to the psychopathic ward of Santo Tomás.

When roommate number one left the room, roommate number two came over to advise me to return the comb, brush, mirror, toothbrush and powder, towel, soap, and washcloth I was arranging on my bed table and the small shelf by my bed. "Put everything in the drawer to your table. This place is full of kleptomaniacs. If you leave anything out it will disappear," she advised. "How many women are there in Remedios?" I asked, assuming that only women would steal from other women's rooms as the men are at the other end of the verandah. "There are only twelve women here now in this building," she

‡Small, booth-like shops usually operated by indigenous shopkeepers.

told me, "and there are three or four kleptomaniacs—that's why they are here. Half the women here are crazy, you know." But I had already surmised this, so the other announcement didn't shock me. "Don't talk to that woman sitting there on the porch in the blue dressing gown. If you notice her she will never leave you alone. And there is a crippled lady who thinks the Japanese are persecuting her person-ally . . ." But I went out for a drink of water from the electric cooler I had noticed outside the door.

Roommate number three, a white-haired hunchback, has been sit-ting on her bed glowering at me with eyes steadily glued upon me, as though I were myself a lunatic endangering her very life by my pres-ence. What a place! And I asked to be sent here for complete rest and relaxation, to find out the cause of a continuous fever and to regain some of the weight lost. Supper was dry rice (full of husks) and white beans cooked with tiny pieces of carabao meat and garlic—and water to drink. We do have tea at Santo Tomás. Already I'm homesick for the accustomed and sane—if noisy—surroundings of "home."

October 30, 1943. This morning I loved "home" the more. A Filipino vendor passed down our verandah before breakfast with warm puto, little round rice flour, water, and baking powder cakes; sour, sticky and unpalatable without sugar, but better than nothing. I ordered two, at ten centavos each. I opened my suitcase and took out my purse to pay the vendor. Ten of the twenty pesos I had brought to Remedios with me were missing. In spite of the warnings I had received I had neglected to lock my suitcase when I went for a walk around the walls enclosing the building, formerly the Malate Catholic Girls School (for Filipinos) at dusk. Of course one of my three roommates took it. To-day I lock my suitcase and take the keys with me when I leave the room.

November 1, 1943. Beth and Clay are with the Roeders while I'm in the hospital. They came to see me yesterday dressed in brother and sister suits. (Beth in dark green pleated skirt with white satinette blouse. Clay in pants of same material as Beth's skirt and identical tailored blouse.) On their heads they wore Swiss milkman's skull caps—black felt with a red felt loop on top and embroidered flowers on one side. The caps were identical except the one on Beth's blond hair had the three letters A.C.S. Mrs. Roeder, accompanying them, wore a Swiss peasant's dress of dark green print, crisp white organdy guimpe* and ruffled organdy apron. Each child carried a few long-stemmed spider lilies and asparagus fern—held stiffly in front of them so flowers wouldn't crush. My heart swelled with pride and joy so full I couldn't answer when an elderly lady near me asked, "Who are the little Swiss children?" Flowers forgotten, the children rushed into my arms. Mrs. Roeder picked up the ones that dropped on the floor and I tried to straighten the blossoms mangled in the contact.

We sat on a bench on the basketball court back of the hospital Main Building. I learned that the picturesque caps had never really been worn by Swiss youth and that the A.C.S. stood for Automobile Club of Switzerland (the Rotarians are at work everywhere). Beth and Clay are given a candy each night if they have behaved themselves during the day, Mrs. Roeder told me. Only once have they failed to receive the bonus—not because they haven't played in mud because they have, and not because they didn't spill Auntie's powder, because they did powder themselves from head to foot with her favorite face powder— but they did not receive candy the day they bathed the two new kittens in the toilet bowl, nearly drowning the kittens and causing great distress to the pet mother cat. The children are getting goat's milk at the Roeders' and are happy and looking well.

Planes just skimming house tops on air patrol over Manila.

Filling stations on every other corner of Manila now—minus gas tanks—eerie Japanese signs and below in small letters, "Police Station." Japanese soldiers sit or stand awaiting an emergency. This is the "Free Philippines."

Mrs. Cook amuses me with stories of what has passed by Remedios— where she sits on the balcony all day and watches passersby. Lovely funerals she has seen from her perch—five coffins of one family at one time. A Filipino man, his wife, and small son shot on the doorstep as they entered their house one block from Remedios. Shot by guerrillas

---

*Yoke of lace, worn with low-cut dress.

who had come from hills for that purpose because the Filipino was cooperating with the Japanese. Both he and his wife were working in the Japanese war office in Manila. The child was shot by accident. The father of the dead woman rushed from his house at sound of shots and dropped dead at sight of the murdered trio. Next day the mother of the dead woman and widow of the suddenly stricken father died also of a heart attack. The family of five were buried from Malate Catholic Church around the corner from Remedios.

Another pretty funeral Mrs. Cook loves to talk about is that of a young Filipino girl of good family who was working in a restaurant to bolster family losses by bombing and fire. A Japanese soldier entered and began making advances to her. He attempted to kiss her. She screamed. The soldier pulled his sword from hilt and slit the girl's throat from ear to ear and calmly walked from the restaurant. This girl's cortege also passed by Remedios with the band of funeral musicians, enormous wreaths of purple, crimson, orange, and yellow artificial flowers, and professional mourners, as became the dead of a family of prestige. No charges were ever made against the soldier. Other well-to-do Filipino families hastily withdrew their daughters from public places where they were trying to "do their bit" in these war times.

Japanese going by singly or in groups in cars and on horseback, always officers in white gloves (white gloves annoy me). Many pass on beautiful Australian horses (besides which the caramota horse seems like a toy animal) which wealthy Filipinos, Spanish, and American families were bringing in for racing at the new Santa Anna Race Track and for private saddle horses. Each palatial Philippine residence before the war must have stables as well as formal gardens, tended by a Japanese gardener and, as well, a Chinese amah (in conventional garb of white coolie coat and black satin trousers) to take children for daily walks. Australian horses, Scotch terriers, Chinese cooks and amah, Japanese gardeners, were necessary assets of well-to-do Filipino in his homeland. Only his houseboys and lavendera were Filipino helpers.

Have marveled at seeing tiny Filipino babies with both ears pierced and simple gold earrings run through the earlobe openings. Girl babies of even poorest families usually have ears pierced also—for perhaps she will be beautiful, marry wealth, and her husband provide her with earrings (which must go through the ear). The Indian woman of high caste, however, pierces not her infant daughter's ears, but her nostril. In such an opening, closely hugging the nose of many of Indian women seen on Manila's streets, glistens a diamond (the only ones seen now, as jewelry, even rings, have gone into hiding and safekeeping for the duration of the war) or a tiny gold star. Between the brows of other majestic Indian women stands out a red or a gold star indicating caste and marital status. There is something soothing in the slow poise of these most dignified of foreigners on Manila streets.

Yellow arm bands on Greek and Italian citizens, never interned but marked as something between enemy and friend, the Greeks of the P.I. so branded since the occupation of the Islands by the Japanese, and the Italians also numbered and banded since the surrender of Italy.† To appear on the streets without this badge, and be caught, means imprisonment or death.

An occasional red arm band—an American, British, or Dutch—an "enemy alien" out of internment on a specific pass for a specified time (which must always be in alien's pocket), on way to outside hospital for treatment not available in Santo Tomás, to visit sick relative at outside hospital, to buy supplies for Santo Tomás, or for similar reasons.

Taia Maru back in Manila early in November after carrying 150 American and Canadian internees, with other American citizens, from Japan and Shanghai to Gao, Portugese port on the African coast, where Taia Maru passengers boarded another ship for U.S. (route undisclosed) and Japanese exchange internees who just landed at Gao from the U.S. boarded Taia Maru for trip back to P.I. and Japan. At Gao, Taia Maru also took on American Red Cross supplies for military and civilian prisoners in P.I. and Japan.

Pictures of Taia Maru as she lay at anchor in Manila Bay, a handsome grey ship with huge crosses on her smooth sides, appeared in the Manila Tribune. From her holds were unloaded foodstuffs—("Luxury foods in small, individual packages, not thousands of sacks of wheat

---

†Although Rome was not liberated until mid-1944, the Italian government accepted the unconditional surrender demands of the Allies on September 28, 1943.

flour or tons of corned beef, as we hoped," said a member of Santo Tomás Executive Committee)—and a small amount of clothing. The food and clothing will be distributed equally between civilian and military prisoners and will probably be given out at Christmas time.

Nina Roeder, lovely Swiss girl who has Beth and Clay at her home while I am at Remedios, passed the pier while the unloading of the Taia Maru was in progress. The happiest faces she has seen for a long time, she said, were those of one hundred fifty American soldiers taken from one of the smaller military prisons in Manila to unload the cargo assigned to Americans. The thin, usually haggard faces of these men were aglow with the temporary freedom afforded them. They had seen nothing but prison walls for almost two years. It was their first entrance into the world—guarded and still prisoners, it is true— so that even memories of normal human activity were becoming uncertain.

Nina Roeder and other Swiss and Scandinavians (particularly the Danish) are making small bags from jusi (hemp fibre) or handker- chiefs (four corners tied together) from old dresses and other dis- carded clothing to hold a bar of soap, a package of cigarettes, and perhaps a pair of string hand-knitted socks, or a jusi shirt for each military prisoner. The cotton cloth handkerchiefs in which the little gifts are tied may be used by the soldier not only as a handkerchief but a washcloth or a too-small towel. For word has come from military prison camps that towels, as well as wash clothes and handkerchiefs, are unknown to the soldiers. American soldiers are at the Port Area (mechanics), Engineer's Island, Bilibid Prison, Park Avenue School (800), Nichols Field, as well as the largest prison at Cabanatuan.

So different from enthusiasm of Mrs. Roeder and her fellow neutral European friends is that of an American woman, in room with me at Remedios, a super hypochondriac who stuffs herself from morn to night and whose hips, twice as broad as her ample shoulders, show the sedentary, housecoated life she has led, supported by a frail, ane- mic daughter whom I had met in Santo Tomás. Someone had told this American of my husband's death in Cabanatuan, the largest of all mili- tary prisons in the P.I. She asked me, a stranger, if this were true. I said, "Yes," and started to leave the room, not wishing to discuss such a personal matter with her. She called me back with this thrust, "Of course, any man who joins the army has a right to expect to die the most terrible of deaths." Later I thought, "She is more cruel than any Japanese soldier faced on the battlefield by my husband. He fought to protect you and me," I wanted to say from a shattered heart, but I could not enter the conversation. Instead I threw my shoulders back, took a deep breath, and went for a walk up and down the pavement of the laid-out tennis court, in the moonlight, at the back of the hospital. The fresh stillness of the night, the glory of the heavens—nature is always kind and is sometimes more humane than humanity.

November 11, 1943. Armistice Day in the U.S. Just another day in the P.I. People are talking of the steady advance of the Russians and the railroad strike in the U.S.‡ "Is it possible," Mrs. Roeder asked me in her quaint French accent, "that the strikers not only want more wages, but really want to prolong the war so they can collect the wages for a longer time?"

"Yes, this is possible, but I hope not true."

In Remedios there is a blind Russian, homeless, cared for by a sick American internee who reads to the Russian, feeds him, and thus helps pass days for both.

I also have come to know well an Austrian girl, 26 years old, whose husband is in Santo Tomás, an American she married in Europe six years ago. They were in Manila when Japanese took the city. The girl's husband told her to claim German instead of American citizenship so she would not be interned. In this way she could stay outside in Manila, look after the house they were just beginning to furnish and the business they had started. She could also send him food into Santo Tomás. Five months after her husband entered Santo Tomás, the

---

‡Throughout the war, a degree of tension existed between organized labor and the federal government. Labor demanded wage increases to meet rising prices; the government, fearful of even more inflation, sought to limit these demands. In 1943 two major incidents—a coal strike and a threatened nationwide railroad strike (to which EHV is probably referring here)—emphasized this clash. Since strikes in the U.S. during the war caused a loss of only one ninth of one percent in total working time, it is safe to say that despite contemporary concern these episodes were not overly significant.

young Austrian wife found herself cheated out of her husband's business which she turned over to a group of Spaniards who approached her, after her husband's internment, to join her in carrying on the business. Without funds and separated from her husband, the wife appealed to the Japanese for internment. Her previous denial of American citizenship made her ineligible. Alone, she became desperate and sick. An attack of pleurisy sent her to the Philippine General Hospital in Manila. Weak, convalescent, she was dismissed for incoming patients whose names crowded long waiting lists for admittance. Mr. Duggleby, the kindhearted internee representative of outside internee patients, discovered her and took her to Remedios. For two months she has been convalescing there and Mr. Duggleby is trying to have her interned with her husband. So in this one small Remedios Hospital a Russian and an Austrian are being kept alive through the largesse of Santo Tomás internees, though it is true most Santo Tomásians don't know of these benefactions.

One day as a crippled man, Mr. Starck, came hobbling down the porch to where I was sitting beside the railing I asked him, "Why is it that all of the Japanese soldiers who pass daily are whole, no pinned-up or loosely hanging pants legs, no empty sleeves as one would expect from soldiers who have been at war for six years, many of them having come from China? Not one young Filipino have I seen who shows evidence of front line fighting. Where are the maimed?"

"Madam," Mr. Starck said in his most serious voice, "you will never see a Japanese soldier on crutches or with an empty sleeve. With my own eyes I have seen a Japanese officer shoot through the brain a Japanese soldier whose leg was severed but who had every chance of living without it. From the Japanese military hospitals the dead are carried to nearby incinerators for cremation. Any Japanese soldier who loses an arm or leg has no hope except to go here. A maimed soldier is of no use to militaristic Japan. A Filipino attendant at one of the crematoriums told me of seeing the body of a legless man, tossed, still alive, with the other bodies to be burned and the ashes returned to Japan. The legless soldier grabbed, with weak arms, a Japanese standing at the edge of the crematorium pit. With his foot the Japanese attendant pushed the maimed soldier down among the stiffened bodies of his comrades and the door of the incinerator was locked before the furnace started."

"The Japanese," Mr. Starck went on, "will not let Filipinos see shell-shocked, horribly scarred bodies of Filipinos whose wounds are the result of Japanese gunfire. These men are in guarded hospitals. The malaria cases and the dysentery cases are released and returned to their Filipino families with a pat on the back and funds from the Japanese who court their favor—but not the Filipinos who can never be of use to Japanese on their own front lines, where they hope and expect to place every young, able-bodied Filipino before this war is over."

I think Mr. Starck knows what he is talking about. With a Danish flag pin on his shirt he goes about Manila freely on his crutches when he feels strong enough. (Mr. Starck, a former ship's steward, had to give up his career when gangrene caused amputation of his left leg, near the hip.) He has made many Filipino friends since the beginning of the war and goes in and out of their homes at will. The Japanese cannot molest him legally.

Mrs. Roeder, who goes everywhere on a bicycle, as do many men and women, says Japanese drivers have often tried to run her against the curb because of her white face, whether she's neutral nationality or not. She dismounts from the bicycle (which goes in street traffic, not allowed on sidewalks) when she hears a truck coming. Priests, in long white or black robes, go by pedaling girls' bicycles, without a center rod, so their robes can fall gracefully.

November 14, 1943. A typhoon of #8 intensity—the highest ever recorded in the P.I. The center of the typhoon passed at 3:00 A.M. when the dead calm, which so deceives those who do not know the actions of typhoons, preceded the reversal of the winds which blow with as great velocity in one direction as the other. Torrential rains fell for three days and nights until water in the streets rose to waist level and hastily constructed bamboo rafts (bamboo poles tied together with strips of rattan) replaced motor and horse driven traffic.

Muddy water flowed over steps and floors in lower parts of Remedios where a few tuberculosis patients and others (elderly couples living together because one or the other is incapacitated and the less sick one acts as practical nurse) were housed in temporary quarters back of the main hospital building. To reach the toilet, internee women had to go through water above their knees, as toilets are lower than bedroom floors. Entire city was thrown in complete darkness. Many electric wire poles toppled. Telephone wires snapped in the terrific wind, water mains were broken open by falling trees and floods. The gas supply for the city, last public service to be discontinued, dwindled to nothing as water rose above the furnaces burning coconut husks to provide Manila with its most popular cooking fuel.

At Remedios, a few semi-sick internees rose at 2:00 A.M. in the blackness and rain and with candles and crudely made lamps (made of a piece of cloth stuck in coconut oil) went to the flooded kitchens to begin breakfast of cornmeal mush, on charcoal. They must also prepare, for immediate consumption, perishable foods which were kept in the electric refrigerators of the hospital, now that no current rendered hospital refrigerators, as well as stoves, useless. On one native charcoal stove (a large clay bowl open on one side for ventilation) seven gallons of mush were prepared and breakfast was served as usual. Only there was no coffee, the day after the typhoon.

Lunch was boiled rice, nothing else; supper, boiled turkey (sent as gift to hospital from Filipino friends) and rice. More charcoal stoves brought in from outside and additional coconut oil lamps made living a little easier, the greatest annoyance being the shortage of drinking water. A generous supply of mung beans and more turkeys, as gifts, tided us over until water receded sufficiently for markets to reopen. Fruits, vegetables, meats, and eggs were doubled in price as result of difficulties of transportation, an expedient use of the emergency for a spurt in the steady flow of prices upward.

Deaths in Manila and the provinces from the wind and floods were high. A caratella* filled with passengers drove into the overflowing Pasig River in the darkness and all were drowned; a doctor and nurse venturing out in the flood were pinned in their car when the strength of the flow overturned it, and the bodies could not be removed until

*carretilla—wagon.

the following day. Filipino children playing and swimming in the streets were sucked into open manholes of the city sewage and drainage systems. Complaints have been made of the danger of these open holes, large enough for repairmen and inspectors to enter, and from which the iron-grated tops have been removed, to be sold for scrap iron, used as grating for charcoal stoves or for other uses—just one small evidence of the pilfering of wartime. It is estimated that hundreds of children lost their lives by stepping into, or being drawn by the water into, these holes while streets and sidewalks were submerged.

Shanties, many of them amateurishly and fragilely constructed by their owners, suffered greatly and though the water reached the top step of several of the Santo Tomás buildings, none was flooded. The architects and landscape artists had so placed the buildings of the university on filled-in knolls that water drains from, not toward, any of the buildings.

Mrs. Roeder's house was flooded and goats and chicken were brought into the house to save them. Beth and Clay were the only ones in the household who enjoyed the flood, when with noses pressed against window panes (glass panes a novelty to them) they watched the rising water eagerly. When garden, roadway, and steps were inundated to a depth greater than height of the car (the house was built with a garage underneath) and water came level with porch, Beth said in great glee to Clay, "Look what the Japanese have done, put all this water here." The Japanese have been blamed and credited with many things but hardly a typhoon before.

Half of rice crop ruined by typhoon. Crop near harvest and wind and rain destroyed it. Daily rice ration cut 20% immediately by Japanese.

The barter system is returning due to terrific inflation in prices resulting from the typhoon, and temporary suspension of business of all kinds. A Filipino came to the home of Mrs. Roeder with a fat chicken. "How much?" asked Mrs. Roeder. "A secondhand dress," replied the Filipino. "I have no dress," said Mrs. Roeder, "but I shall pay you a good price for the chicken." "No, gracias, I want only a dress. There is no material on the market, and besides, I sold my clothing ration card to buy food and I have no points to buy clothes if I had cash. I must exchange what I have to sell for clothes. *Buenos tardes.*"

December 2, 1943. First sight of Manila Bay since the war, when I went to San Juan de Dias Tuberculosis Hospital in an ambulance for fluoroscopy. I was in the ambulance with a T.B. patient from Remedios who was in the last stages of both T.B. and amoebic dysentery, an unfortunate combination of diseases, for treatment of one aggravates the other.

On the Boulevard there were Japanese soldiers sitting at leisure on the inner breakwater of the bay, smoking and chatting, no Filipinos in sight. The American High Commissioner's House protruding into the bay, a big winged white mansion set in a garden reclaimed from the water, with Japanese lettering above the beautifully grilled iron gates at the entrance to the grounds. This is the house from which Sayre and his family fled before the arrival of the Japanese in Manila.

The Elk's Club, Army and Navy Club, Bay View Hotel, Taza de Oro tea room, Luneta—Manila's largest and best known park, the place for all large public gatherings, with its platform above the spacious lawns from which Quezon addressed the multitudes through amplifiers in pre-war days and from which Tozyo and Alunan now coerce crowds to the pro-Japanese Greater East Asia co-prosperity way of life.

The beautiful lawns of the park now are pitted with holes and trenches deep as a man's knees. There are six concrete pillboxes or air raid shelters under construction on the grounds around the Finance Building.

December 8, 1943. Second anniversary of G.E.A.† war and also Obligation Day in Catholic Church—anniversary of Immaculate Conception of the Holy Virgin Mary and Saints Day for the thousands of Marys and Maries who have been baptized in the Catholic faith.

Yesterday I came from Remedios Hospital to the Internee Children's Home of Holy Ghost College. Racked with fever and pain, having been in bed two days stuffed with aspirin and quinine (which for the

†Greater East Asian.

first time in my life I took simultaneously) in an effort to stop the attack doubly quickly, I got out of bed to report for duty in the kitchen of Holy Ghost. Mrs. Roeder can no longer keep Beth and Clay. She cannot find in the markets sufficient food—it is not a question of money, the food is simply not to be had at any price, particularly since eggs, carabao milk, fish, as well as meat, have been commandeered by the Japanese army, which increases daily in numbers in the Philippines.

It is rumored (I shall soon find out) that food for children is better at Holy Ghost than at Santo Tomás—so I have asked for a transfer of Beth and Clay here. Could not bear the thought of the children's coming here unless I was here to help them get adjusted, and to meet the internee women in whose care they will be. Holy Ghost is in sight of Santo Tomás, considered a part of Santo Tomás, staffed by volunteer internee workers—about 28 women to care for 80 children—with paid Filipino helpers to do children's laundry, cleaning of buildings, and heavy work in kitchen.

Many of children in H.G.—who vary in age from babies of a few months to twelve years—have only one parent. Some are orphans; the fathers of many are military prisoners with mothers dead or interned in Santo Tomás. Some of H.G. children have invalid fathers and mothers unable to take care of them. All are enemy aliens—i.e., they are of American, British, or Dutch nationality.

Every second Tuesday is Parents' Day at Holy Ghost and parents who live in Santo Tomás are brought over in the camp bus to spend the day with their children at H.G. The parents arrive about 10:30 or 11:00 A.M. and stay until 3:00 o'clock. As Holy Ghost has no funds except children's food allowance from Santo Tomás, the visiting parents cannot be furnished lunch, so they come with food baskets for themselves and children and with gifts for children. The lunches are opened under the trees which dot the back playground, and little groups of mothers and fathers and children eat rice flour bread sandwiches and drink unsweetened calamanci juice, as little boys and girls confide to anxious parents all that has happened since last visitors' day.

The Santo Tomás bus was late yesterday because it had to go to Santiago Prison to pick up five Catholic priests, being released from there by Japanese for internment in Santo Tomás, before bringing parents to Holy Ghost. The priests had been imprisoned in Santiago for acts definitely non-neutral and considered injurious to Japan (such acts being getting caught carrying messages to military prisoners). Santiago is a prison, not an internment camp, and all who have come from there speak of it as a dark, dreary, damp dungeon. The parents who watched priests get out of the bus at Santo Tomás said priests were pale, thin, frightened, hungry, and dirty, and each carried the sum of belongings left him in a little cloth bundle—the cloth not much larger than a man's handkerchief. When the parents arrived late, what shouts went up from excited children, and what wails when bus departed at three o'clock.

Christmas Eve, 1943. Last minute cookies to be made from rice and peanut flour and candy from pinocha—a dirty, dark brown semi-circular sugar cake, only sugar for sale. The Baguio pine Christmas tree in the combined staff room and office was adorned with streamers cut by the children from bits of colored paper picked up here and there and with assorted broken ornaments held over from pre-war Christmases. There were no electric lights, the tree seeming pathetically stark in the cold glare of uncovered ceiling electric lights.

At 4:30 rushed to shower before changing clothes wet with perspiration from work in kitchen and from tropical heat of day—to put on short sleeved white linen dress for children's party. We were determined to be happy and gave a noisy outward show of joy that we did not feel in our hearts. There was fried chicken for the children's supper (native Bantam-size chickens at ₱10 each) and loganberry pie, from canned fruit stored in the convent bodega from before the outbreak of war, for everyone's dessert.

The Christmas party—staff and H.G. children only—at 6:30. Carols, "Jingle Bells" the favorite, sung by all children, with "Oh Come All Ye Faithful" by fifth and sixth grade pupils sung in Latin. Staff sang "First Noel" in parts, then children were given toys by Mrs. Gump, who explained that Santa himself was absent this year. Toys (rattles, horns, drums—all noisemakers and all stamped "Made in Japan"—made a din which only got under control with shouting of "Refreshments!

Refreshments in dining room." Seventy children stampeded to the dining room for hot chocolate, cookies, and candy before being directed to their respective bedrooms on the second and third floors.

At 8:30 the last child was quiet—if not asleep—because they were all told they would be up early for the big day at Santo Tomás on the 25th and the staff party began. Native lemon juice, a locally made, synthetic blackberry juice, ice cubes and a red-ribbon-bedecked bottle of London distilled dry gin were put on Mrs. Gump's desk, which became our bar. A portable Victrola belonging to one of the staff was brought out and the few old, old dance records in H.G. were played again and again. We twenty to thirty women danced with each other, we laughed, we joked, we gulped eagerly the gin allotted each of us, and at 11:30 some of us went too soberly to bed to weep in solitude from misery no longer controllable, while others went to midnight mass in the chapel within the grounds.

December 25, 1943. Children's shrill voices joined church bells and chimes cutting the early morning air, in the still fresh darkness of 5:00 A.M., before the rising of a lazy tropical sun. The church bells had been ringing since 4:00 A.M. For nine mornings I had been wakened by them—the nine four-o'clock masses of the Christmas novena announced to all Catholic Manila by bells, trumpets, and orchestral music in front of all the churches able to employ musicians. I lay abed trying to distinguish Clay's voice from others in his room directly above mine, shouting as they pulled cheap toys from their little socks. I was glad I could lie abed while someone else dressed him for Santo Tomás, for my head was splitting. Every time I had closed my eyes during the night I had seen Jim. I had heard his voice, I had felt his presence. The Filipino night nurse called beside my mosquito net, as she did every morning, "It's six o'clock, Mrs. Vaughan." This was the time of my kitchen duty—Christmas or not. I would not see my children until after a cup of strong American powdered coffee (from the comfort kit) and perhaps then I could smile more whole-heartedly at their glee.

"Hurry children! Stop your noise and crying or you will be late for the bus to Santo Tomás." So were the milling, excited tots rounded up, checked and rechecked and filed into the camp bus, Holy Ghost workers giving a final pull to Betty's sock and a last swish at Billy's unruly hair. For the Holy Ghost staff wanted their little charges to be pleasing to their parents who awaited them at Santo Thomás.

Another roll call and check-up at Santo Tomás gate, where Japanese guards bowed and demanded a bow in return from adult occupants of the bus. Large group of Filipinos across street from camp gate with Christmas packages for internees, waiting for signal from guards when packages could be delivered to inspection sheds to be searched for notes, sugar, rice, and other forbidden items not allowed to pass in or out of gate.

Inside Santo Tomás a group of internees stood the required distance from sawali fence waiting for the packages we had seen uninspected on outside. Most of those waiting were "squaw men," the name given Americans who have married Filipino women. Many of them are "old timers," men over fifty who came out as young men and who have become fathers, with or without benefit of clergy, of a large number of mestizo progeny. These Filipino wives and mistresses have been faithful in sending in cooked foods to the internee fathers of their children. It is this group of women and children who are classed as "non-internables" and who have become such a problem—clamoring that they are starving in Manila and have no right to be separated from their husbands, though when given a choice of internment when Santo Tomás was opened they disclaimed American citizenship and boasted of their freedom and its privileges.

I saw no change in appearance of people since I left Santo Tomás for Remedios Hospital two months before. Everywhere there were physical evidences of the typhoon and flood—trees blown down, shanties roofless or toppling at queer angles. There was no evidence of Christmas—nothing that we associate with December 25th. Lunch at shanty of Phyllis (they fell heir to shanty when woman owner went to Los Banos to join husband) and sat in folding chairs with tired children through siesta hour—for there was no place to lie down. At three o'clock we were in front of the Main Building with hundreds of other children and parents to await arrival of Santa Claus through sawali gate. (Santa, an internee, had been given permission of Japanese to go outside gate to put on his robes and come in dressed in full regalia.) The gate opened and in he came, sans reindeer, sans sled, sans shoulder pack. Toys had already been placed on long tables arranged in the hot afternoon sun—tables bearing the ages of the recipients of toys, one year, two years, three years, four, and up to school-age children. Uniform toys were on each table—new kapok-stuffed animals for infants and toddlers, wooden blocks (unpainted) in pineapple cloth bags and wooden cutout animals for boys, and stuffed dolls for little girls; for next group, pineapple cloth bags holding pencils, crayons, and notebooks for older children. Children followed curt directions of the Christmas Committee to line up according to ages and were ready to file by gift-laden tables silently and unemotionally at signal to march. Toys were handed to children by the committee members. Santa stood on a small table bearing a miniature two-foot-high Christmas tree and doggereled the internees as follows before the distribution of gifts began:

Next year I hope to see you
In your home or residence
And may we not meet again
Behind a sawali fence.

Tired and wilted from the long day, the heat, the noise, and the confusion, we gladly got into stuffy bus to bring us back to Holy Ghost. Many of smaller children were crying from fatigue and hunger (no candies or foods distributed to children) and all anxious to return to our living quarters, where supper awaited us. A frozen ice, the children had been promised for dessert; a shower, bed. I had not heard a "Merry Christmas" all day, nor a word of the Christmas carols we associate with the day.

My unhappiness was accentuated when the Holy Ghost bus passed San Beda College, on property adjoining that of Holy Ghost Convent, for it was here that Jim sat at his desk in the Quartermaster's Office during that short period in December 1941 between the attack on Manila and the evacuation of the city by the U.S. Army or the U.S.A.F.F.E. Here Jim slept, ate, and did his small part in the transportation division of the army to try to stay the overwhelming advance of the yellow imperialists. In the buildings of San Beda he left his suit-cases, I have been told by his friends, containing the white linen suits I helped him pack, the new silk pajamas I had given him for his last birthday, his washable mess jacket and black evening trousers, the monogrammed sports jacket, and even the leather shaving kit whose containers I always checked and filled with proper lotions, pastes, and powders before each trip. The traveler's shaving kit was my very first gift to Jim; he was my fiance then and it was our first celebration to-gether of his birthday. His surprise and appreciation of the gift were so genuine—a genuineness so characteristic of his nature. When Jim pre-pared for the fateful trip to Manila, he took with him many articles, for personal as well as practical reasons. These articles were left at San Beda in a room still occupied by soldiers who have little use now for linen suits, mess jackets, monogrammed sport coats, or even shaving kits—for the Japanese are, as a rule, unbearded. From San Beda, in sight of my room at Holy Ghost, my husband marched off to Bataan, and from Bataan to his horrible prisoner's death at Cabanatuan. The sights and the sounds from the former college grounds and the U.S. Army grounds—now a Japanese arsenal—twist my heart into knots. What a Christmas, I thought, and next year, and the year after—Jim gone—no home for the children or myself. What is there in the future but other Christmases as bleak, as barren of joy, perhaps next year also barren of the cheap identical toys the children had handed them in the glaring sun from an unsmiling, self-conscious Christmas Commit-tee member?

At Holy Ghost we are in the very center of Japanese and Filipino military, political and social activity—so much so that the Holy Ghost staff often wonder if its internees will not be moved or absorbed into Santo Tomás.

The Japanese brought Christmas to the Filipino children of Ma-nila—in a loudly advertised party held on Thursday afternoon, De-cember 23. Newspapers, posters, and the radio announced to all the Islands the generosity and kindheartedness of the Japanese—a party with free toys and food for the Filipino children who might not other-wise enjoy this time-honored Christmas custom.

From our third-floor staff rooms at Holy Ghost we watched the
excited children line up in front of our building for the short march
diagonally across the street to the entrance to the lawns of Malacañang
Palace,‡ Quezon's former home and now occupied by the Japanese,
where the party was to be held. More and more children came—two
o'clock, three o'clock, three-thirty—the sun was scorching hot, there
was almost no shade from the few coconut palms here and there
along the quiet roadway. At last the palace gates were opened and the
youthful brown horde milled inside the grounds. A voice over a loudspeaker called for order and announced that the President of the Islands would give a speech of welcome. The last thing the tired children wanted was a speech, but two years of a military regime have
taught them something of the necessity of patience and obedience.
Speeches, patriotic war speeches, and at last the prizes for which they
had come, free toys and food.

From our windows we watched the entire afternoon pass. We saw
the disgruntled looks on the faces of the "youth of Manila and the P.I."
as they came away from this affair. In their hands the small boys and
girls carried the cheapest of Japanese celluloid toys—small animals
and dolls so poorly constructed that many were mashed in or dis-
membered before the children left the Malacañang grounds. And the
food—for which they had waited so patiently—candies, perhaps, or
fruit? No, each child was handed out a small bag of raw camotes
(sweet potatoes). The starving *tao*,* the day laborer in the rice paddies
or sugar cane fields, nibbles raw camotes because he can afford nothing better. The children of the P.I. do not look upon the raw camote as
a delicacy—it is a sign of poverty and is recognized as such throughout
the Islands.

To be extolled to give all to country, to sublimate self, and all personal desires and all luxuries—and to be handed a Christmas gift of a
beggar's portion of raw potatoes! The stoicism of the Japanese is not

---

‡More than simply Quezon's former home, Malacañang had served as the summer
residence of the Spanish governors-general, the early American governors-general, and
continues to serve as the executive mansion of the Philippines today.
*Person.

inherent in these tropical peoples, especially in the children. They went home from the party angry, feeling they had been betrayed and deceived.

There are rumors that Holy Ghost is to be closed and all children and staff members here interned in Santo Tomás. This is an old and a recurring rumor—like the repatriation rumor which flares up with great force periodically when "it is sure that we will all be repatriated, negotiations are again under way." There might be basis for the rumors concerning Holy Ghost. The institution is too much in the center of Japanese and Filipino military, political, and social activity in Manila. San Beda, the Japanese arsenal over the wall where our property ends, Malacañang Palace (center of political intrigue, within a stone's throw), and the former German consulate—a massive three-story stone structure—look eye to eye with us when we gaze from our front windows or verandahs. When the staff sits on our third-floor porch away from the noise of the H.G. children (who are not allowed in staff quarters), we are often startled to see Japanese officers on the third floor of the ex-consulate staring straight across at us. Sometimes they rudely examine us through binoculars and point and laugh. We've learned to pay no attention, but sometimes at night when a large crowd is gathered we watch them through their open windows as they drink and toast and sing their gay Japanese songs.

Only a very narrow street separates us from the quarters of the Philippine Constabulary Guards who patrol Malacañang. The Filipino guards amuse themselves by calling down from the windows of their barracks to the Holy Ghost children at play in the "small gardens" of the grounds. The wall around the playground is low here and the children climb up on it to watch the guards drilling or taking sitting-up exercises before the building in which they sleep.

The buildings of Holy Ghost Convent are out of the traffic of Manila. Malacañang was built away from the hustle of the capital—on the banks of the water-hyacinth-coated Pasig River. Holy Ghost Convent, San Beda College, Centro Escolar Catholic School facing San Beda were purposely all built in the "quiet" section of Manila. This area has now become a military drill ground. Now that only the Japanese have automobiles and transportation of all kinds is so greatly reduced, due to rationing of gasoline and to the cost of feed for caramota ponies, the wide roadway these buildings border is used by Japanese troops and Philippine Constabulary for drill practice and for mustering of outgoing and incoming Japanese troops.

Yesterday hundreds, perhaps thousands, of Japanese soldiers marched past, their bodies looking too small and short to carry the heavy shoulder packs strapped to the arms of each. Sticking out over each pack as high as the head of each soldier was a bunch of dry yellow native grass, the soldier's camouflage. When squatting or lying on the ground or when sticking his head out of a trench, the tufts of grass would give this army the appearance of a field of waving yellowed brush.

When the soldiers march by, hours at the time, someone always asks, "How many are there?" and no one has ever bothered to count. Someday I shall count for five minutes and then compute the number passing in one day, but the information is so useless. Sometimes the fully equipped soldiers march four abreast toward the Manila Bay piers. At other times (often in the dead of night) there is the tramp, tramp, tramp of countless feet marching steadily and endlessly away from the bay in the direction of San Beda. At night the sound has become no more distracting than the tick of a clock to which one has become accustomed. The quarters of the Holy Ghost Children's Home might well be moved from an area so pregnant with signs of war.

There were happy people at Holy Ghost on Christmas, war wives separated from their husbands but who had messages from them. There was Mimi Slater, whose husband Lt. Jimmy Slater, Engineer Corps, prisoner on Corregidor, managed to have put into the hands of Mimi, via a brave and foolhardy Filipino messenger, a bundle delivered to the H.G. front door and marked "Merry Christmas to Mrs. Slater." Inside the newspaper-wrapped bundle was a handful of Philippine silver dollars (Heaven alone knows where he got them!), two bookkeeper's pencils—one red, one blue, for his two little daughters here, twenty Japanese pesos, his December salary, and a long, long letter to Mimi.

"Do not worry about me," he wrote. "There are only twenty-two American prisoners, all engineers, who run the light plant, the waterworks, and do other jobs for the Japanese, and we are too valuable to them to be mistreated. I live in a solid, decent structure. I have all the clothes I can wear, soap and other toilet articles left behind in great quantity when our Army surrendered here. I have all I can eat—carabao meat, native vegetables and fruits. In other words, Mimi, I have all the unimportant things of life. You know what I mean. When this is over I'll make it up to you, my darling. The things we'll do together." Mimi read the letter this far to me. Her voice broke here and she read no further. I understood.

The second honeymoons all these separated husbands and wives are dreaming of, living for. My reunion with my Jim, how many hours I had spent planning it.

Another happy Holy Ghost staff wife was the one who received a bracelet, smuggled from Cabanatuan, a gift which showed hundreds of hours of patient workmanship. Pre-war Philippine ten-centavo pieces had been linked together to encircle the wrist. These had been scraped smooth on one side, and the story of this prisoner and his wife had been etched in the plan of the coin markings. The first coin showed a ship sailing east, the second showed lilies encircled by a wedding ring (the couple were married in Manila), the third coin depicted Manila being bombed, the fourth showed prison walls, the fifth showed a cross and a star, the last one showed a ship sailing west. I asked about the meaning of the fifth coin in the bracelet. "Andy says my faithfulness, my smuggling small gifts and messages into Cabanatuan, have made it possible for him to carry on. This he depicts by the cross and the star. Sentimental, perhaps, but then we are both that way. Of course, the last one shows our departure for the States. How happy this bracelet has made me!"

Old friends at Holy Ghost: Sister Luciosa, who was so good to Clay when he was sick with tetanus serum poisoning in Bacolod Camp; the Waters children here, Bill, George, Mary Alice, while their mother recovers from dengue fever and dysentery at Santo Tomás. Dr. Waters spent the day with them on Parents' Day and we had a glorious day together—lunch on porch of staff quarters overlooking the Convent garden with five children. Lunch came from Red Cross kits which were distributed a few days before Christmas. These kits were nicest surprise since internment, a luxury and at the same time a life-saving necessity. The total of three big identical boxes (each weighing 48 pounds) for which I signed contained the following when all were opened and sorted:

Klim—9 pkgs (1 lb. ea)	Toilet soap—20 small bars
Milko—3 (1 lb. ea)	Amer. cheese—12 (1 lb. ea)
Coffee—11 (¼ lb. powd)	Prunes—12 (1 lb. ea)
Cocoa—2⅚ (12 oz. ea)	Cube sugar—5
Preserves—10 (6 oz. tins)	Choc. bars—24
Butter—47 (3¾ oz tins)	Bouillon—24 servings
Pâte—12	Other meats—64 tins (beef,
Chopped ham—6	salmon, luncheon meat)

The Japanese had shaken kits around so contents of different ones varied slightly. Forty packages of cigarettes (Chesterfield, Camel, Old Gold) had been included in each large kit box when it was packed and sealed in the U.S. for delivery to war prisoners. These were removed by Japanese, who opened and inspected every kit because the label of the Old Gold cigarettes was offensive to them. The label bore the following:

FREEDOM

Our heritage has always been freedom.
We cannot afford to relinquish it.
Our armed forces will safeguard that heritage
If we, too, do our share to preserve it.

All cigarettes were removed from all kits as a penalty to us, but such a protest was raised at Santo Tomás—a formal, written protest addressed to the International Red Cross handed to the Japanese Commandant by Santo Tomás Executive Committee—that the Japanese returned the cigarettes to internees, giving forty-two packages to each adult, none to children.

All military prisoners and civilian internees received kits and cigarettes, a large bath towel, and a bottle containing 100 capsules of multiple vitamins (Nutri Caps) containing vitamins A, D, B_1, B_2, and C, dosage two a day. What thrilled us as much as the gifts themselves was the recentness of date on acknowledgment cards included in each kit (did the Red Cross think we'd be permitted to send these individually?) and stamped on the label of the vitamins. The former was February 1943, the latter was May 10, 1943. Only eleven and eight months ago, no time at all when we have been cut off from all contact with the U.S. for two years.

January 24, 1944. Across the garden to Music Hall of Convent proper to hear Schubert's Unfinished Symphony on Victrola records through radio loudspeakers. Delays in changing records on hand-winding portable Victrola, chattering and snickering of handful of Convent boarding students (Filipino girls), almost painful pleasure of this beautiful symphony. Closed my eyes to cut out school girls, and closed senses to sting of mosquitoes to lose myself in melodious strains of winds and strings. The symphony is too short. The staff of Holy Ghost Children's Home, music starved, left with the request to the Sisters in charge of the Convent that we be asked over again when other records (borrowed) are available.

February 3, 1944. "It's true," said the director of Holy Ghost Children's Home. "This institution is to be closed by order of the Japanese Military Authority, and all internees here must return to Santo Tomás by the tenth of the month." This return of internees to the sawali walls of Santo Tomás was part of the initial transfer of internees from the Japanese civilian authority to the military on February 1. From February 1 we were no longer considered "civilian internees" but "war prisoners" and should be treated as such. A complete severance of communications between prisoners and the outside world was the primary concern of the military upon taking charge.

On the morning of the tenth,† Holy Ghost was abuzz at 4:00 A.M., lights on, iron beds (U.S. Army property with cross guns and swords at head and foot) being knocked down (by women internees, of

---

†Although dated February 3, this entry obviously was written after the move from Holy Ghost to Santo Tomás on February 10.

course), last minute tampipies‡ being tied, mattresses, and mosquito nets being rolled and fastened and labeled. There was a rush for mothers to dismantle their children's beds, also to see that springs (what a luxury after the wooden slats on which we slept at Santo Tomás) and other parts of beds were securely roped together. Seventy-five children crying at being wakened so early and frightened by noise of amateur female hammering and rushing about trying to calm children, when aflutter themselves like a headless chicken. Breakfast bell at 6:30 (somebody remembered to ring it) and before all had finished, first bus from Santo Tomás (with 20 men internees who had volunteered to help with baggage and children) arrived, for loading first cargo for Santo Tomás.

Carried in my lap—for want of a safer place—100 eggs in clay rice pot, eggs in a solution of lime and boiled water (50 duck and 50 chicken) so they would not break.

Back to the Annex, headquarters for infants and children in the back yard of Santo Tomás, and I knew when the large gates closed behind the bus carrying the capacity load of internees, closed on its rusty, squeaky hinges, that I should not leave the confines of my prison again until freedom and peace came to the Orient. We were in for the duration. Mrs. Roeder kissed me good-bye at Holy Ghost the day before we left. "I shall see you the middle of 1945," she had said. "That is," she mused softly, "if we are all alive then. I am not sure that we shall all see it through."

March 1, 1944. February was a month of continual change in Santo Tomás, every change to the discomfort of internees. We find that being war prisoners, under the jurisdiction of the Japanese military, is quite a different matter from being civilian internees under the old set-up.

The first move of the Japanese was to close the package line. This meant that hundreds of internees who had received food daily from friends, relatives, servants, or restaurants outside would have to secure and prepare own food in camp. To make room for the Holy

‡Chests or trunks made of palm leaves.

Ghost and other internees being re-admitted, women had been permitted to move to shanties and many of these women got out charcoal stoves and learned to prepare meats and vegetables bought at camp canteen. The order closing the meat department of camp canteen and the discontinuance of meat from camp kitchen menus is working a terrible hardship.

In the Main Building a few people were using electric hot plates, percolators, and grills, and electric irons were in evidence in every room at some time during each day. The order of the Japanese that all privately owned electric and gas appliances (there was gas in chemistry laboratory room), including electric razors and fans, should be turned in to the Japanese authorities put an end to this type of luxurious living. We are to go unpressed, and for cooking—it's the native charcoal earthenware pot stove or nothing.

Having discontinued the sale of meat and the serving of meat in camp, the next food order of the Japanese discontinued the sale of rice bread in camp—except of maximum of one-eighth of small loaf per day to children and those on the sick list.

There have been rumors that all cooking in Santo Tomás is to be stopped. No charcoal is being permitted to enter the camp, so whether cooking will die out for lack of fuel or by order of the Japanese does not matter. It is only a matter of weeks till all privately owned fuel in camp will be exhausted—then??

The food served on the adult chow line is unspeakably worse than any of us ever feared. Breakfast—corn and rice mush, tea and coffee on alternate days, three spoons of sugar per week. Lunch—boiled whole grains of corn and boiled rice, seasoned only with salt. Supper—boiled white radishes (so bitter they burn the tongue), rice, plain tea.

Two or three times a week a small three-inch bony fish is served, heads with shiny eyes, tail, bones, and all. This most internees cannot stomach, though I have learned to pick up the little fellows by the tail, look them straight in the eye, and bite, spitting out a mouthful of bones after each bite. The bones cannot possibly be picked out before. Whether the inner parts of the fish have been removed I have never asked nor dared examine to find out. Some things are better unknown, and the smell of the horrid things indicates a lack of thorough preparation. The Japanese military have said our diet shall consist of rice, corn, and fish—so it does! From funds borrowed from Swiss, children are fed a few necessary extras.

Discontinuing of the Manila newspaper. News favorable to U.S.A. Two interesting reports of items in a recent issue: Americans have long noses to heat air as it is drawn in in a cold climate. Americans are tall because they have tall legs.

Lines in Santo Tomás are longer than ever, for less is sold and there are more buyers, since nothing can be sent in to private individuals from outside. Stood two and one-half hours in sun to secure one pint of peanut oil (190 pints for 4,000 inhabitants of S. Tomás) for frying lime-preserved eggs over charcoal and sticks picked up by Clay and Beth.

Long lines at toilets in morning and evening. Clay sent out before breakfast and told to take his place in line. In a few minutes he came back excitedly. "Mommee," he said, "I can't wee-wee, there is no line." So accustomed to standing in line he didn't know what to do when one or more of the toilets were unoccupied. How the children have become conditioned. Beth takes her little stool and sits quietly looking at a picture book, holding a place in a food line, a peanut butter line, a carabao milk line, for me, until I finish some chore or other, after which I relieve her. She is a dear about this. Clay I cannot trust for "line holding." He wanders off to watch a game of marbles, or follow a stray cat, and space is lost in line if line holder leaves his space. A space or stool must be occupied to be reserved.

A few weeks ago the Japanese Commandant ordered that all lines in S. Tomás be discontinued and a scheme be worked out whereby internees could secure what was wanted without wasting so much time prior to the distribution of the desired articles. The reason for the Commandant's interest was not fatigue and waste of internees' time from their own personal affairs demanding their attention, but because too few men were answering calls for volunteers to set out the hundreds of banana trees sent to camp, to go in parallel rows across the former west baseball diamond and golf course. Men who were standing in lines were also needed to plant mongo beans* between banana rows, to set out pechay,† camotes, talinum,‡ which would become part of the camp diet. Volunteer internee labor squads were also needed to construct a run for 400 ducks which are to be interned also. Since the move of 800 able-bodied men to Los Banos earlier there has been a shortage of labor in S. Tomás for the ordinary daily chores necessary to the care of 4,000 people—the preparation, cooking, and serving of food. Sanitation clean-ups of buildings and grounds, patrol and guard duty to see that internees do not go too close to walls, that camp property is not stolen or defaced, and that the necessary repairs to camp property are made. These labor jobs and the innumerable clerical workers who keep the daily records are essential to an organization of this size—the camp time-consuming requirements plus necessary personal activities incident to camp life.

March 11, 1944. Our first blackout under Japanese supervision caused a twitter of optimistic excitement. A period of "alert" from 12:00 noon yesterday to 12:00 noon tomorrow with complete blackout tonight was declared by the Commandant. Being on "alert," we found out, means no passing of internees between buildings except on necessary business. Mothers must keep children in sight at all times, and emergency kits consisting of a towel and a few food supplies must be kept handy. Why the towel, we weren't told—whether to stop flow of blood from possible air raid wounds, whether to use as a pillow if forced to sleep on floor, or covering for babies from night air. Can do almost anything with it, except eat it. Children were in bed at dusk as there would be no lights for undressing and other preparations for bed.

My Scotch roommate minded the blackout less than the rest of us in the room, for while we sat in idleness, exhausting our inner resources, she carried on the knitting of the sock which was always in

---

*Mung beans.
†Chinese cabbage.
‡Green, leafy, spinach-like vegetable.

her hands. My Scotch friend, like Mrs. Miniver's aunt of the same national background, either "spun thread from her fingers like a spider producing a web, or else she plucked wool from the air" (Mrs. Miniver).* However, the click of needles ceased as suddenly as the flow of our thought when air raid sirens pierced the even blackness of the still night. We had not been told there would be sirens—in fact, we had been instructed repeatedly by the Safety Department that the air raid warning signal in S. Tomás would never be used for practice, that it would be sounded only in event of the real things. A moment of absolute silence followed the piercing shriek, then such a clatter of folding chairs and running feet as women sitting on small porch or on ground just outside the Annex collapsed chairs and rushed to cover in the rooms where their children slept. Air raid practices and blackouts will be frequent from now on, the Japanese have advised us.

That I may better pass the evening hours of total darkness, I have learned to knit also, though it doubtless will be many blackout nights before I become proficient enough to utilize my handicraft in the darkness. A more urgent need for my knitting is the creating of a pair of socks for myself so I can wear the new States oxfords which were a recent gift from Uncle Sam. Along with the food kits distributed before Christmas came shoes for men, women, and children (strangely, the large sizes for children and small sizes for men were missing—whether an error in packing in U.S. or whether these sizes fitted Japanese and were removed by them, we don't know). There were socks, underwear, cosmetics, gowns and playsuits for the women; pajamas, dresses or materials for the children; towels, handkerchiefs, sheets, sewing kits. Of all the articles I received, none pleased me so much as a ten-cent comb, for I had broken my only comb and there was no way of replacing it. There were women's sizes in socks but these were exhausted before my turn at the supplies arrived. The new shoes are a luxury—but the stiff leather requires socks to prevent blistering.

*A collection of sketches published in 1939 by British author Jan Struther describing the everyday life of a middle-class Englishwoman at the beginning of World War II. The book was well received and eventually made into a movie starring Greer Garson. Obviously, however, EHV refers here to the book.

April 1, 1944. Promptly at 6:30 A.M., as usual since beginning of 8:00 o'clock roll call, music begins over loudspeaker, to be interrupted by cheery voice, "Good morning, it's 6:30," and continuation of music. This morning the record was "Farewell to Thee," for the heartily despised Japanese lieutenant who lives in the former Santo Tomás bodega is leaving, to be replaced—we hope—by a Japanese not quite so hard-boiled. We wondered if the lieutenant caught the significance and sarcasm of the adieu. His parting thrust, however, turned the tables: no more cooking in shanties or outside buildings, except in areas under the trees designated by the Japanese. Frail bamboo platforms erected under nipa roof, no sides, for placing charcoal stoves (now fueled with green, smoky wood). What frantic fanning of the little openings in the clay pots which serve as stoves, what gasping as smoke poured into faces of all nearby cooks. There was a fight between two "blinded" women, each blaming the other for fanning smoke into her face. A gust of a breeze and all cooks in the wake of waves of smoke scattered, leaving blackened pots to boil over and cause more smoke and more confusion.

The Taia Maru was a wonder ship, a dream ship, for us upon her return to Manila. On March 3 packages to internees from the U.S. were delivered. Almost every internee had at least one package from family or friends in U.S. For Beth, for Clay, and for me were smashed parcels in war prisoners' collapsible cardboard boxes. The name of the sender gave me a thrill—Mrs. W. M. Jernigan, Greensboro, Georgia, my sister from whom I had not heard, nor from anyone else in the U.S., since the Japanese occupation of Cebu back in February 1942. In Ernestine's own handwriting were customs declarations: towels, toilet articles, color books and crayons, articles of clothing, combs, toothbrushes, gum, canned foods, cards. What a thrill! Lovely silk underwear; my favorite toilet soap, creams, face powder, new dress, panties and socks for Beth, a real boy's suit for Clay with socks to match, prunes, powdered soup, chocolate, hard candies, and gum (which the children had never seen and Clay spat out when it stuck to his teeth). Bridge cards to pass the time (if she only knew how little time there is to pass that way).

Unloaded with the packages were many bags of mail. We now await letters which we have been told have been in the censor's office for many months.

On April 6 the letters were distributed. I received eight. One from Ernestine telling of her own son born since the outbreak of war, of her work with the Federal Bureau of Home Economics in supervising study in southeastern states under Dr. Day Monroe and Dr. Louise Stanley, a continuation of work I left at time of decision to come to P.I. One from Jim's mother, from two brothers (one in Georgia and one in California, neither actively in war work at time), from close friends. "Today is Jim's birthday," began Mother Vaughan in her letter dated August 28, 1943, the only reference to her son. "Jim is reported missing," inserted Ernestine in her long and surprisingly (for the strict censorship) satisfying letter. I knew they would be trying from that end to find out about Jim. So the knowledge of Jim's death will not be a shock for which they are completely unprepared.

April 28, 1944. In the afternoon a trip to a former dormitory which is now an isolation hospital and filled primarily with measles cases. Sign says "Visiting Hours 3:30 to 4:00." Nurse on duty at desk has stepped away, so I slip into wards where Beth and Clay are broken out from head to foot—with some sixty other children.

Saturday, April 29, 1944. Emperor of Japan's birthday. Gifts of food from Neutral Welfare Committee of Y.M.C.A. permitted to come in for occasion were: (1) beef—for stew, (2) chickens—for children and hospitals, (3) ducks—to add to stock on hand, (4) eggs—for children, (5) ham and salami—to flavor fried rice. Filipino wives and children of internees permitted to visit interned husbands and fathers just outside sawali gate for one-half hour. Non-interned relatives came at appointed times and when time was up, left to be replaced by another group of visitors. Three roped-off corridors on ground, formerly occupied by package shed, used by visitors and related internees. Japanese guards marched up and down to see no packages, money, or notes passed between internees and visitors, and other Japanese watched through peepholes in fence with guns poised on boxes ready to fire in case of offense. One internee (old man) going out to see Filipino wife had hat jerked off his head by Japanese because he failed to remove it when passing guard.

Sunday, April 30, 1944. Col. Yoshie, Commandant after April 27. Baseball game this morning at his request. Ball game under way when bespectacled Commandant handed coat to Mr. Grinnell, who accompanied Japanese party of six; also handed him egg shell of raw egg he had just pulled from pocket and sucked, tied handkerchief around head, and relieved internee pitcher. Commandant pitched overhand (out of order in softball, as the game is played in Santo Tomás), then playfully pulled another egg from pocket and pretended to throw this. Laughed heartily at own horseplay. Then called aides to join team when it was his turn to bat. Commandant hit ball and ran to first base. Tired, he called for aide to take his place and run rest of way. This horseplay disgusting to internees, who saw good game ruined. Story goes that before Yoshie took over job as Commandant he talked to Commandant of Los Banos Camp and this Japanese told him in American slang what he learned from his experience, "If you play ball with the internees you will get along all right with them." Good advice, but Col. Yoshie took it too literally.

The new Commandant addressed all internees in blazing ten o'clock sun a few days after ball game. Commandant on stage and internees standing on plaza before Main Building. "Excuse my English," he began, "but I learned it only two years ago." That our interests were his chief concern was the platitude he repeated in different words and always the condition if we obeyed him we could expect better things, "from the bottom of his—his—hurt (heart)." Applause and a bow, which we had been told he demanded as a sign of respect due him, as he closed the speech.

The day after the Commandant's speech he refused to let another gift of eggs to children come in gate, he turned away coffee for the kitchen bought from internee funds, and he deleted bananas from the fruit market list. We have never before had a Commandant with such endearing words and such despicable manners. He is the most heartily hated of all Commandants to date. His treacherous "good-will" is galling.

Sometimes I feel that the children are a millstone about my neck which will drown both myself and them. There are people I must see about borrowing money to buy food for the children—yet I cannot get away from them long enough to dress and must search out the two men I wish to see, Mr. Grinnell and Mr. Pond. On several occasions I have gotten out only a good pair of shoes and only a pressed dress when either Beth or Clay completely demanded both time and attention for some inconsequential matter. It would seem heartless to leave them, yet I postpone and still postpone a matter serious to the welfare of the children. Even after Beth and Clay are asleep at night, I cannot feel free to get out of hearing distance should they call— though I fret and chafe inwardly because of desire for adult companionship of old friends who have asked me to join them in the coolness of the plaza before the Main Building.

A new and popular food in camp—dried squash seed—gathered from kitchen vegetable cleaning tables, boiled and dried in the sun. Slightly sweet and a bit tasty for between-meal nibbles, now that there are no peanuts or sweets of any kind.

Friday, May 27, 1944. Asked Mr. Pond whether there was any truth in rumor that wives and families of military prisoners were to be repatriated soon. Ever since a list of Canadian internees came to S. Thomás, through the Japanese, from the Canadian government, to be asked whether they wished to be repatriated by Canada if and when transportation became available, repatriation rumors have developed thick and fast. A few women who have husbands in Cabanatuan have gone so far as to pack, so sure are they of repatriation soon. "There is absolutely no basis for the belief that military wives and widows, or anyone else, will be repatriated in the near future," Mr. Pond said.

Mr. Pond, former employer of my husband, has done nothing for me or children since outbreak of war. Today I asked him whether he would transport the three of us to States in accordance with Jim's business contract. He said the U.S. Government would take all internees to States. "Shall you pay us the value of transportation if the children and I cost your company nothing to get to States!" Being a keener business man than a kind one, he gave me no answer, but dismissed me. "I wish you would be so kind as to discuss with Mr. Alger in the U.S., when the war is over, my husband's choice between a raise in salary and home leave and our rejection of the salary increase in favor of transportation home. Do you not think that, under the circumstances, the children and I are entitled to the value of the salary increase my husband refused in order to have the home leave, which now you do not expect to give us!" "There is nothing in the records of which you speak" was his final answer.

May 30, 1944. Dental clinic here held for internee children three to seventeen years. Dentists here wish to prepare a paper on conditions of children's teeth, as two and one-half years of unusual food and eating habits should be evidenced in teeth which are forming. Malformed teeth and decayed teeth are common among Santo Tomás children, and prior to the present dental check on all internee children nothing was done in way of examination or check-up on children's teeth, the few dentists in camp finding their hours of free service being completely filled with emergency work for adults. Never were conditions for the observation and study of a particular group of children more perfect. Never in the history of the U.S. have conditions been so perfectly controlled for a study of the bodies, the teeth, the mentality and the behavior of a group of American children. How some American psychologists would like to be dropped, with their questionnaires and notebooks, and chart papers, in our midst! But they had better remember to bring a few cans of corned beef and a few chocolate bars to sustain them during the course of their study, for they might find themselves too hungry to conclude what they might begin. And if they found their subjects a bit lean and lethargic they would understand why.

June 5, 1944. Children with garlands of acacia and hibiscus blossoms chase after a salogubron (large black insect) which, when caught, is tied by the leg with hemp thread and affords amusement as it flies around overhead in circles—like green-backed June bug in Southern U.S.

While children play, the Commandant and the Internee Committee struggle with each other over whether children and adults should engage in any recreational activity calling for expenditure of energy. Committee contends that since sugar has been cut from camp ration, and meat served only rarely in minute and undiscernible quantities in vegetable stews, that on our present diet of starches (rice, corn, dried beans), free of sugar, meat and fat, internees do not have energy for unnecessary activity. Doctors have pointed out to Commandant steady loss of weight of internees as food ration has been steadily reduced week after week (three cups of coffee per person during month of June), no bananas for breakfast many mornings, and corn mush without sugar and without fruit is hard to down. Yet that alone must sustain us through the room cleaning, laundry, etc. of morning until we get boiled corn and rice (nothing else, often) for lunch.

Commandant says loss of weight is due to worry of internees because of separation from families, separation from home, worries that accompany internment, and loss of weight not due to insufficient food provided by Japanese—therefore try to enjoy internment as much as possible and play baseball, have boxing matches, acrobatic dancing classes, etc., which the committee recommended be stopped on present diet.

To keep going, I give children and myself half of mush allowance at 7:00 A.M. and we eat other half cold at 10:00 A.M. when pangs of hunger come, whether we eat full allowance at breakfast time or not. Nibble raw cincomas (turnips) between meals when we can buy these in small camp market where all produce is sold on ration basis—today's basis being one cincoma for three people per day—not much nibbling on that allowance. No peanuts for more than a month, no camotes in market. We used to eat cold boiled camotes between meals as there was no fat for frying for more than six weeks.

June 6, 1944. Manila Tribune: "Hitler Spares City of Rome." The evacuation of Rome has been ordered by Reichfuehrer Adolph Hitler to spare the Eternal City from the ravages of war. Hitler should get a crown of glory in heaven for his kind consideration for the Eternal City!

The paper pointed out Rome had no military value to Germans, in fact they had planned to evacuate it since November last year, but stayed on to protect precious relics there at great cost and handicap to themselves. In getting Rome, we, the Allies, got a millstone around our neck which the Germans were glad to pass on to us. (Wonder if anyone is fooled by such shallow propaganda?)

June 7, 1944. In *Tribune* for today (which Japanese let re-enter camp beginning May 1) opening of long-talked-of "second front" in France on night of June 5 is mentioned,† with little comment save that our losses were heavy and that Germans had been waiting for us so long they were glad at last we had come.

June 12, 1944. Gift of raw peanuts from Y.M.C.A. One kilo for six persons (one-half kilo for three) roasted in camp, great treat.

June 18, 1944. Large iron caldron cemented to kitchen floor in Annex with space between concrete floor and caldron for charcoal. Gas practically a thing of the past. Food for central kitchen for weeks now cooked by charcoal in caldrons in dining sheds. Electricity still available for cooking, but most of camp stoves were, unfortunately, gas.

This month the newspaper (*Tribune*) has been stopped. Three strands of barbed wire ordered placed on top of fence around Santo Tomás by the Japanese, and an inner fence one and one-half meters high ordered constructed ten meters within main fence. The Japanese are determined to make further efforts to cut us off from contact with the outside world.

Area cleared by removal of shanties turned over by Japanese to internees for private gardens. I applied for garden and was lucky enough to draw one. My garden plot weeded, drained by ditches, I prepared myself with tools borrowed from camp. My desire in securing garden was to plant peanuts, as these grow easily in P.I. in any season, yield a big return, and provide a food rich in the oil so lacking in our diet. My garden (as everyone's) is 4 meters by 11 meters.‡ As rainy season is just

†After long delay, Allied forces finally invaded Normandy (France) on June 6, 1944, providing the "second front" which the Soviets had urged since their entry into the war in mid-1941.

‡EHV's garden measured 157.48″ × 433.07″ or approximately 13′ × 36′.

beginning, peanuts must be planted in hills eight to ten inches *above* ground level. Peanuts require five months from time of planting to gethering and there are those who say I will never harvest my crop— that the war will be over before that time. Optimism keeps us going, but I'll wager we will still be in S. Tomás for Christmas, and if Beth and Clay and I have fresh peanut butter, my labor shall not have been in vain. Onions and corn are up between the peanut hills, these crops maturing so much more quickly than peanuts that they will be out of the way before peanut vines cover ground. Fresh, tender corn-on-the-cob with hot butter—what a dream delicacy! The thought spurs me on with gardening.

Scarcity of materials causes Santo Tomás 1944 styles to be dresses, blouses, shorts, with fronts of one color and backs of another, or yokes of one, sleeves of another, and body of another. Only remnants of cloth left in the last round, not enough of one color for a full dress. Some of combinations of plaid and plain are attractive, particularly solid color dresses with pinafore set into dress instead of over it. Nightgown dresses of white, pink, or baby blue crepe seen everywhere—made from baggy gowns from the U.S. All dresses are made with square neck and gathered skirt.

June 22, 1944. Commandant gave written order to the Internee Committee that it must have internees build barbed wire extension on top of fence, put sawali on wire fence separating Seminary Chapel from Santo Tomás grounds, fence separating gym from rest of grounds (now that gym has been evacuated) and low barbed wire fence ten meters inside fence surrounding camp. The committee protested ordering internees to perform this labor, as they are occupied fully with camp duties necessary to their own welfare and these fence construction jobs do not pertain to welfare of internees and should, therefore, be performed by Japanese labor. Commandant said internees must do work or else. . . . Inside fence will cut off gardens, but gardeners will be permitted to go ahead with work during specified hours. Fence may prove a boon keeping children and looters out—as peanut plants are disappearing, being pulled up and taken away.

Another batch of letters distributed. One told of plagiarism of title

Lorenzo the Magnificent to *MacArthur the Magnificent*. To those in the P.I. there is nothing glorious about MacArthur except the brass of his uniform.* Filipinophile because it paid him a salary and perquisites into the thousands of U.S. dollars, as well as pesos per month. He was thought of in the P.I. as shallow, incompetent in all matters except the game of politics. Without exception the comments on the book have been critical, many by internees who lived at the Manila Hotel with him and who have watched his whole career prior to and under Quezon's tutelage. The title indicates that the author (unknown, but it sounds like a romantic woman, enamored by external gloss of the man) did *not* get the information for the book from P.I.

July 4, 1944. Official inspection today by a Japanese prince (rumored to have come from Korea) and all internees ordered to be in or near sleeping quarters from 9:30 A.M. until inspection party—due to arrive at gate of Santo Tomás at 10:20—has left camp. All clothes drying on lines at front and sides of Main Building to be removed. No mattresses or bedding to be sunned on grounds during inspection. No lines to be formed and all lines (vegetable and fruit market lines and lunch chow lines) suspended until departure of "guests." No food (bananas, papayas, pineapple, cincomas, mangoes, avocadoes—all in season and kept from one market day to next) to be left where visitors could see it. Small tables in hallways where food usually kept to be cleared or food covered. All work stopped except "necessary" jobs and men must wear shirts at work, except fire stokers for outdoor charcoal stoves. So we spent an inactive morning, crowded in our overstuffed rooms with curtain drawn across door, in the hope the inspecting party would not enter and cause us all to rise from beds, where we sat, and bow. At last the party arrived, seventeen Japanese, in polished boots, with shining scabbards. One slightly taller than rest, wore

---

*EHV's disparaging view of General MacArthur was widespread among Americans in the Philippines both before the war, when he served as military adviser to the Commonwealth government between 1935 and 1941, and during the war when they believed that he had abandoned their cause. Filipinos, however, were more split in their opinion—some highly critical, others almost worshipful. The book EHV refers to here was Robert Considine's *MacArthur the Magnificent*, published in 1942.

yellow ribbon across right shoulder and tied with long loop on left side. Surely he was the prince for whom this quiet, orderly, artificial morning of inactivity was forced upon us.

At the usual 8:30 P.M. news broadcast a message from the Commandant was read to internees, thanking us for our good behavior and advising us that the inspection party was well pleased with Santo Tomás.

July 5, 1944. As a reward for our good behavior on the 4th, like little children we were given a sugar plum. An old American film, *Dance, Girls, Dance*, starring Maureen O'Hara, Louis Hayward and Ralph Bellamy. Cinés we are still permitted to have, but no more stage shows. On Saturday night, July 1, the Santo Tomás Stock Co. (headed by Dave Harvey and made up principally of the camp men's chorus) put on a minstrel show. There were blackened end men, the interlocutor in high hat and grey trousers, the chorus in white trousers and shirts and coats with huge gold paper lapels. There was an imitation of Al Jolson and a little black Sonny Boy, there was a medley of love lyrics ("Margie," "Sweet Sue," "Mary Lou," and "Mary") sung in turn by a men's foursome. The most popular jokes of the comedians were the localized jokes. "In what town will there be a hot time in the old town tonight? In Memphis, St. Louis, New Orleans?" "Naw, suh, not any of dose places. In Paris." (Our troops are marching Paris-ward.)

"What exercise are you taking now, Rastus? Is ya on de baseball team? Does ya play soccer? What does ya do for recreation?" "I'll tell ya, Mr. Interlocutor, what I does. I has taken up a new recreation dese days. I's taken up fencing." (Referring, of course, to the building of the fence to cut off the gym from Santo Tomás and putting up a sawali fence between S. Tomás and the Seminary grounds—work now under way by internees, much to their disgust.)

But there was a catchy little song which brought down the house. As much as the internees liked it, the Japanese (who have "listeners" at all programs) disliked the song. The next morning, after the show, the Commandant's office called for copies of the words of the song and for a written apology signed by the four men who sang it and by Dave Harvey. When the guilty ones asked the Japanese why they must apologize, they were told by the Japanese that the song criticized the food at Santo Tomás and that internees were never supposed to criticize the camp in any way. The Japanese sense of humor failed to see the humor in the song. As penalty for this little bit of fun there are to be no more stage shows on the plaza, and no speeches without first being submitted to Japanese for censorship. Even Sunday sermons, now delivered on the pathway toward the front gate in front of Main Building, are to be submitted in writing before being delivered.

July 8, 1944. With 8:00 o'clock roll call dismissal signal, came the announcement: West side of front campus from stage to gate and from center pathway between two nipa pavilions westward to gym "out of bounds" today. Truckloads of people coming into gym for "temporary internment" there. Four hundred and seven American and British Protestant missionaries with their families, who had been free in Manila on permanent religious passes, and a large group of Catholic priests (from Atenio)† and nuns from Holy Ghost Convent and the American order of Maryknoll Sisters in their distinctive garb. The latter order has the reputation of being a superior type of woman, superiority in intelligence and in worldly goods being recommendations for entrance in the Sisterhood. The Maryknoll nursing nuns in Manila have always held the respect of the community.

Baggage, mattress rolls, and beds were dumped from trucks on muddy west area ground (there was heavy rain during night preceding). Men, women, and children were rushed into gym to avoid communication with Santo Tomás internees. In the gym they must have stood or sat on the floor—for there were no chairs, and the bedding and beds were soon reloaded on other trucks and taken out of Santo Tomás for Los Banos. Food, corn stew and rice, was taken from our kitchen to the gym (lunch and supper) and the kitchen was asked to have breakfast mush ready for this gym group at 2:30 A.M. on Sunday morning. After a night on the floor, modest nuns with no privacy for disrobing, the mixed religious group, including the most anti-Catholic

†Ateneo de Manila, Jesuit university established in Manila during the Spanish colonial period.

of the Protestant missionary group in the P.I., left by truck for Los Banos before day.

Sister Lucy and Sister Ann (who had been in Bacolod Camp) asked to be transferred to Los Banos with other sisters from Holy Ghost. These two lone nuns in Santo Tomás are cut off from rest of sisterhood and find it embarrassing and at times unpleasant here. Their request was refused, and they were told to return to their stuffy little room in the tuberculosis ward of the isolation hospital where they have been assigned to camp duty.

Father Harvey (canon missionary of the Manila Episcopal Cathedral of Saint Mary and Saint John—so Episcopal that the church carries the flag of England in its chancel) saw his wife and daughter come in with group going to gym for day's stopover before being interned in Los Banos. He asked the Japanese if he might not go to Los Banos with his family or else his wife and daughter be kept in Santo Tomás. His request was refused and Mrs. Harvey and daughter departed for Los Banos, leaving husband and father here.

Departing religious group given banana and hard-boiled egg, and fifty-odd children given compressed soft rice and sugar for eating on trip.

Prices of articles have reached heights almost unbelievable and continue to soar:

Sugar ₱250.00 per kilo (second grade, unrefined)
Cocoa 150.00 per half pound package
Facial Soap 50.00 per cake
Cigarettes 25.00 per pack

In the market: papayas ₱5.00 to 8.00 (pre-war 20¢), mangoes ₱1.50 each, avocadoes ₱1.20 each, string beans ₱9.00 kilo, eggs ₱2.00 each, bananas ₱.30 each (rarely for sale), casava flour ₱20.00 kilo.

People saving cooked rice left over at kitchen, drying it in sun and putting it through meat grinder to make coarse rice flour. They say that the cooked, dried, ground rice makes as good flour as the uncooked. Whether rice has lost anything in cooking is not known, but rice in the P.I. is not cooked as in the U.S. Rice is put on in cold water and cooks until dry, then removed from fire and eaten (no washing in colander after boiling and then steaming as my mother did in Georgia).

Suddenly everyone in Santo Tomás has money with which to buy in market. The Internee Committee is giving in the form of cash relief ₱50 per month for each adult without funds, ₱45 and ₱40 for each child, depending upon age. Therefore a family of five may secure over ₱200 per month. The catch is that in the gift the committee will exact its toll and profit. If the U.S. pays internees cash for cost of internment to us, at what rate of exchange will this money be deducted? The committee, personally putting up the cash, may come out of this millionaires.

Physical check-up of all children in Santo Tomás. By far majority of children underweight. Beth five pounds short of U.S. age-height-weight standard charts, and Clay three pounds underweight by same measure. Children often complain of headache and of being "tired." There are frequent cases of fever following normal exertion of play—even the children can't take it anymore.

July 14, 1944. "It Looks Like Rain" was Bastille Day awakening theme. We're expecting the fall of Paris today, but there is no news in camp but rumors running rife.‡ It has poured in torrents for five consecutive days. My peanuts are a mass of brilliant yellow blossoms. The cannas outside my window are flapping wet leaves and end-of-the-season blossoms against the wooden and cracked glass panes (some have been broken and replaced by wooden shutters). How handy large packing boxes containing Red Cross supplies were! Feather-like acacia petals are like soggy little puffs trampled by rubber boots and bakyas into the muddy ground. Hibiscus bushes are dropping the scarlet bows which adorn their tresses, to discard frivolity and concentrate wholly on the tremendous growth in this time of tropical deluge. The dry, cracked earth sucks in noisily, avidly, and unashamedly the refreshing rains which pour down its parched gullies and dry stream

‡In reality, Paris was not liberated until August 25, 1944, although EHV's assumption that this was a goal of the Allies at the time is accurate, and perhaps accounts for this overly optimistic expectation on the part of the internees.

beds and cover its whole body in a cool, exhilarating bath. Plants move visibly with life and growth. In the forests I am sure the huge vines which entwine the native trees and swing themselves from branch to branch and from tree to tree stretch themselves as they awake from a thirsty sleep and extend themselves as the rains awaken and bring life to them.

In the room children suddenly quarreling with each other, and with me, climbing on beds which are barely holding together from broken springs and lost nails and screws which cannot be replaced—restless, irritable at having their energies cramped in a tiny space too small for normal outlet and expression. A certain amount of motion, accompanied by a certain amount of noise, seems an absolutely unquenchable and undivertable part of a child's day.

The Thursday afternoon and Sunday morning classical concerts (in playhouse during rainy season) are a wonderful release from the tension of the room. Yesterday, Thursday, July 13, I slipped out in scarlet flannel jacket (baby blanket dyed) while Beth and Clay were still asleep in siesta for an hour of Brahms and peace. After ten minutes of glorious melody, however, the loudspeaker became quiet and there was only the dripping rain from nipa eaves. Shortly thereafter a dripping announcer came into the damp, dirt floored pavilion to tell us that the wires between the broadcasting office and the playhouse had become crossed in the rain and wind. The short-circuit resulting meant no concert today.

Back to the room and an hour's joy, while the children slept, in a little worn, much-handled book published in 1908, *The Master of the Inn* (by Herrick)*, which I had picked up in the camp library. The copy I had announced fourteen editions back at beginning of the century, and I can understand why, though the little book has long since been forgotten in the U.S. for it is not ancient enough to be a classic, nor modern enough to be "new."

Another little bit of pleasant reading on a rainy evening, after Beth and Clay again tucked away under U.S. Army mosquito nets in U.S. Red Cross pajamas, *The Sister of the Angels* by Elizabeth Goudge, the story

---

*Robert Herrick, American educator and novelist.

of an eleven-year-old girl. And even after a day of dead-fatigue from
being cooped up in a few square feet with my own two, it's a pleasure
to read of the irresistible ingenuity and charm of childhood.

July 15, 1944. Received today the *Red Cross News* published by American
Red Cross, printed in the U.S.A. and distributed to U.S. prisoners of
war by the International Red Cross Committee. (Like "Americana"
from the *American Mercury* of H. L. Mencken.)

Copy received today is dated September 1, 1943, Vol. 1, No. 1, a
seven-page onion-skin typewriter-size paper, with news from each
state. Then there is a short editorial in which Norman H. Davis† says to
war prisoners: "A bulletin of news about your welfare, containing
news of life in the camp, also is published by the American Red Cross
and mailed monthly to the families of all United States prisoners." We
wonder what Mr. Davis really knows about Cabanatuan, Bilibid, and
other military camps in the P.I. To think that Jim's mother is getting a
rosy, cozy, little chatty message each month about the son she thinks is
a prisoner in the P.I. How appalling! But such is the rosy propaganda
of war. Keep smiling! Keep the home folks happy and comfortable, so
wheels of war machinery may keep oiled with the gore of someone's
sons and husbands and some children's young fathers.

From Georgia comes this news: "Georgia: Georgia's peach crop was
estimated at 16 percent of normal. Lt. E. M. Johnson of the Atlanta Fire
Department was elected president of the State Association of Fire-
fighters. Fifty cases of whiskey were stolen from Jimmie's Place at
Vidalia." That is all.

Mississippi: Mrs. Frank Hill, 21, of Biloxi, gave birth to triplet girls.
Paul Cato, a member of the Senate, married Miss Alexander, of Mont-
rose, a member of the House at Jackson."

Thoughts of homeland in these items from Virginia. "Crape myrtles
were in bloom in Suffolk. . . . Richmond's mimosa trees were attacked by a soil fungus disease for which no known cure exists."

Baseball scores as of August 24, 1943. No mention of legitimate

†American diplomat and financier. During World War II Davis served with the American
Red Cross until his death in 1944.

stage. (Wonder if Noel Coward enlisted or was drafted at his age in this war.) Of the cinema, we learn that *Andy Hardy's Blonde Trouble* was filmed in part, at least, on the University of Nevada campus.

Mention of flowers from Virginia brought to mind flowers of the P.I. that have no odor. Even the roses are odorless and it has been truly said, "The flowers have no perfume, the birds have no song, and the women have no virtue." The latter two accusations I will neither defend nor deny, but the absence of scent from tropical blossoms has been a deficiency which I repeatedly attempt to disprove by smelling blossoms which experience should have taught me cannot and do not give off the expected sweetness which is their due. Here, while nature has been almost too lavish with her paint and the size of her canvasses, she has withheld herself from the distillation of floral fragrance.

For days I have wanted to write a sonnet of hate—for during these rainy hours, days, weeks, I find myself closeted in the sight and sound of a creature so revolting to me that I cannot sleep even when darkness shuts her from my sight and sleep from my ears, for I still cannot turn in my bed without a sigh from her whom I thought asleep, for our beds touch at the ends with only a foot-wide passage between. The sudden memory of the red hills and streams of Georgia diverted my attention. How fickle is the mind—and how interchangeable the emotions of hatred and love, though internment has made me like certain types of people less and love nature the more. For nature is kind, and humanity is not always so. Pettiness, malice are human vices with no counterpart in nature. Yet one must live in a semblance of harmony with his fellow men, for not to do so is so offensive to nature herself that we call a life of maladjustment and chosen hermitage un-natural.

Back to my hate—the appearance (which she cannot help and which, except for the grace of God and straight-legged ancestry, I might have) sickens me. I might stand with my knees a good eighteen inches apart and be unable to bring them closer—but I wouldn't insist upon wearing shorts another twelve inches above my knees had nature been so unkind. Yes, I'm catty! She's forty-five years old and besides the short shorts she has tightly twisted curls (she curls them on her fingers) hanging around her middle-aged shoulders, and her daughter's pink hair clips in her hair. She has small, close-together, popped eyes which are always focused on others' property and affairs. Her ears protrude through the curls, pulled out by nature, as if she has strained to eavesdrop what was intended for ears of others—for no piece of news does she embellish and retell so quickly and so avidly as that verbal tid-bit which was intended solely for other ears. In other words, she is a meddlesome, gossipy, middle-aged adolescent, whose puerile mind and malicious tongue have done more harm and caused more unhappiness than time can heal. I loathe the sight of her, yet she is my roommate for internment, I suppose, and I must look at her every hour of every day.

July 18, 1944. Copied these prices today from bazaar run by Santo Tomás, an exchange where internees with something to sell may offer it to other internees—with 10 percent going to the Relief Welfare Committee for aid to indigents:

Playing cards	₱ 38.50
Camay soap	27.00
Lifebuoy soap	33.00
100 yd spool	
black cotton thread	22.00
Scott toilet tissue	100.00

July 20, 1944. Solomon in all his glory was not arrayed as one of the Santo Tomás males freshly come from the distribution of knitted undershirts sent in by the Japanese for sale to internees. Violent orange, red, fleshy pink, purplish blue (no white ones) in the batch of ₱2.10 Japanese bargains.

Eighteen hundred fifty yards of blue denim were also sold to men lucky enough to draw buying permits for pieces large enough for shorts (Material so thin, however, decency demands that the shorts be lined). Eight hundred and fifty women have drawn sales permits for four yards of "daisy fields." "Acres and acres" of perky, yellow-centered daisies peeking from maroon, green, pink, blue petals will shortly appear in playsuits, blouses, skirts, housecoats, dresses, children's sunsuits, and infants' diapers—not to mention men's outer-

and under-wear. Though cotton textured "daisy fields" are for sale to women over 16 years only, there are no specifications as to the use. As in previous distributions of cloth, wives will donate theirs to shirtless husbands, and mothers will share materials with offspring of all ages. Price for a four-yard length is ₽7.20.

Could the nurse giving plague injections today possibly have been correct? Beth, Clay, and I went up to S.T.I.C. Public Health Office on the mezzanine floor of the Main Building today at 9:20 A.M. for the sixth consecutive visit to the same place at the same hour of the day, same day of the week, to wind up a series of two dysentery, two cholera, and two plague injections with a week's rest between each pair. The shots, Japanese serum which we all feared until we felt no after-effect except that of dull needles, were perhaps after all only water as many people suspected. This series was ordered by Japanese Commandant in "deep concern for internees' well being." After the sixth injection today, as the three of us turned to go down the wide mezzanine steps, I said jovially to the nurse, "Thank you. We've been to see you for six Thursdays. I don't suppose we'll be up again for injections. Good-bye." "Oh, I'll be here to punch you for the next round six months from now. We'll probably begin the whole series over again then. The Japanese said these serums offer only six months' immunity." Back again in six months! My whole day was depressed for I'm not sure I'll be sane after six more months of internment—and there seems to be no injection to prevent mental disability.

Internment is really getting me down—with that always hungry feeling and the continual fight with myself not to raid the comfort kit box and eat a whole tin of butter with a spoon or turn the key in a can of cold, greasy, delectable corned beef while the children are sleeping. My responsibility for my children—for whom the canned goods must be conserved until that "just around the corner" where the Yanks are hiding comes within earshot—gives me not only that lean and hungry look, but lean and hungry discomforts as well. From the feeling inside me I wonder if my stomach is not falling out of place and all the organs in my abdominal cavity shifting here and there in a movement of protest at neglect, and to call to my attention as forcibly as possible their functioning—a functioning which in normal times is perfect, as judged by complete lack of attention drawn to the organs themselves. Now, I'm all stomach, intestines, heart (from gas pressure), kidneys. It's annoying and disconcerting to find one's horizon a blank wall of pain, when attempting to look above, beyond, and outside this flesh and its bone masonry (mostly bone now) which houses the spirit.

Prolonged imprisonment has wrought changes in my mind also. I believe I'm becoming paranoid with persecution complex complete. Two years ago I became convinced that my upbringing, my background had ill fitted me for concentration camp. Circumstances during the past months and years have but strengthened my conviction in this regard. People still push my wet clothes off the public clothes line to make room for their own wet ones, they shove in ahead of me in chow line when I have stood, holding my tray and dishes, for an hour so I might be early in line and early through the meal in order to be early in another line, perhaps the canteen where I'm permitted to buy one-eighth kilo of cornstarch on my ticket today—with the children's bath time past due.

The war had better end soon, though, for if I remember my psychiatry correctly, paranoids become dangerous in the last stages of the disease. By the time the next semi-annual series of injections comes 'round, if we're still interned, I shall be in the last stages. For the sake of all internees in my path, I trust that the nurse's prophecy doesn't come true.

There are two events, one man-devised, the other God-given, scheduled for the coming half year which incline me to believe the nurse's prophecy false. These coming events which cast before them a golden shadow of hope for us are (1) the November presidential elections in the U.S., and the fourth anniversary since the outbreak of war in the Far East, (2) a Christian faith in the importance of the Nativity. Roosevelt is too good a showman not to realize the political advantage of a streamer headline effort to bring direct succor to his imprisoned countrymen, women, and children before testing his popularity at the polls. And God in His mercy, seeking no end except the good inherent in the deed itself, cannot look down upon us indefinitely without compassionate relief.

July 22, 1944. A new *dance*—far superior to the Lambeth Walk—the Santo Tomás Queue, a winding, twisting line of men and women singing "Cheer up, cheer up, everything's going to be lou-sy!!" while beating in rhythm aluminum cup and plate together.

No bananas on chow line now (none for children or adults), no corn, no sugar. Breakfast consists of a plate of rice and a spoon of watered coconut milk. There is weak tea for those whose stomachs require hot water. Boiled rice contains less food value than corn mush, so the breakfast change was to our detriment, as are all food changes, really reductions, being made almost daily.

Rice without sugar or fruit and without milk—coconut milk they cannot take because it gives them diarrhea—Beth and Clay can be forced to eat only with an effort and then in small amounts. So for breakfast they eat about a half cup each, nothing else. At nine-thirty they are begging for food. Having nothing else to give them I bring out the remainder of their breakfast rice ration and out of sheer hunger they take the starch. Still there is one-third of breakfast rice ration left (and this is the minimum on which a person can subsist) and this I put in an enamel cup and put aside for 7:00 P.M. pre-bedtime snack. Because the cold, gummy rice comes out of the cup in a cylindrical mold and looks different, Beth and Clay call it "pudding." These extra doses of starch are essential to keep the children going. They are both losing weight.

Sunday, July 23, 1944. Freshly washed little leaves, twisting and turning themselves in the sunshine, to shake off the rain which falls from them in glistening drops like pearls cast off one at a time. Below the trees the bright pools of water, then a pearl falls into the pool, setting forth a series of laughing ripples on the surface of the water, touching off a faint musical chime which tingles a series of notes from high treble to bass as the pearl slips down the notes of a musical scale to the bottom of the pool.

Such is a corner of Santo Tomás on a bright Sunday morning after two weeks of unceasing rain. Such freshness in nature is the countenance of the Lord.

May the Lord bless thee and keep thee,
The Lord make His face to shine upon thee
And be gracious unto thee.
The Lord lift up His countenance upon thee
And give thee peace   (Numbers 6:24–26)

Such is my wish for all mankind today. My cramped soul expands
until it almost bursts itself with joy in the freedom of the outdoors
after two weeks confinement in a dungeon not unlike Hell itself. Beth
and Clay are learning about the goodness of Christ in Sunday school in
a stuffy little schoolroom on the ground floor of the Main Building,
but I shall commune with nature herself and fine "good in everything" today.

Not only have the elements (torrential rains and blustery winds)
heightened the tension of confinement the past fortnight, but the Japanese themselves have made new efforts to force upon our attention
our prisoner status.

On July 17, during a brief interlude, I was lined up, a number, 0435,
hung around my neck so it stood out starkly across my chest and my
photograph taken by a Japanese photographer. Other internees had
preceded me in this ordeal. Many others will follow. Children under
eleven years are not having photographs made. (Perhaps our captors
are ashamed of having so many of them behind walls.) Our pictures
will be attached to one of the many, many forms each internee has been
required to fill out. Each change in Japanese administration of Santo
Tomás has resulted in demands for new statistics and records. And now
individual photographs. We are Prison Camp #2, we learned, as this
numeral was also tacked on the shoulder of the harassed internee.

July 25, 1944. "Ding, dong! The Wicked Witch is Dead" came the
cheery, childish tune at 6:30 A.M. Could this gay, malicious ditty on
death refer to Hitler? We all hope so, as in this circumstance a single
death might save the lives of million of young men, both German and
Allied, whose approaching conscription age is no cause for birthday
celebration.

August 1, 1944. Rumor still persists that Hitler is dead, and Quezon too.‡ Unfortunate, in a way, that these two, the motivator of this greatest world upheaval and the leader of one insignificant island archipelago republic who had his presidential seat snatched from under him during the struggle, could not see the outcome. Doubtless both men, in their minds, could foretell the end, a factor which may have hastened death.

August 1 to August 6, 1944. The week just passed has been one of the most eventful since internment. On evening of August 1 came announcement like a bombshell—the Commandant has ordered all money in possession of individual internees and in hands of Internee Committee to be deposited in the Japanese Bank of Taiwan, and withdrawals to be limited to ₱50 per month for internee over ten years old and ₱25 per month for children under ten. Reasons given by Japanese for this confiscation and control of prisoners' finances were as follows: (1) Protection against robbery, (2) The money may be increased through interest, (3) The money will not be used needlessly or wastefully, (4) To curb gambling, (5) To steady the economic position of the camp by making money last as long as possible. Obviously these reasons are absurd. Peal of uncontrolled and angry laughter rang out on the plaza as the announcement was read.

Breakfast consists of boiled rice, unadorned, unflavored except for rock salt we may add if we wish. Each internee is given a cup of salt the first of the month to use as he sees fit. By a perverted sense of humanitarian conduct, salt is the only item which has been sufficient. But salt causes thirst and on August 2 we were informed that tap water in Santo Tomás is no longer drinkable and we must boil all drinking water. A limited ration (1 cup boiled water per child per day) is given through Annex kitchen. Small containers may be filled, if one calls at the old camp restaurant site, where gas stoves are still installed with

‡It is possible that the rumor regarding Hitler's death arose from the assassination attempt made on his life by German officers on July 20, 1944. It was unsuccessful, and he did not actually die until April 30, 1945, when he committed suicide in his bunker in Berlin. Manuel L. Quezon did indeed die on August 1, 1944, at Saranac Lake, New York.

uncertain, or no, pressure. My hands are blistered from building charcoal fires and handling boiling water.

Have found use for leaky, porous, earthenware egg preservation jug—for salt. But hot, boiled water must go into numerous small covered and uncovered glass bottles and jars children have salvaged from rubbish heaps around camp grounds where they will play and which they have not subsequently broken.

August 7, 1944. Today a friend, a young handsome Scotchman in the middle thirties (whose wife, Grace, and three-year-old son Ian have been internment-long friends), was taken from Santo Tomás to Mandalucan Psychopathic Hospital. He is hopelessly insane. For several months he has talked of nothing but plans for releasing internee friends from the Japanese. Grace asked that he be taken into Santa Catalina Hospital for observation, she was almost on point of a breakdown herself from daily observation and helplessness to stop grandiose ideas of himself as liberator which steadily took hold of husband's mind. Periods of liberator impersonations followed by weeks of deep depression and gloom. The night of July 6 my friend spent in Santa Catalina coming out of a depression of spirit in which he spoke to no one. He suddenly began to formulate plans for a mass meeting of internees which he would call and in which he would address internees. All night he worked on his plans, not a minute's rest or relaxation. Early this morning he was about camp inviting this internee and that one to his meeting. Later he was taken away.

August 8, 1944. A "picnic" for Beth and Clay is to take a plate of rice with a banana or two, if we're fortunate enough to have them, and go out with spoons and a bottle of water to a tree in the vicinity of the front gate, and after playing with grass and stones there, then sit on the ground and eat the same old thing, which tastes entirely new in new surroundings. Laundry and morning baths for the children are postponed for the day. I take a book or my diary (I don't knit for fun, so leave knitting at home) and if the children don't get into too many fights with other children for space, we have a jolly morning.

Wednesday, August 9, 1944. "It's Three O'Clock in the Morning,"
6:30 A.M. musical today. It is true that Davao was bombed at 3:00 A.M.
yesterday as camp rumor had it. No details but the "back fence radio"
had the news again that Davao was bombed. Glory be!

Today the Commandant's staff met in a foxhole on the front campus
under a large acacia tree across from Commandant's office. Spirits
reached a new high on a low rice diet. We can starve with hope.

On the menu board outside the central kitchen a crayoned cartoon
of someone waving to the world's best known animal cartoon character with the words, "Good-bye, Mickey Mouse," the significance
being that the Japanese money we have been using in camp has been
called Mickey Mouse money because it has no more real value than
children's play money.

August 11, 1944. Beth has whooping cough and we are both exhausted from its effect. Beth is bent double with spasms of coughing.
When an attack comes during the night I jump from my bed and jerk
her into a sitting position before she awakens the fourteen sleeping
occupants of the little room. Last night I stayed awake, ready to jump
at the first whoop. Only ravenous mosquitoes, who seem to be waiting in hordes, to settle on my ankles, toes, fingers and elbows (mosquitoes prefer bony joints rather than the fleshy parts of the body)
keep me from standing watch beside her bed.

A few women in room are considerate about it but Mrs. M. has
sobbed a martyr's groan for the past three mornings. "That child! I
cannot sleep at night for the awful coughing. My health is being undermined by lack of sleep. And of course *all* the children in the room
will get her cough. *Something* ought to be done about it."

The "something" I am having done for her are Vitamin C injections
every second day, ferrous sulphate, and thiamin tablets daily in addition to the A and D and multiple vitamins she was already swallowing
with her breakfast allowance of boiled water. Of course, Clay will get
the whoop also. To try to keep the children separated is impossible.

August 15, 1944. Clay now is out-whooping Beth, for his lungs were
always stronger and his voice louder than hers. In addition to the

vitamin doses they are now having inhalations (they have to put noses in a little tent for this purpose), ephedrine nose drops, throat swabbings, and heavily codeinized cough syrup. There are numerous finger pricks and ear lobe pricks for bloodcount (the white corpuscles increase rapidly with whooping cough). I am sure there is no treatment known to the medical profession which is not being tried on the children. They almost split their throats, and the eardrums of our roommates, as they whoop full blast through the night. The children and I are as popular as a family of skunks in a farmer's hen house. And they say whooping cough usually lasts for six weeks!

August 19, 1944. Correspondence between Commandant (the newest one) and Internee Committee, relative to laziness and indolence of internees, posted on all bulletin boards. The letter from the Commandant opened the subject by writing that on all official inspection trips of Santo Tomás the Japanese had been impressed by the inactivity of internees and excessive amount of leisure time enjoyed by us. Though we did practically nothing to support ourselves, we were constantly asking for more food from the Japanese. The Commandant recommended that internees devote leisure time to gardening (for vegetables and fruits would cease coming when Manila came within bombing area). All internees over 60 and children under 15 should work two hours per day making hemp rope or envelopes for the Japanese (for which they would pay us in sugar, cigarettes, and other commodities we had asked Japanese to supply us). All men and women between 15 and 60 should give an additional (above present work assignments) three hours per day to hard labor in camp gardens or other productive work. The internee working day is to be from 8:00 A.M. to 5:00 P.M. with only Sundays, Japanese holidays, Christmas, and Easter off.

Internee Committee replied with fire. We are not a war prisoner camp. There are many aged, invalids, babies, and young children here who must be cared for by other internees. The majority of able-bodied men were transferred from Santo Tomás to Los Banos last year, leaving disproportionately large number of incapacitated here. All of Santo Tomás' work (heavy work) is now performed by 40% of the internees and this percentage of able-bodied (exclusive of mothers of young children) internees is decreasing daily due to starvation diet. For internees to do additional work on food allowed them is impossible. Also the Japanese have told us repeatedly that sugar is not available in Manila, yet they offer to pay us for work with this commodity so urgently needed. Since it is available (it must be since it is offered as pay) it is the responsibility of the Japanese army to send it to us immediately for purchase by internees at a reasonable cost.

As to the laziness of internees: they put the Santo Tomás buildings in inhabitable shape, giving not only labor but buying materials as well. Internees must have time for personal laundry, for preparing supplemental food, cleaning living quarters, etc.

So the feud is on. The Japanese say work if we want more food; the Internee Committee says feed us so we can carry on with our heavy duties now required of us with our incapacities.

August 22, 1944. The "Abolene" cold cream the Red Cross sent us should have come under the heading of food rather than cosmetics. Most of it has gone into the frying of rich mush and casava flour hot cakes. I recently exchanged my cream for a can of grapefruit juice, the cream promptly going into the larder of Millie Booth, who can turn out palatable hot cakes from rice left over in most any form.

Dress materials sent to the women of S. Tomás were mostly second grade, especially the prints. The solid color Indian Head (Bat brand) has stood up to its name for durability of wear and color, but the prints have shrunk and faded and in many instances have been faulty in weave and in pattern. The children's cotton crepe pajamas are still wearing like iron and look well—slightly faded. The women's play-suits and nightgowns (ugly at first) are without shape or color now. This is for the information of Red Cross, which has given us some good buys and some poor ones—yet we could hardly complain, for as someone has said to complaining internees, "Well, the price you paid was right, wasn't it?"

Air raid shelters have been completed for Commandant and staff and Japanese purchasing agent and his staff. They are oblong trenches dug to one-foot depth, built up to a man's shoulder height, covered with bamboo splits, then the bamboo sides covered with stacked stones and packed with mud, then sodded with grass from what were once beautiful lawns of S. Tomás.

No shelters to be provided for internees, of course. Our lives are unimportant. I am reminded of the boat trip from Negros to Manila, when life preservers and lifeboats were reserved for Japanese in case of an emergency and we, prisoners on the boat, were to look out for ourselves. So now the Japanese shall rush into air raid shelters when the air raid siren sounds while we remain in the buildings (Annex has thin tin roof) or in grass shanties, exposed to shrapnel, bombs, and fire. Our protectors! These Japanese!

September 1, 1944. Japanese self-protection and our exposure to danger has been annoying—but when their efforts destroyed my personal garden I exploded. Next to my peanut patch I secured permission from supervisor of Shanty Area C for the privilege of clearing off one-half a garbage and rubbish dump (shoveling all rubbish into half the area) to plant camotes. Days of hard labor, which often left me too weak to wash perspiration-soaked clothes, and ground was cleared. Another hot morning to cut stems from plants in the camp garden down by the gym to transplant to the prepared ground. Watered and re-watered for many days, camotes showed signs of life and growth. After a month of care and protection, one day I stopped by my garden to pick lettuce for lunch. (Beth and Clay love a "secret" package wrapped in a lettuce leaf—when they eat the wrapping to discover the contents, a banana slice if I have it, or a small piece of panocha, which is put into the mouth whole.)

My camote bed had been uprooted and a foxhole dug exactly in the middle. A hard-packed pathway between garden plots could have been used as a space for the foxhole for the Japanese guard who patrols the wall along Area C, but the guard preferred easy digging within my garden rather than the harder earth beside it.

I protested the destruction of my garden to Mr. Grinnell on September 2. On September 3 Mr. Lloyd, member of Internee Committee in charge of gardens, told me that "the Japanese have stated, upon questioning, that they have no further use for the foxhole dug within your garden. You are at liberty to fill in the hole and begin your garden over again." Such magnanimity! However, I shall not start over again as I have not the strength to expend now on food which will not mature for months. The camotes had a good stand and their wanton and useless destruction by the Japanese has hurt me as deeply as any of the thousands of incidents of the petty wastefulness of this utterly useless and wasteful war.

Withdrew ₱100 from Bank of Taiwan, Santo Tomás Branch, today for use during month of September—₱50 for myself and ₱25 each for Beth and Clay. During August, buying everything my canteen ration cards permitted at prices astoundingly high, I was able to spend only ₱67.40. I did not declare my balance of ₱32.60 today for this amount would have been deducted from my September allowance. I prefer to keep my undeclared "balance on hand" myself rather than in the Bank of Taiwan.

September 3, 1944. Wonder if it is true that lights are on in London on fifth anniversary of war, while we sit in darkness in blackout. For two weeks now we have been in a state of "air raid alert" with nightly blackouts. These blackouts will likely be continued for the duration, we have been told.

Last night sat in darkness in front of Main Building. (After children were asleep. Clay's coughing is better.) Watched most beautiful pyrotechnic display of spotlights—more than twenty of them in a circle around Manila. Their beams crossed and re-crossed to form geometrical figures not unlike snow flakes under a microscope. And then the sound of a plane overhead, and the game of hide and seek with the lights as they flashed here and there trying to find the elusive plane. Unable to detect the plane in the moonless, starless sky, the pilot added zest to the one-sided game by suddenly flooding himself with lights on his plane until he became an iridescent silver bird flitting before a curtain of black velvet. How the long beams of light darted upon the bird and followed his silver course across the sky.

Then, lights off, the bird dipped, turned, retraced his flight and lost his pursuers again. When safe from the eager and frantic lights the playful pilot flooded his plane again to give his pursuers a clue. And the lights all pounced upon him again. What a good time pilot and practicing air-light operators were having—but the complete inefficiency of the ground lights in locating aircraft was obvious. We, sitting within the darkened walls of Santo Tomás, watched the little game with satisfaction for if Japanese cannot find their own planes in darkness, there is little likelihood of locating cautious enemy aircraft.

Tuesday, September 12, 1944. Blackout started August 22. Continuous real air alert (first *real* one) Saturday afternoon, September 9. Second real alert on September 12. On being asked whether American planes were really the cause of September 9 "alert" signal, Mr. Ohashi replied that American planes, flying very high, had been sighted flying north over Luzon. He failed to elucidate further. At last "our own" are within striking distance of us. For almost three years we have waited for the hum of American motors. We haven't heard motors or bombs yet, but the end is definitely nearer.

Last year, I thought, would be Beth's and Clay's last birthday in internment, but they recently celebrated Beth's fifth anniversary and Clay's fourth (three for each of them in concentration camp) with a cake of rice and cassava flour, soda, calamanci juice in water, panocha, nutmeg, cinnamon and two tablespoons of rancid peanut oil baked in a covered frying pan. A frosting of cornstarch and water flavored with a small can of peach jam from the almost diminished comfort kit gave the cake a sickly yellow covering which helped to support the five pink and four white candles left from last year's cake sent into Santo Tomás by the Roeders. Fortunately the Roeders followed the European birthday custom of adding one more candle than actual birthdays—"one to grow on."

Placed yellowish cake on platter of woven bamboo slits (1943 cake arrived on this) and surrounded cake with red lilies. To add another dash of color to already Christmas tree effect, studded cake top with half a dozen green hard candies saved in an air-tight jar from parcel post package from Ernestine in earlier part of this year.

Cake was served to Beth and Clay, Bill and Mary Helen Walker in the Walkers' shanty. Cake rested in glory on crude, rough, homemade child's table covered with a sheet. Children sang "Happy Birthday," and couldn't have enjoyed cake more had it been the real thing. Cala-manci juice in tin cups completed refreshments (which Clay promptly lost in whooping cough attack—I grabbed him from table and rushed him outside shanty).

Four adults had cake and coffee (powdered coffee from kit). The Walkers, G.B.,* and I. Fortunately I had bought birthday gifts for the children before money was called for by Japanese to deposit in Bank of Taiwan—though this was not reason for early purchase as I knew nothing then of Japanese plans for internees.

Some months back Billy Waters, elder son of Dr. Waters, had a birth-day and among his presents (mostly made in Santo Tomás) was a bronze plaque of the Main Building with the letters "S.T.I. Camp, Billy Waters," followed by the date of his birth. Expecting an extinction of bronze I went immediately to the Russian woman who had ham-mered the plaque. The price charged me for each plaque was twice the amount paid a few weeks before for Billy's, though my materials were less expensive and less difficult to get. "The rising cost of living," explained the Russian metal worker. The children were not enthused over gifts, but they are something of which they should be proud later.

Thursday, September 21, 1944. It has happened! Manila has been bombed! A week ago today we underwent two fruitless air raids. So far bombs were falling within hearing distance, but today the real thing happened.

At 9:30 A.M. the sky suddenly blackened with planes as they swooped down from high clouds into the misty morning air below. Immediately heavy anti-aircraft batteries went into action. As these same guns had been practicing since before dawn, everyone thought it must still be a practice, with dud shells and planes in the air—but the planes were *American*. Manila was being bombed and the Japanese were so taken by surprise that the fight in the air was well under way before the usual alert and air raid signals could be given.

When we realized it was the real thing—something for which we have waited for almost three years—with great joy we hastily gathered

*George Bridgeford, a fellow internee from Great Britain.

children together and got under our beds none too soon. A heavy iron cap off an anti-aircraft shell hit the tin roof of the Annex with a terrific thud and rolled noisily down the sloping tin to hit the ground below. Men and women rushed from shelter for this souvenir. A cr-a-a-a-sh and the sound of glass splintering on concrete came from the room directly across a narrow, uncovered corridor from mine. A six-inch iron splinter had pierced the window pane, scattering glass over the room and corridor.

The first put-put-put of machine gun fire, the dull thud and quake of unloaded bombs, the p-s-s-t of shells flying through the air, planes diving, and the steady boom of anti-aircraft guns. How we loved it! The fall of other shrapnel on the tin roof didn't bother us under our mattresses, on the floor. Beth and Clay, grinning, asked for the lollipops I had saved from Christmas for the "first air raid when the Americans come." The children took their little bomb sticks (oblong cubes of wood worn around the neck on a string) from their mouths and put in the lollipops—the first since Holy Ghost Hospital farewell.

Lunch was served in the room, huge pots of rice, a big fish, and a quarter cup of carabao milk for each child. Later some fish chowder (awful stuff) and a hard-tack biscuit was given each adult.

The flow of water ceased almost immediately. Big fires appeared over Manila Bay. (The harbor was bombed and re-bombed.) An oil fire to the south of Manila, and due to the use of water fighting fires, or bursting of water mains, Santo Tomás found itself without water. In an hour the toilets were in terrible condition. There were no pulleys, ropes, or buckets for the wells that have been dug for just this emergency. We had no means of washing children, or greasy dishes which smelled of fish. Many internees discovered themselves without boiled drinking water also. We took all discomforts with a grin. What did these things matter, since our own had come to free us at last?

A few Japanese planes went up to intercept the American attack. Though the planes were too high and the air too hazy to distinguish wing markings, still the American planes were easily distinguished because of the square-cut wing tips as contrasted with the rounded ends of the wings of Japanese planes. Two Japanese fighter planes were shot down by the American raiders rather close to Santo Tomás. A Japanese transport, heavy and bulky, flying low in an attempt to find shelter from the raiders, became easy prey for American bullets. This much only we know.

At 1:50 P.M. American planes returned, and we lay on the floor under the bed until 4:30 when waves of planes left to return to aircraft carrier bases. Japanese "all clear" signal was not sounded until after six o'clock. As darkness came, a glow on the western horizon over Manila Bay outlined the setting sun. This glow was from fires on or near the bay piers. As darkness settled in the east, the western lights heightened and sparks scattered high into the already star-sprinkled sky. Suddenly daylight returned as flames scorched the clouds—it looked like an explosion of a gasoline storage tank. The delayed thud of the explosion indicated anew the difference in time with which vision travels as compared with sound. We settled down to an evening's rest, of course in total blackout.

September 22, 1944. "Pennies from Heaven" came over the loudspeaker in a melodious voice crooning good morning at 6:30 A.M. today. And we rose, stiff jointed, with raw elbows and knees from sliding on the concrete floor getting under the beds, hoping and expecting more highly explosive pennies from our countrymen today.

The pennies began dropping about 9:30, heavier weight and more highly explosive than yesterday.

There was a little water in the pipes this morning and I went to wash-troughs in early morning darkness at 5:00 A.M. thinking I would be the only one out at this time of day with dirty clothes. Other internees, however, were trying to get ahead of raiders. Many scrubbed soiled clothes without seeing them and hung them up to dry not knowing or caring very much whether spots were removed. Women washed hair in slow water trickle, thinking "I'd better get it clean now, we don't know when the water supply will go for good."

Two American planes were hit by Japanese anti-aircraft this morning. One plane exploded in midair—a horrid sight and a more horrible fact if one lets his mind dwell upon the young aviators trapped in the plane. The second American plane hit careened off at an angle, one wing out of control. As the plane lost altitude, wobbled, regained altitude listing heavily to one side, an escort of two other American planes flew close by to accompany injured ship and crew. So the three planes disappeared from sight, but it is likely that if the pilot and crew bailed out they would be sighted and perhaps saved by accompanying raiders.

October 3, 1944. Truck from Baguio Camp arrived camouflaged with pine branches. People in Santo Tomás fought for sprigs of the fragrant pine.

Corned beef twice a week (one-fourth can per person) recommended by doctors, two of whom saw Japanese take food from Corregidor. No market, no fruit, no lunch, no drinks.

October 7, 1944. "There will be an air raid today," said a friend, "because the guards on the camp grounds have helmets on their backs, and three balloons for sound detection are in the air."

Mrs. Greenham went to shower at 6:30 and found a sign saying, "Sorry, reserved for Japanese from 5:00 to 8:00 A.M."

October 19, 1944. Boxes removed from front grounds, supposedly by request of Swiss consulate—or a message from Tokyo.

October 15, 16, 18, 20, 1944. Daily raids, dogfights, parachutes, planes careening wildly, throwing off smoke as they crash unpiloted to ground.† Too far away to tell nationality of pilot or plane. On the 15th four shanties hit by shells, but no one hurt (enamel cup mashed) as most shanty dwellers have outside dirt-and-stone shelters.

Biggest event—Japanese now using Santo Tomás grounds as quartermaster's headquarters, huge cases of supplies of all kinds stacked

†Military activity in the Philippines began to increase in early October in preparation for the planned Allied invasion of Leyte later that month. Much of the air activity which EHV observed was in connection with the landing of MacArthur and his forces in Leyte on October 20, 1944, followed by the noteworthy Battle of Leyte Gulf on the 23rd and 24th. This began the Allied recapture of the Philippines which would continue until the final surrender of the Japanese on Luzon on September 2, 1945.

high as person can reach from unloading trucks. Iron plates, one broken case contained dried apples, all kinds of foods. Internee Committee protested use of Santo Tomás grounds for this purpose. Japanese replied, "It is an insult to the Imperial Japanese Army to say that we might use the internees as a shield." The Santo Tomás grounds are not protected territory, "for the U.S. has never been officially notified that this is an internment camp." We laughed, for mail has all been addressed, the Red Cross sent packages, to Santo Tomás.

On the 18th an air raid for 9½ hours. On the 20th an air raid for 10 hours. Spent entire day in and out from under beds. We all have colds (so does everyone else) from sitting and lying on draughty floor.

November 1944. Spasmodic raids.

December 23, 1944. Went on two meals a day after rice ration cut by Japanese to 200 grams (from 300) per day—breakfast at 8:30, supper at 4:30, no lunch.

Air raids, when flying fortresses, silver, appeared suddenly from morning sky escorted by fighters which looked like midgets in comparison.‡ Dropped a few bombs on Manila, but flew in direction of Corregidor.

December 24, 1944. Neutral welfare committee of Y.M.C.A. sent in a few supplies for Christmas—chocolate, coffee, sugar, a small amount of clothing, four cigarettes, and five cigars.

January 1, 1945. At daylight people out in roadway with broom and dustpans sweeping up rice from broken sack brought in after dark on day before. In middle of morning children still gathering a few grains mixed in sand.

‡On December 17, 1944, U.S. airplanes from Admiral William F. Halsey's 38th Task Force began extended air raids in preparation for the invasion of Luzon which occurred at Lingayen Gulf in northwest Luzon on January 9, 1945. Concerned particularly for Allied internees and prisoners of war, some of the invading forces began an immediate drive toward Manila.

January 7, 1945. Four-motored American bomber (silver) burst into flames, hit by anti-aircraft shell. Parachute also caught fire and body plunged to earth. New Japanese Commandant arrived.

January 30, 1945. On this day eight deaths.

January 31, 1945. Dr. Stevenson, head of internee medical board, sentenced by Japanese to twenty days in jail because he refused to order his staff of doctors to change wording of death certificate of internees from "starvation" and "malnutrition" to other causes. Dr. Stevenson said each doctor diagnosed his patients himself and ascribed causes of death when death occurred. He could not order another doctor to change a diagnosis.

Later in the day other internee doctors were called in and ordered to change all certificates before 6:00 P.M. They were changed.

February 7, 1945. MacArthur in at 10:00 o'clock—in Manila.* Shelled by artillery from concealed hideouts in city. Tower of Main Building a perfect target for long-distance range. Saw girl killed by my door—Japanese bullet.

February 8, 1945. Many deaths saddening. Had our first wheat bread.

February 13, 1945. Nina Roeder nursing in guerrilla hospital for last seven months. Husband, Colonel in U.S. Army, with guerrilla forces. Neutrals pouring into Santo Tomás being murdered by retreating Japanese. Menus: Breakfast—cream of wheat (milk and sugar), stewed apricots, eggs, bacon. Lunch—creamed chicken, buttered spinach,

*General MacArthur's visit to Santo Tomás on February 7 was preceded by the arrival of the 2nd Squadron, 8th Cavalry, U.S. Army, on the evening of February 3. After a short but difficult struggle at the front gates, most of the approximately 3,500 internees were liberated and given medical attention. Two hundred and twenty of the internees were held hostage by the Japanese survivors until their safety was guaranteed; the hostages were freed on February 4. Due to confusion in the Japanese command, Manila was not surrendered until March 4, 1945, after a long and bloody battle. Only the area in north Manila around Santo Tomás and Malacañang Palace was secured by Allied forces at the time of the internees' liberation.

mashed potatoes, canned peaches, milk, candy bar. Dinner—cream of tomato soup, buttered peas, vanilla pudding, milk.

February 14, 1945. Other dishes served—chili con carne, string beans, fresh braised beef, mixed vegetables. Also we were given toilet soap, toothbrush, tooth powder, cigarettes, gum, and chocolate bars. Men were given razors, blades, and shaving cream with one supper. With every breakfast a tall can of evaporated milk.

February 20, 1945. Recorded a broadcast for WSB Atlanta (radio) to Ernestine, Aunt Helen, Hortense, Mother Vaughan, Aunt Susie, and Aunt Fannie.†

February 22, 1945. Memorial service for Mr. Grinnell, Mr. Duggleby, and others.‡

February 25, 1945. Thanksgiving service.

March 3, 1945. Filipinos scrubbed (for pay) bathroom floors, walls, and toilets. Japanese currency—Mickey Mouse—no good.

March 7, 1945. Saints' Day of Santo Tomás. A Catholic holiday, special mass in Seminary.

†Internees were invited to record messages for local radio stations in the U.S. as soon as facilities were available in Santo Tomás. Greetings to families were the general focus of these messages. In her first letter written after liberation, EHV told her sister Ernestine Jernigan, "I can send only one letter at this time." The letter is dated February 6, 1945. "I weigh 90 lbs. now, only skin and bones, for we have really nearly starved the past four months," she wrote. In a second letter to her sister, written three days later, she said: "We've been shelled by hidden Japanese artillery since I wrote, and sixteen internees were killed outright, one within a foot of me. . . . Of course [the Army] got the Japanese— and the food we are receiving! For the first time in three years we had BREAD, just plain, sliced wheat bread, but Beth and Clay almost cried they thought it so good. We'll have butter and jam on bread later, as they say our shrunken stomachs can't stand too much at one time."

‡When it became apparent that the American forces would soon enter Manila, the Japanese commandant of Santo Tomás ordered the four top Internment Committee members shot. This fact, although suspected, was not confirmed until after liberation and the memorial service to which EHV refers was in their honor.

LEYTE
1945

Friday, March 9, 1945. At 12:30 over loudspeakers was read a list of names of people to be ready to leave at 1:30 with not more than 50 pounds of baggage each.* Had gotten children's lunch, not mine. Began mad rush of packing. No one ate. Rushed to plaza before Main Building to form last Santo Tomás queue to fill out forms for weight, etc., before boarding trucks for Nichols Field Airport.†

Open truck ride through Manila. No large building left, theaters, hotels destroyed. High Commissioner's home (built on reclaimed sea land at great cost) shattered ruins. Bodegas at piers, roofless, blackened walls. Large residences all burned, cars parked along highways burned. Burned hangars at airport, destroyed planes on edge of field (whether American or Japanese, could not tell), men busy with drills, cement, patching bomb and shell holes in concrete runways.

"If you need a little Philippine Island money for the trip, the Red Cross can let you have it," said a young officer as we stepped aboard a plane to carry us to Leyte—a C-47 carrying 20 passengers each. Some went on 40-passenger planes.

By time approximately 150 internees were boarded it was 3:20 P.M.

*EHV, Beth, and Clay were among the first internees to leave, undoubtedly because of the children. Other internees stayed on in Manila well into April since the "mopping up" took longer than expected.
†American airfield three miles south of Manila.

It is a two and one-half hour flight to Leyte (Tacloban)‡ and we arrived about 6:15, after dark. We flew 150 miles per hour. At Tacloban there were coffee, fruit juice, and cookies for hungry internees.

Baggage checked again, in darkness, and on trucks for a long dusty ride to our quarters—women and children to one camp, men to another—on Orange Beach. Assigned to tents (with concrete floor) for fourteen people. Out to open-top showers for bath in cool starlight with coconut palms in sight high above walls of showers. A hasty supper and away to bed on army cots with clean white sheets but no pillow.

Saturday, March 10, 1945. Awakened at 6:30 by army nurse and told breakfast at 7:00. Then began long physical exam. Given American broom to sweep tent.

Case history taken, ears, nose, throat examined. Chest X-rayed, blood count, stripped for thorough examination. Reflexes checked.

C.I.C.* to give names of persons who collaborated with Japanese and persons (neutrals and Filipinos) who assisted internees. Gave names of Simke and Lenhart as helping us. Signed paper for C.I.C. that I would reveal no information concerning escapes from camp or information about internment.

Signed promissory note for $825.00 ($275.00 each for Beth, Clay, and me) to repay U.S. Government for passage from P.I. to undisclosed port in U.S. Sent 10-word cable to Aunt Susie.

Beth stepped on centipede first day—barefooted—and Clay's vaccination gave him fever.

Monday, March 12, 1945. Soldiers kind to children. Gifts of candy, crackers, chewing gum, so much that I had to beg boys not to feed Beth and Clay for they would not eat in dining room.

Soldiers took children bathing out in ocean. How they loved it! I got barefooted and waded on beach. Amphibian truck came by on huge rubber tires and we all got on for a sea ride. Bobbed on waves while

‡Capital of Leyte Province, on the northwest shore of San Pedro Bay, 355 miles southeast of Manila.
*Counterintelligence Corps (U.S. Army).

soldiers in group and internee women in playsuits and dresses dived for swim

Red Cross clothing given out. Beth and Clay given wool plaid jackets (really girls' dresses which I cut off for jackets) and in pocket of each was a little stuffed animal (duck, dog) and a little stuffed doll, made by American women for refugee children. Should have liked for New Jersey Red Cross women who made the toys Beth and Clay received to see children's faces light with joy at these unexpected gifts hidden in the pockets. Little animals will return to U.S. with us—for we left what toys the children had at Santo Tomás.

Sailed from Leyte on S.S. Admiral Capps on March 18, 1945, arriving in San Francisco on April 8, 1945.

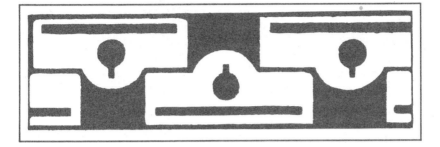

INDEX